FRENCH RIVIERA

DUMONT GUIDE

FRENCH RIVIERA

by
ROLF LEGLER

translated by
RUSSELL STOCKMAN

STEWART, TABORI & CHANG
PUBLISHERS, NEW YORK

FRONT COVER:
Villefranche (Jon Prime)
BACK COVER:
Cannes (Allan A. Philiba)
FRONTISPIECE:
The town of Solliès

Library of Congress Cataloging-in-Publication Data

Legler, Rolf, 1945–
The French Riviera.

(DuMont guide)
Translation of: Côte d'Azur.
Includes indexes.
1. Riviera (France)—Description and travel—Guidebooks.   I. Title.
DC608.3.L3813   1985   914.4′904838   84-2540
ISBN 0-941434-60-5

Copyright © 1982 DuMont Buchverlag GmbH & Co.

Published in 1986 by Stewart, Tabori & Chang, Inc., 740 Broadway, New York,
New York 10003 under exclusive world-wide English language license
from DuMont Buchverlag GmbH & Co.
All rights for all countries are held by DuMont Buchverlag GmbH & Co.,
Limited, Cologne, West Germany.
The title of the original German edition was
Côte d'Azur: Frankreichs Mittelmeerküste von Marseille bis Menton
by Rolf Legler.

The Practical Travel Suggestions were prepared by John Sturman.

First printing, 1986

Distributed in the United States by
Workman Publishing, 1 West 39 Street,
New York, New York 10018

Printed in Spain

CONTENTS

MARSEILLES

THE PROVENÇAL COAST

LES ALPES MARITIMES

EXCURSIONS INTO THE INTERIOR

PRACTICAL TRAVEL SUGGESTIONS

MARSEILLES

THE CITY AS PHOENIX

FEBRUARY 1, 1943, WAS A BLACK DATE IN THE HIS-
tory of the oldest city in France. On that
day, the German occupation force began to
blow up the old part of Marseilles, which
they were unable to control. Two days later, the Swiss journalist for the *Gazette de
Lausanne* reported: "The detonations have
stopped. The silence is complete. I encountered no one on my walk through the deso-
lation except for cats, who seem determined to stay. In the falling darkness the
whole scene took on the hallucinatory
grandeur and eeriness of a modern-day
Pompeii." In his book *Midi*, Archibald Lyall
summed up the report: "Massalia had been
destroyed."

THE MYTH OF THE CITY'S FOUNDING, AS HANDED
down to us by various Greek writers, is a
far happier story. Nann, the king of the Ligurian Comacines who had settled here,
had a lovely daughter, Gyptis. In his castle,
which presumably stood on the elevation
of Allauch, some 7 miles north of Marseilles, he was making preparations for her
wedding. According to local custom, it was
up to the princess herself to choose her
groom from among the assembled suitors,
symbolically indicating her selection by offering him a cup of wine.

At just this time two ships from faraway
Phocaea, a Greek colony in Asia Minor,
docked in the inlet of Lacydon, now the
Vieux Port. They had been dispatched to
found trade settlements here on the Ligurian coast and were richly laden with gifts.
The leader of the delegation was a young
man named Protis. These new arrivals were
promptly invited to the wedding celebrations and turned up at the castle at the very
moment when Gyptis was to select her future husband. Without hesitation she approached the good-looking stranger and
presented him with a cup of wine. As a
wedding present to the young couple, King
Nann gave the Phocaean Greeks the hill of
Accoules on the north side of the harbor
basin, where Marseilles was to come into
being. The history of Massalia thus begins
with a marriage for love.

BETWEEN THE MARRIAGE OF PROTIS AND GYPTIS and the Nazi bombing of old Marseilles lie roughly 2,500 years of rich history that had a decisive effect on the development of the West. Marseilles is today the second largest city in France and the largest port in the Mediterranean; the Germans could not destroy it; neither could Julius Caesar's conquest of it in 49 B.C., nor the Saracens' razing in 838 A.D., nor the Great Plague of 1580. Marseilles has survived to become a legend of continuity and indestructibility.

THE CITY'S HISTORY

MARSEILLES, LIKE ALL OF LOWER PROVENCE between the mouth of the Rhône and Toulon, bears no evidence of its Paleolithic past due to an extreme fluctuation in the level of the Mediterranean. Only after the last ice age, which ended about 9000 B.C., did the shoreline settle at its present level. Previously, the shoreline near Marseilles ranged from 325 feet above to 650 feet below its present level, a total discrepancy of nearly 1,000 feet; the islands now lying near Marseilles were once the peaks of small foothills.

In the Mesolithic period, an independent civilization of hunters, fishers, and gatherers appears to have arisen to the east of the Rhône delta. Traces of this culture are scattered around the Etang de Berre (La Montade, Istres, Ventabren near Roquepertuse) and on the foothills of L'Estaque (Châteauneuf-les-Martiques). Tombs and ceramics from the Neolithic period have also

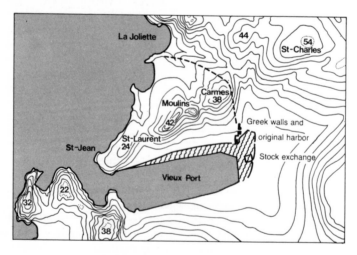

Topographic drawing of Marseilles.

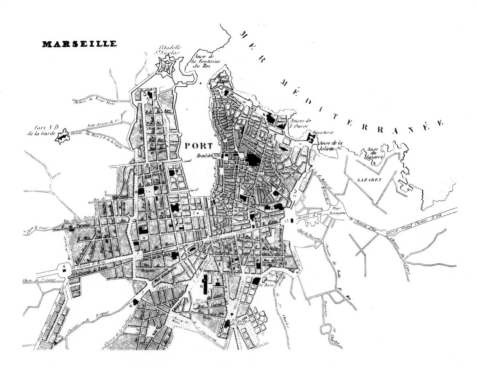

Map from Abel Hugo's France Pittoresque *(1835).*

been found in this region. The simplest explanation for the lack of such finds in Marseilles is the fact that it has been densely built over repeatedly so that all possible earlier historical traces have been destroyed.

Current scholarship suggests that the Phocaeans were not the first Greeks to engage in commerce or set up trading posts on the Mediterranean coast of France. Since the middle of the Bronze Age, we can be certain that there were contacts between this area and the eastern Mediterranean. Then, as recently as the first millennium B.C., the Iron Age began in the Mediterranean region, bringing new populations and technologies to the area. The new metal appears to have first been introduced through northern Italy. Tomb finds in the valley of the Arc (northeast of Marseilles, southeast of Aix-en-Provence) lie close to iron mines and production sites, and they reveal skeletons of a tall people with a distinctive ritual of burial. This ritual, the skeletons, and the shapes of the iron objects discovered here are unlike those that were of "Celtic" attribution. Perhaps these finds in the Arc valley are the first concrete traces in Provence of the enigmatic people known as the Ligurians, who cannot have been a more homogeneous or closed ethnic group than the

"Celts" of the early Iron Age, or Hallstatt period (ca. 800–500 B.C.), who lived north of the Alps.

The equestrian graves of Mailhac and quite recent finds at Le Pegue, in the central Rhône valley, assure us that peoples from north of the Alps penetrated far to the south. This is our first evidence that the valley of the Rhône had become a main route for economic and political contacts between northern Europe and the Mediterranean.

With the beginning of the Iron Age, new peoples enter onto the stage of Mediterranean history as the Phoenician monopoly on Mediterranean commerce began to be challenged. The Phoenician settlements in North Africa started to formulate independent policies. At the same time, the Etruscans and Greeks—especially the Corinthians from the Peloponnesus and the Ionians from Asia Minor—had developed increasingly into powers to be reckoned with. The tradition established by the Phoenicians' travels into the western Mediterranean and possibly beyond was continued by the Greeks, whose voyages are documented from at least the eighth century B.C.

In the seventh century B.C., it was chiefly seafarers from the Greek island of Rhodes who actively traded with the region that is now the south of France, and they seem to have founded commercial settlements by this time. The name "Rhône" (*Rhodanus*) likely derives from the Rhodians, as do such place names as Rhodanusia (a legendary city near Arles), Mont Rodinac (near Allauch, the fortress of King Nann), and Rodanas (the ancient name for St. Maximin). Rhodian ceramics from the seventh century B.C. have been discovered in the lowest excavation strata at Le Pegue, St-Blaise, and around the Fort St-Jean in Marseilles. Fernand Benoit has given the name of Paleopolis to this pre-Phocaean Marseilles. Admittedly, these excavations around Fort St-Jean and analysis of them are still incomplete.

Aristotle, Strabo, and Justinus all agree that the Phocaean Euxenes (ca. 600 B.C.) discovered the ideal natural harbor of Marseilles and was granted—possibly by King Nann—a concession to establish a trading colony. Massalia, the name given to the new colony, is presumably derived from two Ligurian words, *mas* ("house" or "premises") and *salia* (for the Salians, the natives who lived there). It appears to have been intended to be a courtesy to the Salians, with whom the Greeks hoped to establish trade. Phocaean Massalia experienced extremely rapid growth, soon eclipsing all of the other Rhodian settlements (St. Blaise, for instance). Attracted by its uniquely favored location, a new flood of immigrants arrived in 542 B.C.; Persian expansionism had forced the people of Phocaea to evacuate their homeland en masse. Many of them settled in Massalia, and soon the city's trade with the heart of Europe reached a first peak. The civilizing influence of Massalia on its neighbors cannot be overrated. The Celts and Ligurians altered their whole way of life. Their first settlements were founded sometime after 600 B.C., and from this exposure to Massalian customs, they began to use money as a means of payment and to worship the Greek gods. Ceramics and handicrafts from Massalia became prized articles of trade.

Then in the fifth century B.C., the city's commerce suffered a distinct recession due to a revolution in the Celtic world north of the Alps. The transition from the heterogeneous Hallstatt civilization to the more uniform La Tène culture brought with it a new thrust of Celtic expansionism.

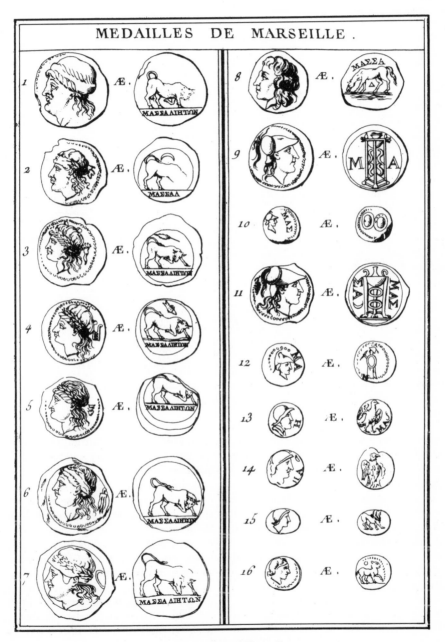

Ancient coins of Massalia.

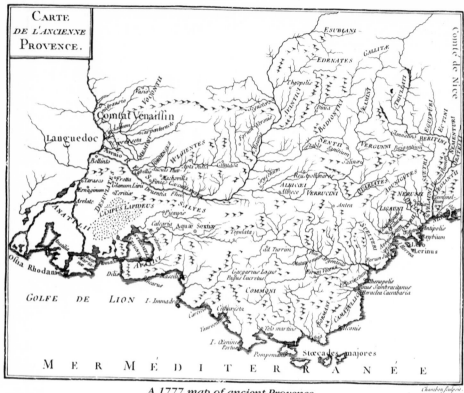

A 1777 map of ancient Provence.

The destruction of trading posts in the Rhône valley and the blocking of this route by the Celts put a major dent in the commercial activity of Massalia. Alpine passes replaced the Rhône as trade routes, and Spina temporarily supplanted Marseilles as a bridgehead and reloading point until it was sacked ca. 400 B.C. But Massalia repulsed a Celtic invasion and embarked on a new trade policy that included the founding of settlements such as Olbia (Hyères), Antipolis (Antibes), and Nikaia (Nice). Massalia recovered its preeminence.

The fourth century B.C. witnessed the height of the development of Phocaean Massalia. Two Massalian seafarers made

voyages of discovery in this century. Euthymenes passed through the Pillars of Hercules and sailed as far as Senegal. Pytheas, however, deserves even greater admiration. He too sailed beyond Gibraltar but then turned northward, sailing around Britain, visiting Cornwall, discovering Thule (believed to be Norway or Iceland), reaching the Arctic, and finding there a frozen sea. From his report, the *Periplus*, which survives only in fragments, it is clear that he not only had his eye on a sea route to the tin in Cornwall and the amber in the Baltic but was pursuing scientific goals as well. Whether or not he discovered that the earth is round, as many scholars assume he did, Pytheas must be numbered among history's great explorers.

Also in the fourth century B.C., the sea power of Carthage began to pose a threat to shippers of the western Mediterranean. The natural opponents of this Punic ascendancy were first the Greeks and then the Romans. Massalia, though, clung to its neutrality until the First Punic War, when its fleet, supported by Roman ships, defeated the Carthaginian fleet near the mouth of the Ebro. Moreover, the hostile stance of Massalia may have forced Hannibal to route his troops across Mont Genèvre instead of marching along the coast, leading to major losses from his army in the Second Punic War.

Thus Massalia helped to save Rome, and a short time later, Rome returned the favor. Toward the close of the third century B.C., the Celts had again forged southward, in a new wave of invasion, until they stood outside the very gates of Massalia. Not being a land power, Marseilles turned to Rome and asked that rising power to ensure peace in the interior.

In 123 B.C., Sextius Calvinus not only destroyed the capital of the Salians (Entremont), but settled for good at the base of the demolished community, founding the Roman settlement of Aquae Sextiae (Aix-en-Provence) in 122 B.C. Four years later Domitius Ahenobarbus established the colony of Narbonne. In other words, the Romans stayed and prepared to build for the future.

The Massalians continued to rule their traditional sphere of influence: the Mediterranean coast from the mouth of the Rhône east to Monaco (Herakleia Monoikos). They did not object to the fact that their Roman allies took responsibility for preserving peace in the land. But when Massalia (Massilia under the Romans), feel-

ing it owed as much to Pompey as to Caesar, attempted to remain neutral during the Roman Civil War, Caesar besieged the city for six months. In view of the city's long-standing loyalty to Rome, upon his victory Caesar punished Massalia relatively lightly: he took away its walls, its weapons, a portion of its fleet, and its possessions (except for Nice and St-Tropez). The role of trading center fell to Narbonne and to a lesser degree to Arles and Fréjus. For 300 years after that, Massalia remained an island of calm—such calm that it was a favored place for the banishment of high officials. (It was here that Petronius wrote his *Satyricon*.)

NEXT TO NOTHING IS KNOWN ABOUT THE origins of Christianity in Marseilles. The first bishop we hear of, Oresius, took part in the Council of Arles in 314. In the fifth century, after Arles had ceased to be the capital of the ruined Roman Empire in the

Attic red-figured hydria *from the excavations behind the Stock Exchange.*

West, Marseilles was again able to surpass this ancient rival. In about 415, St. Cassian founded the monastery of St-Victor in what had once been the quarry for the ancient cemetery south of the harbor. Despite the turmoil of the times and a variety of rulers, Massalia's harbor enabled it to continue its commercial activity to a modest extent until after the sixth century. Then a decline set in, and Massalia became a mere town, too small for its ancient walls. However, Marseilles was still one of the few intact harbors on the French Mediterranean coast, so all important ambassadors to the Frankish king—the popes in Rome, caliphs in Bagdad, Basiliscus of Constantinople—landed here. When the Arabs came to dominate the Mediterranean, they brought Massalia to economic and then physical ruin. In 838, they attacked, conquered, plundered, and destroyed the city. After 1,500 years, Massalia had died.

But roughly 150 years later, after the Saracens had been driven out of the Massif des Maures, Marseilles arose again like the phoenix from its ashes. By the close of the ninth century, Marseilles was transformed into a viscounty independent of Arles. At the end of the tenth century, the offices of the viscount, the bishop, and the abbot of St-Victor were for a time in the hands of a single family, the descendants of a certain Arlulf. Bishop Honoratus, the brother of Viscount Pons, distinguished himself not only by rebuilding his diocese, but by initiating the rebuilding of the Abbey of St-Victor in 977. The peace enjoyed by Provence in the eleventh century favored the development of a completely new Marseilles. A patent issued on July 28, 1094, by Raimund of St-Gilles and his wife, Douce de Provence, exempted all boats and barges of St-Victor from tolls on the Rhône and the Durance. In the twelfth century, Marseilles once more maintained extensive commercial contacts and its own trading posts throughout the Mediterranean, although it certainly did not enjoy the preeminence it had in antiquity. The dimensions of its cathedral, Notre-Dame La Major, the nature of the contracts it made with Genoa, its very late appearance as a self-administered commune, its nonparticipation in the First Crusade, and other facts further indicate that Marseilles was merely one of many medieval cities along the northwestern shore of the Mediterranean. The most important port in southern France at this time was St-Gilles—and the Italian cities of Genoa and Pisa were even more significant.

When the male line of the local ruling family died out with Barral in 1192, an open conflict broke out between the city and the powerful Abbey of St-Victor, ending in a wave of anticlericalism. The people rejected the claims of the monastery, exiled the bishop, and proclaimed a free commune, or city-republic, whose short-lived existence was recognized by the two feudal lords of Provence, Raimund Beranger V and Raimund VII of Toulouse, as late as 1225. Marseilles was not to find peace in the thirteenth century, however. First came the terrible Albigensian Wars, in the course of which Marseilles, like many of the other larger communes of Provence, took the side of Raimund VI, who had been robbed of his lands and was willing to guarantee the city's freedoms. Marseilles continued to be a self-determining republic until the death of Raimund VII in 1249.

Beginning in 1246, the legal feudal lord was Charles of Anjou, and this dour ruler made short shrift of the free republic. In the subsequent wars of the Sicilian Vespers between Anjou and Rome on the one hand and Catalonia and Ghibelline Genoa on the other, Marseilles had the most powerful seaports of the western Mediterranean as its opponents. Added to its loss of independence and its entanglement in the war between Anjou and Aragon in the fourteenth century, further blows struck the city. First, the Christians abandoned the ports of Egypt and Syria, which had again become Moslem. Second, the Rhône valley lost its importance as a trade route because the Italians established more direct shipping lanes to England and Flanders; accordingly the Champagne fairs, crucial to the economy of the Rhône valley, became insignificant. And, when the papal court established itself in nearby Avignon, Italian merchants and moneychangers moved there from Marseilles, rendering Marseilles a minor port of Avignon. Worst of all, though, was the raging plague of 1348.

In short, from the first half of the fourteenth to the middle of the fifteenth century, the proud but long-suffering harbor city seemed headed toward almost certain death. Yet Marseilles would not expire. Although its affiliation with the sphere of Anjou had brought on this decline, it was, oddly, virtually the last of the Anjou line who became the guardian angel and savior of Marseilles (discounting the insignificant interlude of Charles of Maine).

In 1423, Alfonso V of Aragon, unable to capture Naples, conquered defenseless Marseilles and plundered it out of pique. However, the Anjous could not hold Naples either, and in 1442, King René the Good withdrew from his Italian possessions, deciding rather to devote his whole attention to his own county of Provence.

In 1444, the dauphin Louis paid an official visit to the city, which accorded him an enthusiastic reception. In the same year, Jacques Coeur, the treasurer and adviser to the French king, transferred the headquarters and fleet of his far-flung commercial enterprise from Montpellier to Marseilles. And four fairs were established in Lyon These events were crucial to the development of Marseilles.

The measures adopted by René the Good were no less significant. In 1447, he established two annual ten-day fairs in Marseilles, and he began to make the harbor secure militarily. Although René was twice married, he died in 1480 without heirs. His successor, the sickly and childless Charles of Maine, followed René to the grave less than a year later, but not without first making his will completely in accordance with René's own wishes: the heir to the county of Provence would be the royal house of France. According to the prevailing feudal law, this bequest was thoroughly possible, but it was bound to cause anger, for, since 1031, the ultimate sovereign and feudal lord of Provence had officially been the Holy Roman Emperor. The anger was compounded in the first half of the sixteenth century by the fact that two such irreconcilable rivals as Francis I, who was personally offended at having lost the election for emperor, and Charles V opposed each other. The Provençals, and particularly the people of Marseilles, however, approved of the choice of their beloved king and stood loyal to France—admittedly with a constant eye toward the preservation of the freedoms conceded to them by the counts of Provence.

Twice Charles V attempted to press his legal claims to Provence by force; twice he was obliged to back off by the determined resistance shown by the city of Marseilles (1524 and 1536). After the first sally (under the leadership of the Connétable de Bourbon) Francis I built the Château d'If and another fortress on the Piton de la Garde (below the present-day Notre-Dame-de-la-Garde). And in the Plan-de-

Marseilles in the sixteenth century.

Fourmiguier—the marshy plain at the east end of the ancient harbor basin, where the city's main street, La Canebière, begains today—he erected stables, dockyards, and arsenals. Thus, the commercial port of Marseilles became a military harbor as well. Charles V could only document the empire's claim to Germany, Italy, and Burgundy through his forced election as King of Burgundy/Arelate in Aix in 1536. The Massalians' hopes that their longstanding quasi-autonomy would be preserved were dampened by the Edict of Joinville (September 1535) and the Decree of Villers-Cotterets (August 1539), both of which demonstrated that the French king felt little gratitude for the loyalty of the people of

Marseilles. On tne contrary, it was apparent that he was determined to force the incorporation of Provence into France at all costs.

The behavior of the people of Marseilles during the Wars of Religion throws a telling light on their character. Engaged in commerce for centuries, this city was cosmopolitan, accustomed to living with people of all races and beliefs. Quarreling about questions of faith was foreign to it, and above all troublesome for commerce. In 1560, when the religious wars began to ignite in France, the citizens of Marseilles sent a deputation to the French court with assurances that they intended to live and die in the Roman Catholic faith. In the three years after the Battle of Lepanto, the Massalians were the only merchants of Christendom admitted to the court of the Ottoman Empire. When Henri IV, the descendant of a Protestant king, ascended the throne, the people of Marseilles responded with the assertion that they would never serve a heretical king. It was a convenient and welcome excuse for them to secede from France, and once again Marseilles proclaimed itself a republic. But what had been unacceptable to Charles of Anjou was certainly not going to be countenanced by Henri IV. In January 1596, the city's dream of independence was ended.

Provence tried to free itself from France for the last time in 1660. But Cardinal Mazarin was too strong. With his crushing of the Fronde rebellion, he had already brought about the consummation of absolutism. He advised Louis XIV to crush the impertinent Marseilles from his base in Toulon. The loss of independence must have seemed more important than the "punishment" of seeing Toulon become the most important military port on the Mediterranean. (Being a military port had not been their own idea in the first place.)

The wealth from the trade that flowed through the harbor had encouraged the city, at that time still quite medieval in appearance, to undertake major urban changes. However, the political situation, the Provençal insurrection, and the temporary money shortage which necessarily followed, prevented the realization of most of the planned improvements. Had they been carried out, these projects, proposed by

View from Le Sieur Tassin's Atlas *(1686).*

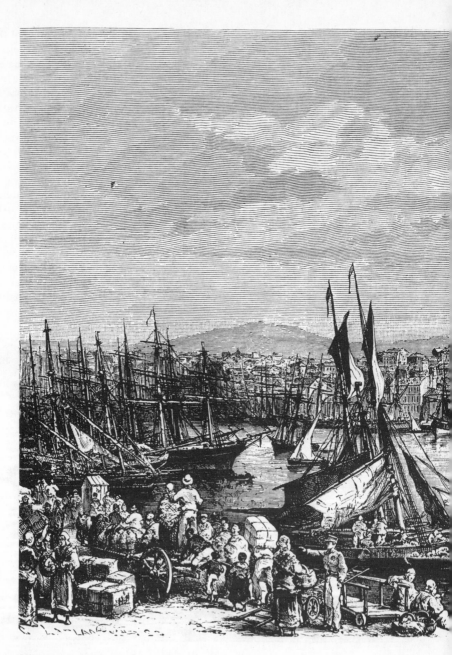

Nineteenth-century depiction of the Vieux Port.

Pierre Puget among others, would doubtless have given Marseilles the look of a splendid Baroque city.

In the late seventeenth century, responding to the needs of the times, Marseilles opened itself to world trade. Overseas colonies, filled with exploitable riches, had been established. Despite the competition from cities like Bordeaux, Nantes, and Le Havre, which were more favorably situated for Atlantic trade, Marseilles was able to regain its preeminent position. The ancient metropolis of the Phocaeans had become France's most important international port.

This development was temporarily interrupted by the French Revolution. In its very essence bourgeois and plebian, Marseilles played a quite significant role in this uprising. As in Aix, the citizens had chosen as their deputy the enfant terrible of the Provençal nobility, the fulminating orator Mirabeau. As it happened, he chose to represent Aix. The Jacobins of Marseilles who went to Paris in 1792 enjoyed great influence there. In that same year, a young Alsatian staff officer, Roger de Lisle, composed a battle song for the Army of the Rhine. When the citizens of Marseilles celebrated the departure of a troop of 500 volunteers to support the Revolution in Paris, some of the men sang this hymn. Their compatriots liked it so much that when the force marched into Paris, all 500 of them sang the song with so much youthful vigor, zeal, and enthusiasm that the Parisian passersby stopped to listen to the melody as though electrified. The Revolution promptly adopted this battle song as its anthem. Because the volunteers from Marseilles had introduced the hymn to Paris, it came to be known as "La Marseillaise." Today it is the national anthem of France.

After Marseilles recovered from the bloodbath of the Revolution and the Reign of Terror, its position in the Mediterranean began to rise again. Its status was especially enhanced by the conquest of and founding of a French colony in Algeria under Charles X. But wealth of unsuspected proportions came only in 1869, when the Suez Canal was opened and the Mediterranean became a fast and cost-effective route to the Indian Ocean and the Far East. No other city profited more from the Suez Canal than Marseilles did. Nearly all of the buildings that dominate the city—Notre-Dame-de-la-Garde, the cathedral, the Stock Exchange, the Palais Longchamp, the Gare St-Charles—date from the period between the second half of the nineteenth century and the beginning of World War I.

AN APPROACH

From the Arc de Triomphe via Notre-Dame-de-la-Garde to the Vieux Port

IN SPITE OF ITS FORMER PREEMINENCE AS A seaport, Marseilles today is most likely to be approached by land. Even in the seventeenth and eighteenth centuries, visitors to Marseilles described a city with two faces, one for the sea and one for the land. The modern superhighway from Aix-en-Provence to Marseilles attests not only to an advanced and efficient control of traffic, but moreover to a sense of Baroque vistas, for, from St-Antoine on, the road leads virtually straight ahead toward the Arc de Triomphe, with the landmark, Notre-Dame-de-la-Garde, in the distance. One should head directly for this basilica, for virtually nothing can help the visitor gain a better understanding of this pulsing city than the grand view from here, the highest spot in Marseilles. The original face of Marseilles is presented to the visitor in unparalleled beauty: the sea, the offshore islands, the rugged cliffs of white limestone, and the Vieux Port (Old Harbor), the nucleus of France's oldest city.

Coming from Aix, it is simplest to take the exit marked Vieux Port. From every other direction it is somewhat more complicated to do so, but nevertheless one should watch for the signs for either Centre Ville or Vieux Port. From the Vieux Port, drive south from the Quai des Belges along the Rue Breteuil, and follow the signs to Notre-Dame-de-la-Garde (some signs display only the silhouette of the church,

without any legend). A right turn off the Rue Breteuil onto Boulevard Vauban brings one to the Rue du Fort du Sanctuaire, which leads up to Notre-Dame-de-la-Garde. This church, built in a neo-Byzantine style by Espérandieu in 1864, is a sacred emblem of Marseilles. In its crypt, there is a marble *Mater Dolorosa* by sculptor Jean-Baptiste Carpeaux (1827–1875).

After one has enjoyed the unforgettable aerial view from Notre-Dame-de-la-Garde, it is time to turn to the Vieux Port. Any tour of the city ought to begin here, just as the city itself did.

On the Quai des Belges, near its intersection with the city's main street, La Canebière, there is a large brass plaque in the pavement stating that in 600 B.C. the Phocaean seafarer Protis set foot on land at this spot. (Actually, in Protis's time, the shore lay several hundred yards to the north; also, this portion of the Vieux Port was then a marshy swamp and therefore the least likely of places to land a ship. It was only by draining this swamp in the Middle Ages that the Valois kings could build docks and arsenals for their navies here, on the so-called Plan-de-Fourmiguier.)

*T*HE ANCIENT CITY

THE DEMARCATION OF THE NORTH SIDE OF THE Vieux Port (see map, p. 26) is the elongated ridge of Accoules, which consists of three hills sloping upward toward the east: the Butte-St-Laurent (79 feet) in the west, the Butte des Moulins (138 feet) in the center, and the Butte des Carmes (125 feet). This ridge was the wedding present given by King Nann to the newlyweds Pro-

tis and Gyptis. On the Butte des Moulins, the Phocaeans erected temples to their two chief deities, Apollo and Artemis. An enormous, elegant Ionic capital discovered at the foot of the Butte-St-Laurent may have come from the Temple of Apollo, perhaps dating back to 500 B.C. At the base of this acropolis lay the city proper, roughly a hundred yards inland from the present-day

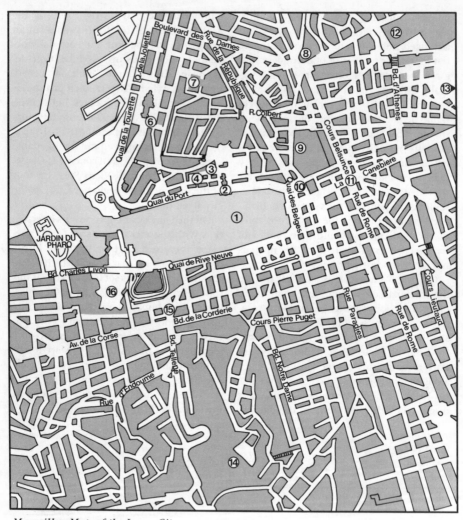

Marseilles: Map of the Inner City

1. Vieux Port
2. Hôtel de Ville
3. Maison Diamantée
4. Musée des Docks `Romains
5. Fort and church of St-Jean
6. Old and New Cathedrals
   Notre-Dame La Major
7. Vieille Charité
8. Arc de Triomphe
9. Greek excavations behind the stock exchange
10. Stock exchange
11. La Canebière
12. Gare St-Charles
13. Palais Longchamp (just off the map to the east)
14. Notre-Dame-de-la-Garde
15. St-Victor
16. Fort St-Nicholas
17. Park and Château Borély (off the map to the southwest)

Quai du Port. The boundary between the upper and lower city ran approximately along the modern Rue Caisserie and Grande Rue and consisted of two districts separated by the *agora*, or marketplace (Place de Lenche). The Phocaean city thus formed an elongated triangle bounded by Bassin-de-la-Joliette and Fort-St-Jean, the Vieux Port, and the Butte-St-Charles (the site of the train station). The relatively superficial descriptions of the city by ancient authors (Avienus, Caesar, Strabo), according to which the city was washed on three sides by the sea, have hardly seemed accurate until quite recently. (The so-called Wall of Krinas has been known since 1913, but it was, incomprehensibly, dated to Roman times—second century A.D.) In 1967, however, ruins were uncovered (see map, below) during construction of an underground garage behind the Stock Exchange, excavation of which has been in progress ever since and is by no means complete. The most important findings so far are:

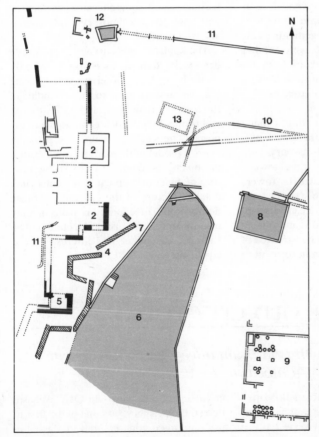

Marseilles: Map of the excavations behind the stock exchange.

1. *Wall of Krinas*
2. *Towers*
3. *City gate with remains of a stone-paved street*
4. *Foundations of the Older Wall*
5. *South tower*
6. *Horn-shaped harbor basin*
7. *Quay wall*
8. *Water reservoir*
9. *Dry docks*
10. *Water conduit*
11. *Drains*
12. *Basin*
13. *Terrace ornamented with triglyphs*

1. The Butte des Carmes, contrary to previous belief, stood within the Greek wall.
2. The ancient description of the "horn-shaped" harbor of Massalia has been confirmed. Where the church of St-Ferréol and the Stock Exchange now stand, the harbor bent northward, nearly as far as the present-day Cours Belsunce. Thus Massalia actually was surrounded by water on three sides.
3. The theory that the Wall of Krinas dates from Roman times has been refuted. This section of wall, fortified with three square towers, is constructed of pink-colored stone from La Couronne, fitted together in a fashion typical of the Hellenistic building of the period, and dates from the same time as the wall of St-Blaise—the third or second century B.C.

Thus, these excavations provide a much clearer picture of ancient Massalia. A wall of pink-colored Hellenistic masonry, with right-angled segments and three towers, ran toward the east. Between the towers was a city gate; the remains of a street, from Roman times, paved with stone are also apparent. A few steps east of this are foundations of an older Greek wall constructed of white limestone. A harbor basin adjacent to it extended like a horn to the north and was contained by a fourteen-foot quay wall. Two stone stairways led down to the water, which, with a depth of nearly nine feet, provided anchorage for the largest ships. East of this was a square basin with a capacity of more than 9 million cubic feet, which was connected to an aqueduct and dates from the same period as the Wall of Krinas. It probably was intended to supply fresh water for departing ships. To the south, one can clearly make out the remains of extensive dry docks. Additional drains, aqueducts, and streets lie to the north of the harbor basin. A square terrace ornamented with triglyphs was almost certainly a funerary structure.

The Roman period survives at the Musée des Docks Romains (see map, p. 26), directly behind the Hôtel de Ville. During foundation work prior to the rebuilding of the Vieux Port quarter after 1946, the remains of a Roman dock complex were exposed. The small museum here provides maps, a model of the harbor, and a display of objects, in addition to this visible remnant of the Roman epoch, that paint a quite detailed picture of the city under Roman domination. The exposed remains of a Roman theater to the east of the church of St-Laurent may be of less interest for the layperson.

*T*HE OLD CITY TODAY

Hôtel de Ville—Maison Diamantée—La Vieille Charité —Cathédrale La Major

THE BUILDINGS ALONG THE QUAI DU PORT TODAY are not particularly inspired architecturally. Speed and lack of money served as the architects of this "new Old City." Auguste Perret, the designer, was one of the first to use reinforced concrete, but in Marseilles he did not provide a glorious example of modern architecture. He was capable of doing better, as can be seen from Notre-Dame at Le Raincy, the Théâtre des Champs Elysées in Paris, and in the reconstruction of Le Havre. In Marseilles, however, one sees a striking contrast between Perret's architecture and the old *Hôtel de Ville*, the showpiece of the harbor front (see map, p. 27). The Nazis considered only a very few buildings worth saving in old Marseilles. The Hôtel de Ville was one of them, as were the Maison Diamantée and the Gothic House.

Even though the Hôtel de Ville was spared by the Germans, it has endured numerous mutilations and alterations in the course of its 300-year existence. A predecessor of the Hôtel de Ville was begun as early as 1653, but it never managed to rise above its foundations. Only in the 1660s, after the city was brought back into the kingdom of France for good, did peace and commercial stability return to Marseilles. As early as 1663, Pierre Puget submitted two proposals for the city hall, one in a quite Roman, Baroque style, the other considerably more French. Both were rejected.

The city's two official architects, Gaspard Puget and Mathieu Portal, were commissioned to plan and execute the building in 1666; the resulting façade is distinctly reminiscent of Genoese examples. The building consists of a wide middle structure running parallel to the street and two narrower side wings perpendicular to it. This three-part design is repeated on a smaller scale in the three bays of the central section, to which the two bays of each of the side wings stand in distinct contrast. There is also a contrast between the two stories. On the ground floor, the center section and side wings are flush with the sidewalk. But the *piano nobile*, or upper

story, of the middle section is set back somewhat, creating a terrace enclosed by a balustrade along the front and flanked by two towers. The balcony this creates forms a narrow stage on which acts of state could take place. Furthermore, the two stories are decorated differently. The monumental ground floor is two-dimensional, whereas the upper story is more sculptural and suggestive of movement. The architectural and decorative importance of the *piano nobile* is doubly apparent today, since the original Mansard roof, much higher and with two peaks, was discarded in the course of later alterations. The sculptural relief of trophies above the middle window of the grand hall is attributed to Pierre Puget.

ONLY A FEW STEPS TO THE NORTHWEST, BEHIND the Hôtel de Ville, stands another distinguished seventeenth-century (Grand Siècle) building in Marseilles, the *Maison Diamantée* (see map, p. 26). It is listed everywhere as a Renaissance building from 1552 and is alleged to be patterned after the Palazzo dei Diamanti in Ferrara (although the diamondlike cutting of rusticated stone had been used in Provence as early as the late fifteenth century). Most recent theory suggests that this building was constructed later, in 1620, by the supervisor of the city's artillery, the Italian Nicola da Robbia. His choice of a more military style was thus appropriate to his function.

One sixteenth-century building that survives is the Gothic House, at the intersection of the Grande Rue and Rue Bonneterie. It was built in 1535, presumably for the consul Cabre.

THE THIRD OF MARSEILLES'S REPRESENTATIVE seventeenth-century buildings is on the other side of the ridge of Accoules, at the northern edge of the former Old City. This is the *Vieille Charité* (see map, p. 26). It was constructed in 1640 as a hospital for the poor and the aged, following the pattern of the hospice in Lyons. A decade later, the initial building was found to be too small, so Pierre Puget was commissioned to design a generous addition in 1655. Puget did not submit his designs until 1671, and they were not significantly realized before 1679. Gaspard Puget, the older brother, was the city's official architect, but Pierre was definitely its greatest artistic genius. He had a gift for blending the most diverse influences of his epoch in an individual way. He created a three-story rectangular building with an arcaded courtyard that combines Parisian ideas (various designs for the Dôme des Invalides) with Italian influences (Bernini's San Andrea della Quirinal). But in 1688, while Pierre Puget was still alive, construction was halted for lack of funds. The completion of the building in the early eighteenth century did not follow the original plans in all details. Also, the impact of the central chapel, consecrated in 1704, was reduced by the construction of a vestibule in 1863. It is hoped that the present extensive renovation of the Vieille Charité will at least bring out Puget's exemplary influence as an architectural genius.

THE MONTÉE DES ACCOULES IS A UNIQUE STREET composed of countless flat steps. It leads right through the upper town, a section virtually undisturbed by traffic, to the Place de Lenche (the former agora or forum). From here, it is only a short walk to the cathedral precinct. Here the showy *Notre-Dame La Major* rises (see map, p. 26). This structure, built on a cruciform ground plan, 459 feet long and with a cupola rising

a full 230 feet, was one of the most ambitious church-building projects of the nineteenth century. Its architects, Leon Vaudoyer, H.-J. Espérandieu, and Henri Revoil, who designed the interior furnishing, created a model example of historical eclecticism, combining a Romanesque ground plan with Byzantine elevation and Italianate decoration.

Preparatory work for the cathedral's foundation unearthed an important find from the Early Christian epoch in Marseilles, the foundation of a *baptistry* from the fifth century. In ground plan (square outside, inside an octagon supported by columns) it is closely related to many other Provençal structures of this type (at Aix, Fréjus, Cimiez, Riez). Its diameter of 75 feet, however, makes it far and away the largest baptistry in all of France.

THE OLD CATHEDRAL NOTRE-DAME LA MAJOR still stands, but it is overshadowed by its younger sister. The discovery of the foundations of the Early Christian baptistry in 1850 corroborates our assumption that the very earliest cathedral in the city stood on this same site. The name *Notre-Dame La Major* seems to imply the existence of a second, smaller church also consecrated to the Madonna, possibly Notre-Dame-des-Accoules. The Early Christian structure was probably destroyed during repeated attacks by the Saracens, and in the middle of the eleventh century it had to be rebuilt from the ground up. The modest structure proved inadequate for the rapidly growing population of the city, and a century later it was replaced by the Romanesque building that still stands. This cathedral, built after 1140, had a three-aisle nave with five bays, a transept that did not project beyond the width of the nave, and three apses on the east end. A choir bay half the depth of those of the nave connects the transept to the apses. In its ground plan, the broader central apse is a semicircle on the exterior and half of a fourteen-sided polygon inside (typical of many Romanesque structures in Provence). The considerably wider central vault is slightly pointed and is supported by the two lower semicircular vaults of the side aisles, blocking the area that would hold window openings for a clerestory. The most interesting part of the structure architecturally, however, is the crossing, which is crowned by an eight-sided, ribbed cupola resting on pendentives—concave triangular sections formed by the conjunction of the cupola and pairs of opposite arches—above a nearly square opening. These pendentives are adorned with the symbols of the four Evangelists, the only interior sculptural decoration evident. The nearly square base from which the cupola rises is set above an oblong crossing bay in a manner quite common in the Romanesque architecture of Provence: four progressive arches rise, stepwise, from the main arches opening onto the transept, thus reducing the long rectangle to a virtu-

al square. This original solution, possibly first employed in Notre-Dame-des-Doms in Avignon, is also encountered in the cathedrals of Apt, Carpentras, and Cavaillon, and the churches of Noves, St-Honorat-des-Alyscamps, and St-Laurent-des-Arbres.

Notre-Dame La Major underwent radical changes in the fourteenth and seventeenth centuries, which chapel structures were added on the east and north. The most important alteration consisted of a reorientation to the north (for reasons that are unknown today), at which time the surviving east apse, along with the new square apses erected in the fourteenth century, became mere side chapels. The two western bays of the nave were sacrificed during one of these remodelings. Construction of the new cathedral (beginning in 1853) involved the destruction of the cloister, the bishop's residence, and an additional two bays of the nave. Therefore the surviving fragment presents only an incomplete impression of the Romanesque cathedral.

The Romanesque altar of St. Serenus (sixth century), in the chapel of the same

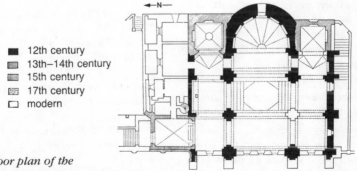

■ 12th century
▨ 13th–14th century
▥ 15th century
▦ 17th century
▢ modern

Marseilles: floor plan of the Old Cathedral of Notre-Dame La Major.

name, is probably the front side of what was originally a reliquary sarcophagus in which the mortal remains of Sts. Cannat and Lazarus were preserved. Local tradition has it that the sculpted figures set in the carved arcade depict these two saints. A sculpted Virgin in a severe and blocky style sits enthroned beneath the middle arcade in the *Sedes Sapientiae* or "Seat of Wisdom." The spandrels between the arcades are decorated with the symbols of the Evangelists, and the capitals, typical of the Romanesque period, are restatements of ancient examples. Altogether this fine Romanesque sarcophagus fragment represents a work of great grace, and, assuming that it was created under Bishop Raimund I who died in 1122, it attests to the high standard of sculpture in Marseilles at the beginning of the twelfth century.

The large, glazed terra cotta relief of the *Descent from the Cross* is attributed to Luca della Robbia. A work that deserves particular attention, the altar of St. Lazarus, who was revered by the Provençals, stands on the north side of the transept. The cathedral chapter had commissioned two Italian artists summoned to Provence by King René the Good—Tomaso di Como and Francesco Laurana—to create this work. Preceding Laurana's *Bearing of the Cross* at St-Didier in Avignon (1478), the Lazarus altar at La Major represents the earliest example of Renaissance sculpture in Provence, although some of the figures — Mary Magdalene and Martha on the semicircular pediments, for instance — admittedly appear to be later additions.

33: Cap Ferrat, Villa Ephrussi-Rothschild (Jon Prime).

34: Villa, French Riviera (Guido Alberto Rossi/The Image Bank).

35: Beaulieu, Villa Kerylos (Jon Prime).

36: Ecclesiastical splendor in Nice (Jon Prime).

37: Augustus Caesar's Trophy in La Turbie (Allan A. Philiba).

38–39: Cimiez, Roman bath ruins (Hugh Rogers/Monkmeyer Press).

40, top: In Monte Carlo (Richard Steedman/The Stock Market). Bottom: Biot, Leger Museum (Richard Steedman/The Stock Market).

41: Villefranche, St. Pierre Chapel (Richard Steedman/The Stock Market).

42: Vence, Matisse Chapel (Bullaty-Lomeo Photo).

43: Maeght Foundation, The Chapel (Gary Crallé/The Image Bank).

44, top: Cimiez, stained glass in the Chagall Museum (Marvin E. Newman). Bottom: Picasso, War and Peace, Vallauris (Marvin E. Newman).

45: Bonnard, Nu devant la cheminée (Giraudon/Art Resource).

46–47: Matisse, Intérieur à Nice (Giraudon/Art Resource).

48: Sculpture at Maeght Foundation (Susan Shapiro).

*T*HE NEW CITY

Le Grand Cours—Arc de Triomphe—La Canebière—Stock Exchange—Palais Longchamp—Gare St-Charles

MARSEILLES IS THOUGHT OF MORE IN TERMS OF its rich past than as a center of art. Compared to other smaller and younger Provençal cities, such as Nîmes, Aix, Arles, or Avignon, it will have less of artistic interest. Of the two most famous artists to be born beside the inlet Lacydon, Pierre Puget and Honoré Daumier, the latter worked exclusively in Paris, and the former's reputation was made in Toulon, Genoa, and Versailles. Puget never enjoyed the status of official architect or sculptor in his own city. His designs for Marseilles's Hôtel de Ville were rejected in 1663. Even after Puget settled in his home town after a final falling-out with Colbert in 1679, Marseilles made no attempt to take advantage of his presence. The building of La Vieille Charité was the result of private initiative, and his magnificent plans for a Place Royale (1686) were never realized due to a lack of funds. Whether the city's pronounced distaste for the monumental, its eye for the practical and leaning toward moderation, reflect the city's merchant mentality (as detractors insist) or whether they are deeply rooted in the Greek heritage of the individual as the measure of all things (as local boosters choose to believe) is impossible to say. In either case, the modern city is doing a great deal toward giving Puget his due recognition—as draftsman, painter, sculptor, architect, city planner, and musician—and disposing of its image as a city only of merchants. Today, Marseilles can certainly point with pride to one area well worth no-tice—the former *Grand Cours*, now the *Cours Belsunce* and *Cours St-Louis.*

IN THE MID-SEVENTEENTH CENTURY, IN A RARE meeting of minds among the Duc de Vendôme (who was royal governor of the city), the city fathers, and the royal engineer, the Chevalier de Clerville, Marseilles—still largely medieval—embarked on a methodical program of municipal expansion and improvement. De Clerville carried out the renovation of the south side of the harbor (Fort St-Nicolas in 1660, the Arsenal in 1666). The medieval land wall was razed, and a new, grandiose street, the Grand Cours, was laid out in place of the former trenches to mark the transition from the old city to the new one being planned. A precedent for this was undoubtedly the Cours Mirabeau (1651), in Aix-en-Provence, which had also taken shape under the Duc de Vendôme. These tree-lined showpieces are unique in the history of urban planning, given the early date of their construction. Each links an old center that had developed haphazardly over centuries to a section conceived of as wholly new. But while the Cours Mirabeau was a cul-de-sac providing the aristocracy of Aix with a pleasant place to promenade on horseback or in fine coaches, the Grand Cours of Marseilles became a main traffic artery, connected with the Arsenal and the harbor via another tree-lined *allée* running into it at nearly a right angle. The official architects of the city, Gaspard Puget and

Mathieu Portal, were commissioned to plan and execute this epochal piece of urban design.

Between 1667 and 1668, Pierre Puget also presented designs in an intensive correspondence with the city administration, which were rejected. But here, as in the Hôtel de Ville, some of the ideas of the greater Puget became incorporated via his brother. Even though it was not possible to realize all of his concepts in the Grand Cours, its ultimate execution shows the undeniable influence of Pierre Puget. His concept was influenced less by the Cours Mirabeau in nearby Aix than by the Strada Nuova (today the Via Garibaldi) in Genoa, where he had lived for seven years. One evidence of his influence on this project, which had been developed in the mid-sixteenth century, is the motif of balconies supported by sculptural figures of Atlas—a touch that established Puget's fame and spread it as far as Paris by his repeating of it for the Hôtel de Ville at Toulon. In Marseilles it was carried out with great originality. In order to remove the *piano nobile* from the noise of the street, Puget raised it to the third floor, so the Atlas figures along the Grand Cours framed the window directly above the entrance rather than the portal itself.

We know how this splendid street actually looked thanks to the fortunate survival of a model of the city, the *plan Lavastre*. Of the splendid townhouses still standing on the Grand Cours, the two best examples are the Logis d'Auriol (where the Cours meets La Canebière) and the Hôtel de Foresta (at the corner of the Rue d'Aix and Rue Nationale).

Today, the Grand Cours can be seen as the precursor of the great avenues of the nineteenth century. As early as the Restoration and certainly during the time of Louis Philippe (1830–1848), the booming city burst its seams and expanded in every direction. The Grand Cours was closed off to the north in 1833 by the construction of a single-opening *Arc de Triomphe* (see map, p. 26) in honor of the Revolution and the First Empire. Its southern extension was marked by the obelisk on the Place Castellane and the Avenue du Prado. The new arteries of this period—such as the Rue Paradis, Boulevard d'Athènes, Cours Lieutaud, Cours J. Thierry, Boulevard Longchamp, Boulevard de la Libération, Avenue R. Schuman, and Boulevard des Dames—for the most part led into open country. However, under the Second Empire, various streets (e.g. Rue de la République, Place Sadi-Carnot, Rue Colbert) were cut through the old city, inspired by Haussmann's alterations of Paris.

A NEW, PULSING HUB OF MARSEILLES DEVELOPED as an eastern extension of the axis of the old harbor and took the name *La Canebière*. This name supposedly derives from *cannabis* (Latin for "hemp"), for it was here that the ropemakers so crucial to the outfitting of sailing ships were headquartered. The city's *Stock Exchange*, erected here in 1860 (see map, p. 26), is now the seat of the Board of Trade and as such is of considerable importance. The Marseilles Stock Exchange is said to be the oldest structure of its kind in France. In front of it, King Alexander of Yugoslavia and the French Foreign Minister Barthon were killed on October 9, 1934, by a Macedonian assassin.

Musée Cantini

SOUTH OF LA CANEBIÈRE, OFF THE RUE PARADIS, IS one of France's foremost museums of contemporary art, the *Musée Cantini*. This

*Marseilles:
La Canebière
in 1840.*

lively and varied collection was begun in 1960 by an acquisitions committee of twenty art historians, critics, artists, and collectors appointed by the mayor of Marseilles. Their goal was to obtain fine works of twentieth-century art, and by 1973 almost 500 paintings, sculptures, drawings, tapestries, prints, photographs, and objects had been gathered. Both Europeans and Americans are represented with a particular emphasis on art by living French artists.

The collection includes works by such "classicists" as Balthus, Francis Bacon, and Hans Hartung as well as works by Bernard Rancillac, Valerio Adami, and others. The outstanding sculpture collection features pieces using both traditional and experimental media. Jean-Claude Gilli, Niki de Saint Phalle, Jean-Claude Fahri, and Pierre-Alain Hubert are represented along with the Spanish collaborate, Equipo Cronica. The museum also houses the Centre d'Information de l'Art Vivant.

The Musée Cantini, in the seventeenth-century Hôtel de Montgrand, was acquired about the turn of the century by Jules Cantini who bequeathed the building to the city of Marseilles. The mansion opened in 1936 as a museum of decorative arts. Today, though the main part of the building is devoted to contemporary art, an excellent collection of rare Marseilles and Moustiers porcelain is also exhibited.

THE PALAIS LONGCHAMP, DESIGNED BY H.-J. Espérandieu between 1862 and 1869, is a magnificent structure. A Baroque fountain, fed by the overflow from the canal which brings water from the Durance to Marseilles, is flanked by two sweeping flights of steps and two colonnades, which lead to twin pavilions. This picturesque palace houses two municipal museums, the Musée des Beaux-Arts and the Musée d'Histoire Naturelle.

The *Musée des Beaux-Arts* is considered one of the finest provincial collections in France with a collection that is particularly noteworthy for its seventeenth-century paintings. The seventeenth century was a

The Palais Longchamp.

golden period for painting in Provence, and many of the best artists from that time are represented in the museum, André Boisson, Bartholémy Chasse, and Gilles Garain among them. A grandiose altarpiece by Michele Serre depicts the *Martyrdom of St. Peter Véron.* The work, completed in 1676 for the Dominican church in Marseilles, is executed in a powerful style strongly influenced by contemporary Italian painting. Portraits worthy of note include Jean Daret's representation of a magistrate and Laurent Faucher's portrait of an abbot.

Perhaps most fascinating is a group of paintings by the leading Provençal artist of the seventeenth century, the Marseillaise painter and sculptor, Pierre Puget. Puget's intimate representations of the *Infant Jesus Asleep* and the *Madonna Teaching the*

Child Jesus to Read are representative of this artist's formal yet delicate style. Altarpieces by Puget tend to be more dramatic, as the *Salvator Mundi* ("Savior of the world") altarpiece, which was commissioned in 1655 by the Confraternity of the Corpus Domini for the Holy Sacrament Chapel of La Major. A large collection of sketches and finished drawings by Puget are also exhibited on the ground floor of the Palais.

As you ascend the staircase to the first floor of the museum, you will see two allegorical murals by the late nineteenth-century artist, Pierre Puvis de Chavannes: Marseilles as a Greek Colony and Marseilles as Gateway to the Levant. Both suggest the illustrious history of the city and are painted in the pale, pastel shades associated with this artist. The compositions reflect

Puvis's interest in classical painting by their use of monumental figures, idealized forms, and friezelike arrangements.

On the first floor are paintings of the Italian, Spanish, Dutch, and Flemish Schools. French nineteenth-century painting is well-represented with works by Thomas Couture, Gustave Courbet, and Jean-François Millet. Of special interest is a large group of works by the famed early nineteenth-century painter and draftsman, Honoré Daumier, who was born in Marseilles but lived and worked in Paris most of his life. The collection is rich in caricatures and political cartoons, rendered in Daumier's sharp, satiric style. Some fine drawings and prints by this master are also on view.

The pavilion to the right of the Palais Longchamp is the home of Marseilles's *Musée d'Histoire Naturelle*. For the anthropology enthusiast and the nature lover, Provençal zoological, geological, and prehistoric exhibits are on view, as are displays of the lush native flora and fauna. A large aquarium stocked with rare fish is found in the basement, and on the grounds of the Palais is a small zoo with both indigenous and exotic animals.

Gare St-Charles

THE MORE THE NINETEENTH CENTURY RETREATS into the past, and the more historians in our century deal with the preceding one, the more it becomes clear that the nineteenth century was a fateful age that fundamentally upset and changed the face of the earth and the conditions of human existence. It was also the century that set the tone for the technological civilization that appears increasingly threatened today. In France, the Revolution was followed by the First Empire and the Napoleonic Wars, which radically altered the political map of Europe. This period was followed by the collapse of the Empire, the Restoration epoch, revolution (1830), the reign of the Citizen King, another revolution (1848), the Second Empire and colonialism, collapse again, and finally a new attempt at a republic. Accompanying the breaking of these political waves were unheard-of technological, economic, and social advances and upheavals that presented new roles and challenges to art and architecture including the altogether unique task of constructing train stations (comparable in our own century to the design of airports). This kind of building was perhaps the most complex and filled with contradictions.

Added to this technological conflict—namely that of tradition versus innovation (traditional means of transportation versus trains; established building techniques versus the use of steel, cast iron, and glass)—was, on the social level, the drifting of the old confrontation between nobility and the economically and politically decisive upper-middle class. This phenomenon was greatly due to new methods of production and to an increasing democratization of the overall structure and was happening even more rapidly than the Saint-Simonists could have dreamed possible. These challenges and conflicts became symbolized by the train station as architectural assignment, one in which technology, art, and organization were faced with an intoxicating "no man's land." The architects were euphoric. They had an epoch before them that required more market halls, factories, warehouses, train stations, and railways than it did triumphal arches or temples.

The train stations of the 1840s were still conceived of as service buildings for the conveyance of the aristocracy and the upper-middle class. However, the expansive development of the rail societies necessarily tended in the direction of transportation for masses of people, and their opening to the lower-middle and working classes led to the hierarchical division into three transportation classes, still evident even today. The propagation of progress, modernity, and capitalistic daring on the one hand and the inclusion of far greater numbers of the lower social strata required a solution in terms of organization and building technology, particularly in adjunct structures such as entry halls, waiting rooms, and ticket counters. The complexity of the task and the use of new techniques and materials necessarily led to hybrid and unorthodox amalgamations so that, even at the close of the nineteenth century, purists like Huysmans could complain that architecture in metal represented plebeian taste carried to the extreme.

The nineteenth century resolved the problem in its own way. Wherever synthesis was impossible, it responded with addition. In the search for functional solutions, and with their own personal preference for the Florentine Renaissance, Duban, Hittorf, and Labrouste created a true archetype of the French train station of the second half of the century. The area lying in front of the technological core (the train platforms) presents itself in the form of a palace façade of many bays. This served to satisfy the desire for splendor and the railway patrons' consciousness of tradition. Even the stations built at the end of the century, Gare St-Lazare (Lisch, 1887–1892) and Gare d'Orsay (Laloux, 1897–1900), correspond to the type created by Hittorf. The "palace" façade of the latter responds especially to the Louvre, which lies on the opposite bank of the Seine. The juxtaposition is significant for such palace façades can take various forms to suit regional structures and historical traditions. Thus, the classicist airs of the train stations of Montpellier and Nancy, though similarly anachronistic, represent local homage to structures from the past: Le Peyrou and Place Stanislas.

However, the actual cores of every train station, the platform halls themselves, presented an image of modernity and progress. Unadorned, they proudly looked toward the future. Innovation in technology—both in the railway as the raison d'être of the complex and in the use of modern materials like steel, cast iron, and glass—resulted in engineering structures belonging to the nineteenth century, logical down to their last details. Yet here too, references and preconceptions creep in that one would at first assume to be quite out of place. In the multiple naves of the platform hall, the light panels of glass, and the spaciousness necessitated in part by the structures' function, there is more than a suggestion of sacred architecture; and this suggestion is not altogether accidental. Faith in technological progress is, after all, nothing but a profane substitute for religion. The libraries of Labrouste were distinctly conceived as temples of knowledge, just as the market halls of Baltard posed as temples to consumerism. Marx was able to pillory the glass palaces of the world's fairs and the glass arcades as cathedrals of commerce, and on June 16, 1846, Théophile Gautier wrote of train stations: "It would be odd if architecture were not to discover the principle of its renaissance in the construction occasioned by the coming of the railways. Every faith has developed the specific form of its temples. The religion of the century is that of the railway."

However, of all of the ornate buildings erected during the vast spending spree of the nineteenth century, one is of particular interest and significance: the *Gare St-Charles* (see map). Built in 1892–1893, the Gare St-Charles can claim to be one of the very first French stations to do away with the pretense of aristocratic or ecclesiastical trappings and present a solution representing the most up-to-date technological developments. While the contemporary Gare St-Lazare and Gare d'Orsay in Paris perfectly realize the combination of palace façade and modern engineering structure with religious connotations, the Gare St-Charles does not even attempt such a fusion, and therein lies the special significance of this structure. The Gare St-Charles is simply a train station. A low, virtually unornamented, three-part façade

does not mask the glass gable of the platform hall behind it. The terrace in front of the station is in no way ostentatious or imposing. The restrained façade is all the more astonishing given its location on the highest of the three elevations of the city. Its very lack of pomposity is in itself monumental.

Although the station is a purely functional work of architecture, its connection to the city via the Boulevard d'Athènes was a showpiece of urban planning. A splendid flight of steps adorned with sculptures, balustrades, and flower beds—an elegant open-air construction of almost Late Baroque charm—connects the St-Charles hill and the city. This counterpart to the seventeenth-century Grand Cours must be seen.

*T*HE CITY TO THE SOUTH

St-Victor—Château Borély—Unité d'Habitation

VISITORS WHO APPROACH BY SEA ALMOST automatically notice the city's landmark, Notre-Dame-de-la-Garde, as soon as they pass through the narrow opening between the fortresses of St-Jean and St-Nicolas and enter the ancient inlet of Lacydon.

Even before you catch sight of Notre-Dame-de-la-Garde, however, you are bound to be struck by another fortress. With a distinct air of menace, its crenelated towers loom against the less impressive

confusion of urban building. This structure used to be known as the *clé du port* ("key to the harbor"), reminding us that the south side of Lacydon, scarcely settled until well into the seventeenth century, was also protected by a wall. With the construction of Fort St-Nicolas in 1660, this wall and fortress became unnecessary. As a defensive structure, the complex was never of historical importance in any case, for in actuality this martial façade conceals a venerable place of worship, the church of St-Victor. It is all that remains of the once-extensive convent buildings of the monastery of the same name.

ST-VICTOR IS SIGNIFICANT IN THE EARLY HISTORY of Christianity in France. Its site, on the south shore of the harbor directly across from Massalia, served as a quarry for the Phocaeans, stone from which was used to construct the oldest walls in the city. In pre-Christian times (second and third centuries A.D.), there was a necropolis associated with the quarries.

St. Victor has been venerated in Marseilles since at least the fifth century. This Roman officer and convert to Christianity is supposed to have been martyred in Marseilles during the reign of coemperor Maximian (end of the third century) and then buried and worshiped near the quarries. In the second decade of the fifth century, St. John Cassian, friend of St. Honoratus and a cofounder of Lérins, settled near the tomb of St. Victor and founded a monastery of his own. Thus, the convent of St. Cassian in Marseilles is one of the three oldest monasteries in Western Europe. After the fall of Constantine III, a Bishop Lazarus was driven out of Aix and fled to join his fellow bishop Proculus in Marseilles. Ultimately he was also buried in the monastery of St. Cassian. An extensive Early Christian cemetery similar to the one at Arles developed around the graves of Sts. Victor, Lazarus, and Cassian in the third century. As early as 440 A.D., Leo the Great was able to officiate at the dedication of two churches within the confines of the monastery of St-Victor, one honoring the Madonna and the other consecrated to Peter and Paul.

Because it lay outside the city wall, the monastery was particularly vulnerable to attacks by the Saracens, and in the course of the eighth or ninth century it was completely leveled. Only after the Saracens had

The Château d'If: Drawing by Thornton Oakley (1936).

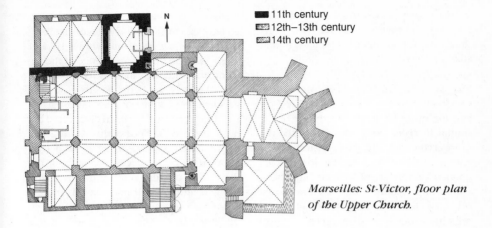

■ 11th century
▨ 12th–13th century
▧ 14th century

*Marseilles: St-Victor, floor plan
of the Upper Church.*

been driven out of the Massif des Maures was a Bishop Honoratus able, in 977, to commission the rebuilding and reconsecration of St. Cassian's monastery. Thanks to a succession of hard-working, exemplary abbots who followed the rule of St. Benedict—Wilfred (1005–1020), Isarn (1020–1047), Bernard (1064–1079), and Richard of Millau (1079–1106)—the monastery managed to surpass even its predecessor in wealth and influence. The first two of these abbots supervised the building of a church, and the later ones were papal legates to Spain, demonstrating the high regard in which the abbey was held by the popes in Rome.

The church built by Abbot Isarn was replaced under Hugo de Glazinis by a considerably larger, Late Romanesque one which is the structure that survives in the present nave. This renovation lasted for at least the whole of Abbot Hugo de Glazinis's term of office (1201–1250) and was probably not completed before 1279. It was considerably larger than the preceding structure, and the entire side aisle required massive

subfoundations. In 1363, after one of St-Victor's former abbots, Guillaume de Grimoard, became the sixth of the Avignon popes, under the name Urban V, a new chapter in the building of the monastery began. The exterior of the monastery church—with its unexpected military appearance—dates from this period.

Though secularized in 1738 and transformed into a college in 1751, the monastery fully expired only after the damages it suffered during the French Revolution. The excavation and reconstruction initiated under Henri Revoil in 1895 was just the beginning of a long process of recuperation.

The lower portion of the exterior wall of St-Victor slants outward steeply, as was the custom in fortress architecture. Above this, the vertical walls are composed of perfectly smooth square blocks of stone with no hint of decoration and with virtually no window openings. At various heights, individual elements of the structure are crowned by battlements.

In accordance with their defensive function, the transept and choir (built after

1363) display a rigorous lack of decoration. The choir walls are as much as 11 feet thick, making its window openings understandably ineffective.

TWO STAIRWAYS LEAD DOWN TO THE CRYPTS, one from the westernmost bay of the nave and the other from the fourth bay of the southside aisle. Here you encounter the more archeologically and historically fascinating part of St-Victor. This lower level contains a warren of chapels, corridors, niches, and chambers that open into each other, all clearly showing that building and rebuilding took place over a very long span of time. The north-south sequence of rooms obviously follows the design of the oldest structure, the memoria or *Basilica*

Notre-Dame. This three-aisle, stone-vaulted basilica with very low side aisles was of quite modest dimensions (only 18 feet long). It stood on the south edge of the ancient stone quarries and was itself partially carved out of the bedrock—its east aisle, for example. Additional graves that date to the third century have been discovered beneath the present floor of this basilica. The church itself appears to have been constructed in two successive phases in the first half of the fifth century, however, and scholars agree that it must have been one of the two structures known to have been dedicated by Leo the Great in 440. It was splendidly fitted out with marble facings and stucco as well as mosaics. In front of the basilica stood a large, high atrium, near-

*Marseilles: St-Victor, floor
plan of the Lower Church.*

1. *Stairs from the end of the
   central nave*
2. *Grotto of St-Victor or St-
   Cassian*
3. *Basilica (fifth century)*
4. *Catacombs and cemetery
   "intraformas"*
5. *Atrium (fifth century)*
6. *Remains of Early Christian mosaics at base of
   arch (fifth century)*
7. *Remains of stucco decoration (fifth or sixth
   century)*
8. *Chapel of St-Hermes and
   St-Hadrian*
9. *St-Blaise Chapel*
10. *Isarn Chapel with tomb
    sculpture (beginning of
    eleventh century)*

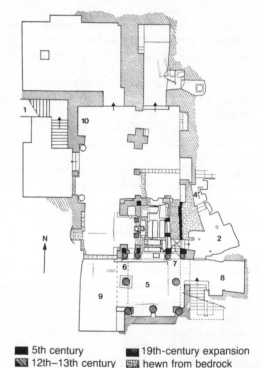

■ 5th century   ■ 19th-century expansion
◣ 12th–13th century   ▨ hewn from bedrock

ly square in outline and presumably roofed in wood. The present atrium columns of different heights are poor substitutes for the monolithic marble and granite columns with splendid Corinthian capitals that were removed in 1802.

The entrance to the crypt of St-Victor lies in the first bay of the eastern side aisle. The relics of the saint are said to be preserved in this catacomb chapel. The capital of the right-hand column, carved directly from the bedrock (probably eleventh or twelfth century), depicts a bearded figure with a bishop's crosier popularly held to represent St. Lazarus. The northern end of this artificial grotto consists of a tunnel-like corridor with more catacombs and a sequence of tombs. The basilica of Notre-Dame-de-la-Confession, the atrium, and the St-Blaise Chapel were all independent structures standing outdoors until the beginning of the thirteenth century. Then, during the construction of the new church under Hugo de Glazinis, they were incorporated into the massive substructure for its southside aisle.

This complex constitutes the largest Early Christian and medieval necropolis in France after the one in Arles. Numerous valuable sarcophagi have been preserved and are now housed in the various chapels of the crypt.

The Abbey of St-Victor houses several important works of art. An exceptional group of sarcophagi carved with pagan subjects is exhibited in the crypts. One sarcophagus represents a scene from classical mythology, the *Forging of Arms for Mars*, and is believed to contain relics of the Holy Innocents. The *Centaur* sarcophagus bears an inscription to Cossutia Hygia and her daughter Julia Quintana, and was reused in the eighth century for the remains of St. Mauront, bishop of Marseilles. A marble al-

tar today preserved in the Upper Church, Chapel of the Holy Sacrament, was probably used in one of the two original churches built by St. John Cassian. It is considered the most beautiful example from a series of early altars preserved in the south of France and is carved with symbolic Christian images.

Medieval objects at St-Victor include a famous wooden sculpture of Notre-Dame-de-la-Confession, known as the *Vierge Noire*. This piece was carved in the late thirteenth or early fourteenth century, and its delicate style and sinuous lines are typical of that period. One of St-Victor's treasures is the tomb of Isarn, abbot of St-Victor from 1020 to 1047. This exceptional sculpture portrays the abbot reclining as if asleep on the tomb's lid. A block with an eight-line inscription is laid over the recumbent abbot as if it were a blanket. The portrait of Isarn is both stylized and expressive, and exemplifies Romanesque sculpture in Provence in that period.

Also housed at St-Victor are several sculptures from the sixteenth and seventeenth centuries. Among them is a bas-relief, attributed to Pierre Puget, that represents *Mary Magdalene Praying* and is kept in one of the crypt chapels.

THE BEST ROUTE TO THE CHÂTEAU BORÉLY IS THE Corniche Président-J.-F.-Kennedy, a shore road which offers magnificent views. The Château was built at the outskirts of the city between 1767 and 1778 by Louis Borély, a Marseillaise merchant. The imposing, three-storied structure, surrounded by extensive gardens which were enlarged in the nineteenth century, on the whole presents a conservative and sedate appearance. Much of the Château's original interior decoration is still preserved. The

A flower kiosk in Marseilles: Drawing by Thornton Oakley (1936).

Salon Louis XVI, the Galerie Parrocel, and the Salon Doré, on the ground floor, all feature sumptuous stucco decorations and ceiling paintings. On the first floor, the Boudoir, the Chambre d'Appart, and the Chapelle suggest the exquisitely comfortable living conditions of the Marseillaise upper class in the eighteenth century.

Since 1862 the Château's ground floor has housed Marseilles's exceptional *Archeological Museum*, which includes important antiquities from Egypt, Greece, Rome, and Provence. The Egyptian collection, among the finest in Europe, began in 1861 with the famous Clot-Bey collection, a gift from the Egyptian merchant of that name who lived in Marseilles. Bronze statuettes, precious jewelry, amulets and scarabs were included in this treasure. Larger pieces of Egyptian sculpture have been added over the years and feature a charming terra cotta, the god *Horus as a Child*. A bronze representation of the cat goddess *Bastet* is rendered in a sinuous, graceful style, and an impressive, black granite sculpture of a goddess holding a scepter and a cross carved with the cartouche of Amenophis III is also of great interest.

Other ancient works of art include a fine collection of Etruscan bronzes (statuettes, vessels, etc.) and figural statues from Cyprus. The Cypriot pieces were acquired from the famous Cesnola Collection which was dispersed to some of the most important archeological collections in the world including the Metropolitan in New York. An outstanding group of ancient Greek vases features examples from the Minoan and Geometric periods. Of special interest are the exquisite Attic red-figured vases with delicately painted scenes from Greek mythology. Works from the Ancient Near East include a richly carved, terra cotta statue of the goddess *Ishtar-Astarte* from Susa.

Today, a particular emphasis of the Archeological Museum is Antique Provence. In 1864–1888, excavations at Marseilles, Arles, Cimiez, Tauroentum, and the sites of other classical civilizations, yielded artifacts from Greco-Roman Provence. Many of these objects are now the prized possessions of the Château Borély. An exquisite marble statue of *Artemis of Ephesus* represents the goddess making a benediction. This masterful work, which may have been made in Greece and brought to Provence, dates from the third or second centuries B.C. The ancient craft of mosaic in Provence is admirably represented by a *Bather* in multicolored stones. This fragment of a larger composition was discovered in the Vieux Port of Marseilles. Finds from Roquepertuse (a site southwest of Aix, near Velaux) are also exhibited in the Borély. Architectural fragments from this once-important Celto-Ligurian shrine include the portal from the sanctuary and a painted lintel. An active special exhibitions program, which has received much international acclaim, presents displays of the art and history of the region during classical and preclassical times.

The Château Borély has not only a wealth of ancient art objects, but also over three hundred drawings (mostly from the French eighteenth century). In the 1960s, the French art critic Maurice Feuillet presented the drawings to the city of Marseilles with the stipulation that they be exhibited in a building from the same period—the eighteenth century. Today, these rare and beautiful drawings are kept in the elegant first floor apartments. Drawings by Watteau, Greuze, and Hubert Robert are in the collection, as well as Fragonard's *Ulysses and Iphigenia* and Boucher's charming *Head of a Young Woman*. Works by Italian artists Tiepolo and Castiglione and Netherlanderish master Pieter Bruegel the Elder are also among the collection's treasures.

FROM THE CHÂTEAU BORÉLY, TAKE THE AVENUE du Prado then turn south at the Rond Point du Prado onto the Boulevard Michelet which leads to Le Corbusier's architectural masterpiece, the *Unité d'Habitation*. The Unité, a large block of flats, was designed in 1946. Here, Le Corbusier's ideas for a revolutionary mass-dwelling unit were realized on a grand scale. With the completion of the Unité in 1952, the concept of apartment houses changed forever, paving the way for the glass, steel, and concrete structures we know so well today.

The Unité comprises 337 apartments with 23 different floor plans. Each apartment includes balconies on both the front and back, and a two-storey living room, which permits an ingenious skip-stop elevator system for the building. The truly remarkable aspect of the Unité is that it is a complete community, including shops and recreational facilities under its one roof. Halfway up, an entire floor is devoted to shops and a post office. The huge roof terrace (43,000 square feet) was planned as an abstract landscape of sculptural forms, and includes recreation rooms, sports facilities, a playground, a wading pool, and a restaurant. This concrete "landscape in the sky" is brightened in spots by polychrome tiles set into the concrete. The Unité is entered through the simple and functional space of the lobby, decorated with an intricate window of brilliantly colored glass.

The best view of the Unité is from the Boulevard Michelet, which affords the picture of the massive building hovering above the ground on its sculptural, weight-bearing pillars. The series of shallow balconies creates a geometric pattern across the horizontal structure and emphasizes the sculptural aspects of the Unité. The exterior design is similar to Le Corbusier's earlier dwelling complex, the Swiss Hostel at the Cité Universitaire in Paris (1930–1932) but is bolder and has a greater sense of the textural. The surface of the Unité, created with poured concrete, was left rough and this texture is further emphasized by the tiny pebbles set into the concrete.

This self-contained community, which stretches upward rather than outward, is a milestone in the design of apartment houses. With its surrounding spacious, landscaped grounds it is, as the architect himself claimed, a "vertical garden city." The Unité d'Habitation, set against its dramatic backdrop of mountains on the outskirts of Marseilles, is both a beautiful, bold sculpture, and a marvelously functional and innovative housing complex.

CHATEAU D'IF

FROM THE HEAD OF THE VIEUX PORT, NOW USED mainly by yachts, motorboats leave every half-hour for the piers of the new harbor basin of *la Joliette* and for the offshore islands of *Frioul* and *Château d'If*. The latter island achieved fame with the worldwide success of Alexandre Dumas's *The Count of Monte Cristo*, whose hero was wrongly incarcerated here. This novel had no factual basis apart from the setting. The fortress has been used as a prison since the seventeenth century, primarily for political dissidents. Its prominent inmates have included the Man in the Iron Mask (whose identity has not been determined definitively to this day), Glandèves de Niozelles, and Mirabeau.

The castle was constructed on orders from Francis I in 1524. Originally intended to protect the harbor, it was fitted out with all the attributes of a medieval fortress. Only a century later, however, it lost all importance as a military structure and was transformed into a state prison. A visit to the Château d'If is an absolute must for every visitor to Marseilles. Even more than Notre-Dame-de-la-Garde, it offers a panorama of the city that reveals its essential char-

acter as a port. Just like Naples and Istanbul, this city's true face is best seen from the sea.

The Château d'If: Drawing by Thornton Oakley (1936).

THE PROVENÇAL COAST

*F*ROM MARSEILLES TO TOULON

*Cassis—La Ciotat—Bandol and Sanary-sur-Mer—Peninsula of
Cap Sicié—Six-Fours-les-Plages—Notre-Dame-de-Pépiole*

THE COASTLINE BETWEEN THE TWO MOST important Mediterranean ports of France—Marseilles, France's greatest trading and industrial port, and Toulon, its military counterpart—offers little of artistic interest. However, it boasts a remarkably varied shoreline, as yet unspoiled by wholesale international tourism, and its Provençal interior is equally well preserved. On weekends, crowds from the two cities flock to this shoreline area, but on weekdays, the landscape is peaceful and relaxing. Driving south along the coast from Marseilles toward Cassis, you will discover with astonishment that only about three miles beyond the Parc Borély, at Cap Croisette, the road abruptly stops. Equally abruptly and steeply the cliffs of the Massif de Marseilleveyre and the Massif de Puget plunge into the sea, forming picturesque, fjordlike bays. This is the coast of the *calanques*, named for these bays, which cut deeply into the rocky mainland. They may best be seen on foot from Cassis or from a boat rented there.

CASSIS, KNOWN IN ANTIQUITY AS CHARSIS OR Portus Charsicis, was surely one of the earliest Massalian settlements along this coast. There have always been important stone quarries here (Calanque de Port Miou) which have supplied building material for Genoa and even the Suez Canal. In addition, Cassis produces a famous white wine. Its enchanting and lively harbor can have changed little since the time of Provençal poet Fréderic Mistral (1830–1914), who celebrated the town in his poem *Calendau*, or since it was discovered by the Fauvist painters Derain, Dufy, Matisse, and Vlaminck at the very beginning of this century. Here, as in Sète and other harbors of the Midi, water tournaments, including events such as jousting from boats, take place in the summer, especially on June 29, the feast day of Peter the Apostle, patron saint of fishermen, between the Quai Jean-Jacques Barthélémy and Quai St-Pierre.

LA CIOTAT HAS ALSO PRESERVED THE IMAGE OF A typical Provençal port. Finds in the Grotte de Terravaine prove that this rocky ridge, which projects far out into the sea between Cap Canaille and Cap de l'Aigle, has been inhabited since the dawn of human history. Of key archeological importance are the grave finds dating from the end of the Neolithic period (3000–2000 B.C.), which clearly indicate a transition taking place at that time from a nomadic hunting existence to a settled, agricultural one. They also reveal the appearance of war in the world. Massalian ceramics from the fifth century B.C. found here attest to early and close contacts between the Phocaean colony of Chitarista and its mother city, Massalia. (The Greek name Chitarista lives on as Ceyreste, a community approximately three miles to the north.)

Altogether, the entire bay between Cap de l'Aigle and La Pointe du Deffend bear traces of dense Roman and pre-Roman settlement. The modern name "La Ciotat" derives from the Latin *civitas*, meaning "city." One splendid find here was a Roman freighter from the late third century, which was carrying a cargo to Provence that included a whole gallery of busts of the emperors and a lead bathtub. When plague struck Marseilles in 1580, all but two or three thousand of its inhabitants abandoned the city. The more resourceful promptly transferred their trading posts to La Ciotat, where shipyards and a deep-sea harbor were available.

Seeing the dramatic cliffs of the Cap de l'Aigle, the bay, and the plain burned to an

View of La Ciotat.

ochre color in summer and fall and lined with rows of palm trees, you might believe that you have been transported to North Africa. In fact, as late as the nineteenth century, people who announced that they were going to the Mediterranean coast in the summertime were often asked: "Why go to the Sahara?"

MODERN *BANDOL* HAS BEEN A POPULAR BATHING resort since the nineteenth century. Together with neighboring *Sanary-sur-Mer*, it forms a sun-filled, cheerful backdrop for what is a tragic story of exile in recent literary history. The Alsatian writer René Schickele moved to Bandol in 1931 for health reasons. Upon the Nazi rise to power in 1933, he urged his persecuted colleagues to join him in the south. Many of them came: Bertolt Brecht, Lion Feuchtwanger, Rudolf Herzog, Hermann Kesten, Erwin Piscator, Ernst Toller, Franz Werfel, Arnold Zweig, and others. For many of them, the Midi was a first stopover on the way to their ultimate destinations in America. Others, though, created major works here including the two Mann brothers. Thomas Mann wrote the second volume of *Joseph and His Brothers* in Bandol, and Heinrich Mann began his magnum opus, the biography of Henri IV, in Sanary.

THE PENINSULA OF CAP SICIÉ, NEAR TOULON, IS archeologically one of the most interesting regions in the *département* of Var, so rich in finds from early history. On its northern side, behind Ollioules and squeezed between the mountains of Le Gros Cerveau and Baou de 4 Oures, are the *Gorges d'Ollioules*, filled with grottoes with Neolithic finds. But the later cultures of the late Bronze and early Iron Ages are also strongly represented. The Peninsula of Cap Sicié was densely populated at this time because

Drawing of Sanary-sur-Mer by Thornton Oakley (1936).

it was rich in ores, which the Greeks and Romans also exploited. At *La Leque-du-Brusc*, the very southern tip of the peninsula, the copper mines were still being worked in Greek times. The dolmen at La Leque, however, points to pre-Greek use of these mines. The word *leque* turns up frequently in names of areas with a considerable number of huge stone monuments. Farther north, for example, in the valley of Siagne, which has a number of dolmens, there is a pass *de la Lecque*. Les Leques, between Bandol and La Ciotat, may have a similar origin, and the word *cromlech* means a row of cult stones placed in a circle. The wealth of ore at La Leque was surely the reason for the founding of the Phocaean settlement of Tauroentum, men-

The Gorges de Ollioules.

tioned by Strabo and suspected by archeologists to have been near present-day *Le
Brusc*. This theory is supported not only by
the fact that a part of Le Brusc is called
Tauren today, but also by recent excavations, which brought to light the remains of
an aqueduct, a Hellenistic wall made of
large blocks of stone, and dwellings of
dried clay and lime. If Le Brusc is in fact the
site of Tauroentum, then it was here, off
the Peninsula of Cap Sicié, that the decisive
sea-battle took place in which Caesar's naval commander, Brutus, defeated Pompey's
fleet, paving the way for Caesar's siege of
Massalia.

ALSO EXPLOITED SINCE ANTIQUITY, POSSIBLY
even before the arrival of the Greeks, were
the iron ores at *Six-Fours-les-Plages*. Directly below the wall of the fort of Six-
Fours, which can be seen from a considerable distance, lies the collegiate
church of St-Pierre. Its foremost treasure is
its location, with a glorious panorama of
the bay of Toulon. Its simple, cubic exteri-
or structure displays an architectural variety that becomes comprehensible when
one learns something of the building's history. The newer and larger church, oriented to the north, was added in the seventeenth century (in the tradition of the
distinctive Gothic of the Languedoc), to a
smaller church, running east-west, dating
from the beginning of the eleventh
century.

You no longer enter through the original
south portal but through the small doorway to the east of it. In the interior, the visi-

tor can see even more clearly how the old and new spaces are differentiated. The masonry and vaulting of the Romanesque church are so advanced for their time that it is difficult to believe the generally accepted dating. The arcaded openings to the side choirs are stepped back fivefold and the abutments outlined. The oculus, a small round window, in the wall above the choir arch and the choir window itself are likewise so clear and precise that one would rather suspect the date of their construction to be the beginning of the twelfth century, a century after they were actually built. Two side aisles flank the nave bay,

and their vaulting runs parallel to the main single-aisle structure.

A semicircular depression on the floor in front of the choir wall marks the location of an older apse wall some eight feet below the present level of the church and possibly belonging to a previous structure from the fifth or sixth century. The altar table, of remarkable size (6.8 feet by 3.1 feet by 7.8 inches), is also attributed to this earlier church. The sixteenth-century polychrome wooden statue in the niche formed by the choir window (now walled shut), depicts St. Peter, the church's patron saint. The south wall of the choir is inscribed

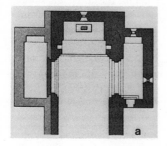

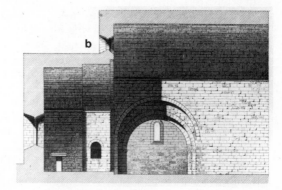

Six-Fours-les-Plages: Eastern portions of the Roman structure.
a. Ground plan
b. Longitudinal section
c. Cross section

with the date 364. Opposite, excavations undertaken in 1967 beneath the west bay floor of the seventeenth-century Gothic church brought to light a baptistry only 6.5 feet in diameter, also dated from the fifth to sixth century. The existence of a baptistry in such a remote church at a time when the right to baptize was reserved exclusively for the bishop raises the same questions as does the baptistry of Notre-Dame-du-Brusc. The mystery of this site is heightened by the presence of Christian grave steles (upright stone slabs) on the wall south of the baptistry, one of which bears the date 369. Was this the site of a building even before the fifth or sixth century?

The newer, much larger structure was built after 1608 north of the Romanesque building. Thus, the Romanesque portion forms the first (southern) bay of the expansion, which was built in a Gothic style unique to southern France.

The church of St-Pierre at Six-Fours contains a wealth of priceless furnishings. Its greatest treasure is the polyptych on the west wall of the Romanesque structure. The contract between the patron for this work and its artist fortunately has been preserved. From it we learn that on August 30, 1520, the artist Jean Cordonnier, called Jean de Troyes, was commissioned to create an altar retable for the church of St-Jean-des-Crottes (to the east of Six-Fours, where the St-Jean campground now stands). The polyptych depicts in two registers a Madonna and Child flanked on the left by John the Baptist and St. Peter, and on the right by St. Honoratus and St. Benedict; the lower register includes a Crucifixion with Saints Martin, Victor, Sebastian, and Margaret.

Also worth mentioning are an *Assunta* of white marble, attributed to Pierre Puget; a wood panel from the sixteenth century; the splendidly framed altar painting behind the main altar, *The Naming of Peter*, by G. Greve (1620); an unusual, highly narrative *Holy Family*; and an altarpiece with a pictorial composition on the subject of the sacred Rosary, in which the central grouping (the Madonna adored by angels, with St. Catherine and St. Dominic) is framed by fifteen medallions depicting in great detail the fifteen mysteries of the Rosary.

(You should check the hours when St-Pierre permits visitors as they are somewhat restricted.)

BEFORE PLUNGING INTO THE LIVELY BIG-CITY turmoil of Toulon, the traveler should make a slight detour to the rewarding church of *Notre-Dame-de-Pépiole*. To get there, first drive along the D 559 back toward Sanary to its intersection with the D 63. After about six-tenths of a mile, turn left onto a small road, easily overlooked, to Les Playes, following the signs to Notre-Dame-de-Pépiole. A priory of Sancta Maria de Sexti Furno is frequently mentioned in the archives of St-Victor and in a document from 1144, is given a precise geographical

Pierre Puget

location, *a ripa Roeppe* ("at the Roeppe River"). Today, in fact, the mountain stream known as the Reppe flows by no more than 300 yards away from Notre-Dame-de-Pépiole.

Looking at this small chapel from the east, one is immediately struck by the natural simplicity of the three apses constructed of rough-hewn, varicolored stone, lined up in a row and tilted slightly as though by the wind. There is something earthy about Notre-Dame-de-Pépiole; it appears to be as old as the land surrounding it. It is generally dated to the fifth or sixth century making it one of the oldest Early Christian structures in France. The first monastic buildings of Lérins may well have looked like this. Yet the apses do not necessarily give the impression of a Christian structure. This former priory church on the Peninsula of Cap Sicié, where ancient ruins abound, was in fact erected on the site of a heathen cult shrine. Beneath the threshold of the church portal, a nearly ten-foot-long sacrificial stone and other indications of the ancient Ligurian culture were discovered.

Though the structure of Notre-Dame-de-Pépiole appears to be quite uniform, its restorers (who did not complete their work until the 1970s) have determined that it was built in three separate centuries. Today, one enters the chapel through the southern doorway, which leads into what, in the eighth century, was a single religious space flanked by two parallel rooms: a martyrium on the left, a sacristy on the right. In the eighth century the structure was expanded to the west by the addition of two bays. At that time, a portico that presumably connected the church and the convent buildings was destroyed. The right-hand altar base is formed by a portion of this last wall. The opening of the side walls and addition of large round arches were not accomplished until the twelfth century.

*T*OULON: PUGET, VAUBAN, AND NAPOLEON

TRAVELERS WHO HAVE ENJOYED THE VIEW FROM Six-Fours have already gotten some idea of the unique geographical situation of the Bay of Toulon. An even better view can be had from atop Mont Faron. But the sight of seemingly endless concrete buildings in the distance should not dissuade the visitor from discovering the heart of old Toulon.

Like Marseilles, the history of Toulon is the history of its harbor, and it is surprising that neither the Phocaeans nor the later Greeks seem to have paid any attention to this bay, so ideally suited to be a port. There are no convincing suggestions that the city existed before the Romans came to Provence. The earliest mention of Telo Martius appears to be in a seventh-century copy of the itinerary of Marcus Aurelius, a source that carries little weight today. Another document, the *Notitia Dignitatum*, dating from the beginning of the fifth century, mentions a *procurator baphii telon-*

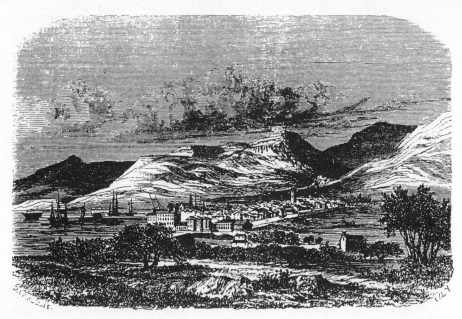

Toulon

ensis, a reference to a state dye-works. The Romans were eager to exploit a quite unique natural resource of the Bay of Toulon: its vast quantities of the murex mollusk, from which a precious purple dye could be produced. Dye was the Romans' chief interest in Telo Martius, and to promote its production and export they established a settlement here with a small harbor as a shipping base, possibly in the early Empire. The dyers of Telo Martius soon discovered that the madder root (alizarine) also yielded the much sought-after dye, even though of inferior quality, and Toulon rapidly developed as a center for the production of purple dye. This radiant pigment was extremely expensive and reserved for the highest dignitaries (emperors, and later, cardinals)—not surprising facts when one considers that between 10,000 and 12,000 murex mollusks were needed to produce a single gram of dye.

However, the etymology of the name "Telo Martius" may suggest that Toulon had a pre-Roman history after all, though not as a port city. The important finds of coins at the sacred spring of St-Antoine at the foot of Mont Faron (from *pharus*, meaning "lighthouse") probably were gifts to the Ligurian deity Telo worshiped there, and whom the Romans associated with their war god, Mars. The name "Telo" developed successively into "Tolo," "Tholon," and finally Toulon.

The history of Toulon as a military port doesn't unfold until the early fifteenth century, when Louis of Anjou used its previously insignificant harbor as a base for his fleet in his attempt to reconquer Naples. When the French royal house came into possession of Provence through inheritance in 1481, Charles VIII took up the Anjou claims to southern Italy and, from then on, the French kings followed an aggressive Mediterranean policy. In 1513, Louis XII commissioned an Italian architect to build the Grand Tour de la Mitre (197 feet in diameter) on the southeast end of the Petite Rade ("small basin") to protect the port, and the admiralty of Provence was transferred to Toulon by Henri II in 1555, although Marseilles was still the largest commercial and military harbor on the French Mediterranean coast. The rekindled desire of the Massalians to break away from France led the French kings to develop Toulon as their chief military port in the region, especially when Henri IV acceded and, later, during the general push toward independence in Provence in 1660. As early as 1595, Henri IV commissioned arsenals and shipyards to produce larger, up-to-date warships here and also made improvements to its harbor (La Vieille Darse). Though briefly occupied during the War of the Spanish Succession, Toulon was further developed by Richelieu for the enlarged French fleet in 1636. In 1660, during a long inspection tour through France, Louis XIV spent twelve days in Toulon and determined to make the city France's permanent military port. He commissioned Sébastien de Vauban to redesign the city, a project that gave rise to what is now called old Toulon.

Vauban was therefore the creator of the new naval base. Pierre Puget, who had been commissioned to submit plans for a new, Baroque Toulon in 1657, lost out. The magnificent caryatids from the old Hôtel de Ville are all that remain of his ambitious plans. This sculptural genius of the south of France in the seventeenth century was stalked by bad luck. His sweeping plans to make Marseilles into a southern Versailles could not be realized for lack of funds, and his plans for Toulon remained equally unfulfilled. After various major contracts had been promised Puget, it was ultimately Vauban, the favorite of the king's new minister, Colbert, who was selected. Vauban's comprehensive Baroque redesign of Toulon was made easier by the fact that a major fire had destroyed much of the old town only shortly before.

Toulon's rise as a military port had a decidedly unpleasant side to it. The great war galleys of the seventeenth and eighteenth centuries were propelled only in part by the wind. The main driving force was provided by thousands of galley slaves who, until they died of sickness and deprivation, were chained to pieces of wood and became a main tourist attraction in Toulon. The scornful gawking of travelers must only have added to the galley slaves' misery. Not only criminals were pressed onto the rowing benches; devout Protestants, opponents of the absolutist regime, and innocent men denounced by *lettres cachets*, or anonymous letters, sat alongside thieves, pickpockets, and murderers. Even when a galley slave's innocence was proven and his release was ordered, as often as not the ships had just set to sea when the messenger of justice arrrived with the papers to save him.

IN THE SPRING OF 1793, THE ROYALISTS' counterrevolution took hold in Toulon. Louis XVII was proclaimed king, and all the Jacobins were thrown in jail. In order to prevent a major bloodbath, Admiral Trogoff had been forced to surrender the port of Toulon to the allied sea-powers under the supreme command of the English Admiral Hood. The reconquest of Toulon became a national priority, a matter of life and death for the young Republic. Not only the harbor but also Fort l'Eguillette was in the hands of the English. This fort controlled the harbor itself and its access to the sea. It was impossible to take the fort by sea, for Hood's fleet lay there, and it could be approached by land only with difficulty. Because of its virtually impregnable position, the soldiers nicknamed it *Le petit Gibraltar*, "the little Gibraltar."

A twenty-four-year-old artillery lieutenant from Corsica, Napoleon Bonaparte, was the first to recognize the key position of l'Eguillette, having determined that the force that held the fortress held the whole city. The new commander of the Republican forces, Dugommier, accepted Bonaparte's analysis. With the few cannons available to him he blasted the English, weakening their resistance, and succeeded in recapturing l'Eguillette. Hood was forced to withdraw from Toulon with major losses. The Republic had won. The pre-

viously unknown lieutenant was promoted to general on the spot. The rise of the great Corsican had begun—in Toulon.

Toulon's role as France's principal military port on the Mediterranean dictated the future of the city, which would not always be rosy. A military port not only protects, but—even when ringed by formidable fortifications—it also attracts any adversaries. In World War II, Toulon was occupied jointly by the forces of the Wehrmacht and the Vichy government. The battle fought by the Allies and the occupation forces over Toulon was murderous, so it is almost miraculous that so much of the old city was spared. Even some of its Provençal charm was preserved. A stroll through the narrow streets and alleys between the Rue Jean-Jaurès, the Place d'Armes, the Arsenal Maritime, the Quai Stalingrad, and the Cours Lafayette is always rewarding, and the walk will reveal that the "old" city is relatively young.

A Tour

WHETHER YOU APPROACH TOULON FROM THE west or the east, the signs pointing to the Centre Ville will direct you to the city's main artery, consisting of Avenue Maréchal-Foch, Avenue Général-Leclerc, and Boulevard de Strasbourg. It is best to park on the spacious *Place de la Liberté* (see map) and explore the old town on foot. From the southwest corner of the Place de la Liberté, the Rue Adolph-Guiol leads to the *Place d'Armes*, a typical example of a French Baroque square. This complex was created as part of the major rebuilding of Toulon carried out under Colbert. The chief architect Vauban must surely have planned to place a monument in the center

of the square, but this goal was never realized.

The Rue Louis-Jourdan leads to the church of *St-Louis* from 1767, whose façade, in the form of a Doric tetrastyle (its portico having three columns), provides an example of academic classicism. In the

Toulon: Map of the Old City.
1. Train station; 2. Place de la Liberté; 3. Musée Municipal; 4. Syndicat d'Initiative; 5. Place d'Armes; 6. Remains of the Old Arsenal; 7. St-Louis; 8. Musée de la Marine, portal by Puget; 9. St-François-de-Paul; 10. Cathedral; 11. Place Victor-Hugo and Theatre.

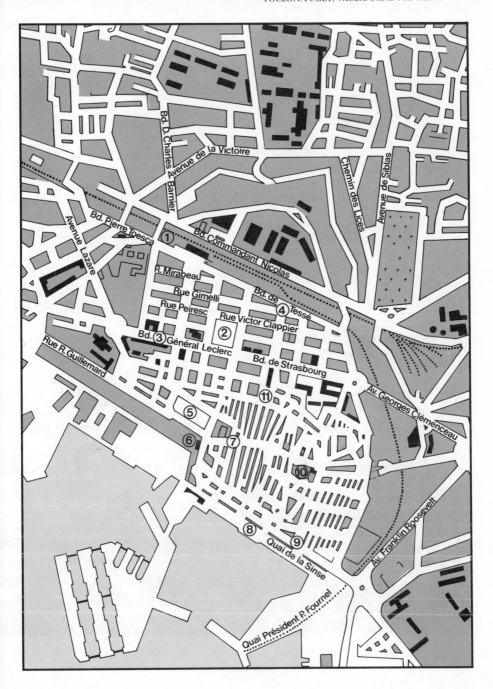

1887 view of Toulon.

interior the narrow frieze is articulated by an alternation of plain metopes and triglyphs (vertically-grooved segments) and separates the repetitious ordination of Doric columns from the dark barrel vault of the nave. The choir wall, dropped down to the level of the capitals of the nave columns, serves as an unorganic, almost violent partition between the dark nave and the light-filled choir rotunda topped by a lantern cupola.

Another street leading from the Place d'Armes is the Rue Anatole-France, which goes straight toward the harbor, passing the remains of the old Arsenal that survived World War II. On the right, two sumptuous Baroque portals give some idea of the structure's original decor.

THE CORE OF THE HARBOR COMPLEX IS THE OLD harbor basin laid out under Henri IV. The bustling activity on the Quai Stalingrad and Quai de la Sinse and in their modern cafés belies the destruction that took place here during World War II. The reconquest by the Allies cost Toulon virtually all of the seventeenth-century buildings near the harbor, the architectural pride of the city including the Arsenal and the Hôtel de Ville. But, miraculously, the crowning treasure of the otherwise totally destroyed Hôtel de Ville, the portal by Pierre Puget (see map, p. 73) survived and now stands on the Quai Stalingrad.

Pierre Puget was born in Marseilles in 1620. At eighteen he went to Italy to complete his artisic training, becoming familiar with Rome, Florence, and especially Genoa. He returned to France in 1645, and his brother Gaspard, a state architect, secured commissions for him. Puget had worked solely as a draftsman, painter, and

Portal of the Arsenal.

The Puget portal.

sculptor in wood before 1656, when he was given the job of decorating the new Hôtel de Ville in Toulon. The marble Atlases that the thirty-six-year-old created shook the art world of his time. The fame of these Atlases reached as far as Paris, particularly impressing Louis XIII's powerful finance minister, Nicolas Fouquet.

This type of portal, flanked by Atlas figures supporting a small balcony in the *piano nobile*, was not original. Puget had certainly seen such works in Genoa (Via Garibaldi, from the second half of the sixteenth century) and in nearby Aix (Cours Mirabeau, begun in 1651). But he adopted this Mannerist decorative form to create a masterpiece of seventeenth-century French sculpture. His Atlas sculptures are not simply ornamental appendages to a showy structure; rather, they are figures bursting with realism and life. They actually carry the entablature of the balcony, with a vitality reminiscent of works by Michelangelo (the Boboli *Slaves*, for exam-

ple). The viewer has a tangible sense of the virtually superhuman effort required of these Atlases. Their heads and bodies display an astonishing individuality. They reminded the people of Toulon of the galley slaves, especially the Moslem prisoners of war, and at the same time, they served as abstract personifications of Strength and Exhaustion. The Atlases alone make a trip to Toulon worthwhile.

AT THE INTERSECTION OF THE AVENUE DE LA République and Place Louis-Blanc (where there is a market every morning) stands the small church of *St-François-de-Paul* (see map, p.73) from 1744, with its slightly curved, two-towered, unfinished façade. Just past it, turn left into the Rue de la Fraternité, which leads to the small but lively Fish Market. Proceed north from here to the *Place de la Cathédrale*. This narrow square is dominated by the eighteenth-century cathedral façade. The dimly lit interior of the Cathédrale Ste-Marie reveals portions of a late Romanesque structure with later additions and alterations. Among its noteworthy furnishings are an *Annunciation* by Pierre Puget; the Baroque rayed gloria (1682) by Charles Veyrier, Puget's nephew, pupil, and collaborator; Corpus Domini Chapel at the end of the right-hand side aisle; and a painting of the *Last Supper* attributed to J. B. van Loo.

On leaving the cathedral, continue west, where the Rue Emile-Zola runs into the Rue d'Alger. Turning right onto the Rue d'Alger will take you through the center of the old city. The nearby *Place Puget* with its exuberant Fontaine des Trois Dauphins (created by Chastel, 1779–1782) is the most intimate of the old city's squares. The larger *Place Victor-Hugo* is dominated on the north by the façade of the pompous theater built in 1862.

*H*YERES AND THE ILES D'OR

Hyères

ANYONE WHO ASSOCIATES A PARADISIACALLY beautiful landscape, a varied coastline, a deep blue sea, a tireless sun, and the subtropical vegetation of the Provençal coast with the Côte d'Azur will find it to be true in Hyères. One of the southernmost cities, along with Bandol and Toulon, between the Rhône and the Alps, Hyères was a favorite spa for the English upper class as early as the eighteenth century, well before the development of Cannes and Nice; the history of tourism along the Côte d'Azure begins in Hyères. The unforgettable view from the remains of its medieval mountain-

top fortress encompasses the Bay of Toulon, the wooded summits of the Massif des Maures, the broad bay of Hyères, the Giens peninsula, and the Iles d'Or.

Hyères was founded in the Middle Ages at the foot of the Colline (hill) du Castéou. The city and its fortress, which like Marseilles had attained quasi-sovereignty in the twelfth century, were finally forced to bow to the power of Anjou. It was a favorite port for pilgrims on their way to and from Jerusalem, and Louis IX (St. Louis) landed here on his return from the Seventh Crusade. It remained popular with British

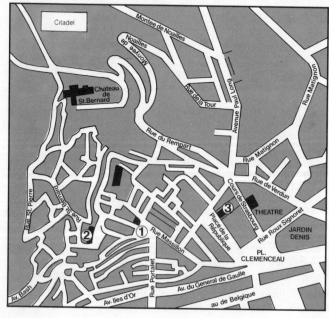

Hyères:
Map of the city center.
1. St-Blaise Chapel
2. St-Paul
3. St-Louis

vacationers as late as the second half of the nineteenth century, when Robert Louis Stevenson, who was frequently sent here by his doctors, wrote of the Mediterranean: "Only once was I happy there, and that was in Hyères."

At around the turn of the century, Hyères fell out of fashion as a worldly winter resort, forcing the city's inhabitants to fall back on their own resources. Happily, nature had provided them with abundant ones: salt along the flat coastal areas (Salins des Pesquiers and Salins d'Hyères), which the Romans had taken advantage of; early vegetables (*primeurs*), fruit, and wine. Hyères also exports palms, subtropical plants, and flowers. Today, this city of more than 45,000 inhabitants has a yacht harbor that is much visited and always full, and the nearby peninsula of *Giens* and the offshore Iles d'Or are favorite areas for day-trippers.

However, tourism is only a secondary industry in Hyères. Thus, the city and its environs have been able to maintain, for the most part, all of the original charms that were bestowed on the Côte d'Azur.

IN THE NEW CITY, THE TWO MAJOR NORTH-SOUTH avenues, Alexis-Godillot and Gambetta and the intersecting Voie Olbia, still represent something of the worldly nineteenth-century spa. The actual old city, though, begins north of the Avenue des Iles-d'Or. It is best to approach it from the southeast through the Porte de la Rade, following the busy Rue Massillon to the square of the same name. Both are named for the court preacher of Louis XIV, Jean Baptiste Massillon, who was born in Hyères (at 7 Rue Rabaton) in 1663.

The most impressive structure on the Place Massillon is the chapel of *St-Blaise*

Hyères, street in the Old City in the nineteenth century.

with its attached tower (see map, p. 78), from the twelfth century. Both are remains of a complex that belonged to the Knights Templar, and today they house the law courts. The nearby collegiate church of *St-Paul* still preserves portions from the twelfth and thirteenth centuries notably its stepped portal which has been heavily damaged. The church was remodeled in the sixteenth century, when its high windows were given the forms of the Flamboyant Gothic style. The low side chapels also date from this phase of construction. Even though the church of St-Paul is open only at quite restricted hours, it is well worth the short walk if only to see the picturesque *Place St-Paul* and its spectacular views.

Of the wealth of religious structures that characterized medieval Hyères, one survivor is the convent church of *St-Louis* on the Place de la République, once outside the city walls. This was once the monastery church of the Franciscan brothers, whose garden lay on the site of the present square. Its construction date is unknown, but the Romanesque façade permits us to place it in the first half of the thirteenth century. On his return from the Seventh Crusade in 1254, Louis IX is supposed to have attended Mass and received the sacrament in this church, which would confirm such a dating. The three symmetrical portals are typical of Provence, whereas the rosette and the arcaded frieze remind us of its geographical proximity to northern Italy. The central section of the three-part façade is only slightly elevated, revealing that the church was conceived as a hall church— one in which the nave and aisles are covered by a single roof. Yet the simple interior, predominantly in the style of the

View from the Place St-Paul.

View of Hyères.

Franciscans, surprisingly contains cross-ribbed vaulting. The bases of the vaults in the central nave clearly show that this vaulting was not part of the original structure; the pointed barrel vault of the side aisles permits us to assume that, as was usual in such churches in France, a similar barrel vault initially covered the nave as well.

HEADING SOUTH FROM HYÈRES ALONG THE N 559, one first passes the hilltop church of Notre-Dame-de-Consolation. This site has attracted pilgrims since the early Middle Ages. The original, ancient statue of Notre-Dame-de-Consolation now stands in the modern pilgrimage church erected in 1957. This structure (architect: R. Vaillant; polychrome sculptures: Lambert-Rucki; glass windows: G. Loir) replaced an older one and demonstrates a concerted attempt to blend ancient rites with modern forms.

At the spot where the N 559 reaches the gulf of Giens and then turns westward stands the isolated and unexpected chapel of *St-Pierre-de-la-Manarre*, possibly dating from the late tenth century. This was the convent church of a Benedictine monastery that was destroyed soon afterward by the Saracens, who erected a lighthouse complex (al-Maner) higher up the slope. The settlement at the foot of the elevation of Costebelle has borne the name L'Almanarre ever since. Graves from the Merovingian period were recently discovered next to the small church.

Finds of Greek spearpoints, Attic ceramics, and Massalian amphorae only a few yards to the west of this church have put archeologists on the track of two cities known in antiquity: Olbia (the "Fortunate One") and, incorporating and lying above this, Roman Pomponiana. Excavation carried out under the direction of M. Coupry has so far uncovered the typical structures of a Greek settlement—city walls, drains, and residential quarters. Two shrines have been discovered, and a marble statue of a healing deity, found in 1909, led to speculation that there were in fact two different cities, a Greek one and a Roman one. The excavations at Olbia—Pomponiana have progressed considerably since then but are by no means complete. The discovery of a Roman city gate leading toward the harbor was the cause for a good deal of excite-

ment. Constructed of massive stones, it incorporates an apotropaic phallus to ward off the evil eye. By Roman times at the latest, extensive use was being made of the salt marshes here, leading scholars to believe that the name *Hyères* is derived from these salt marshes (*aerae*).

Iles d'Or

THE OFFSHORE ILES D'HYÈRES, WHICH THE GREEKS knew as the Stoechades, are remarkable for their beauty. Pliny the Elder, who was familiar with the western Mediterranean, distinguished between the islands of Marseilles, the Lesser Stoechades, and those of Hyères, which he called the Greater Stoechades. The Ligurian name *stoechas* is supposed to designate a specific type of lavender that grows only on the Iles d'Hyères and the opposite shoreline (near Le Lavandou) and was known to possess certain healing properties. The Iles d'Hyères were not given the name *Iles d'Or* ("golden islands") until the sixteenth cen-

tury. The shortest crossing to the Iles d'Or is from the dock at La Tour Fondue, built by Richelieu, on the south side of the peninsula of Giens.

The Iles d'Hyères were separated from the Massif des Maures when the Tyrrhenian Shield sank some 2 million years ago. They were inhabited at an early date, as Ligurian and Greek finds attest. The ancient settlers were followed by Romans, and finally by the monks of Lérins, who were a favorite target of raids by the Saracens. Francis I selected these islands as a royal base for the control and protection of the coastline, creating the marquisate of the Iles d'Or. Al-

Ile de Port Cros: Drawing by Thornton Oakley (1936).

though the inhabitants were exempted from taxation, not enough laborers and farmers lived there. Therefore, the king conceived the notion of protecting the coast from the constant threat of raids by corsairs by commuting the sentences of all criminals willing to settle on the islands. The rocky soil scarcely offered the possibility of profitable cultivation, so the freed prisoners did precisely what their Saracen predecessors had done—they turned into pirates.

Today the Iles d'Hyères are a protected area because of their unusual flora. In 1971, the French government bought up practically all of the largest of the four islands, Porquerolles, for military purposes. The central one, Ile de Port Cros, is a veritable Garden of Eden. Similarly, the Ile du Levant, the easternmost of the group, was once a luxurious garden spot that provided the monks from Lérins with ample produce. Today, though, the island is shared by nudists and the military. For a visit to the Iles d'Or, you must set aside at least a full day.

THE MASSIF DES MAURES

TO THE EAST AND NORTHEAST OF HYÈRES, THE landscape changes dramatically. The rocky coastline from Marseilles to Toulon gives way to softly rolling hills, and the gleaming, at times dazzling brightness of the limestone formations to the west falls into shadow. Even the vegetation appears to change. Everything is several shades heavier, darker, more oppressive—the "dark massive" would be a literal translation of the name *Massif des Maures*. The name of this mountain mass does not come from the Moors, who were better known here as the Saracens, but from the Provençal *maouro*, meaning "dark." Nevertheless, the Massif is linked to the Moors: the dark Saracens, who practiced Islam, were the lords of this mountain range for roughly a century.

The Massif des Maures never reaches a breathtaking altitude. Its greatest elevation, La Sauvette, is only 2,556 feet high. But the Massif des Maures, the Esterel Massif, and the Iles d'Hyères are among the oldest land masses on earth. The Massif des Maures and the Esterel are a single block of porphyry from the earth's distant antiquity. Red and violet porphyry alternate in astonishing color combinations with anthracite, gray gneiss and schist, and green serpentine. As early as the Roman period, these multicolored, primeval stones were an important export item. The unique mineral composition of the bedrock and lime-free water nurture a distinctive flora, and this in turn its own fauna. Umbrella pines, Aleppo firs, cork oaks, Spanish chestnuts, and holly dominate the dense green covering of the Maures and the Esterel. The production of corks for bottles, and processing of chestnuts into *marrons glacés* or unsweetened chestnut purée, are among the main sources of income for the inhabitants of the Maures even today.

THE IMPASSABILITY OF ITS RAVINES AND impenetrability of its band of dense forests made the Massif des Maures, like the Esterel, the focus of countless mysterious legends and also a place of refuge for rebels and outlaws. Lying on important roads, the two ranges became favorite territories for highwaymen demanding ransom money from travelers. The people dwelling along this coast found protection from pillaging Saracen pirates, and galley slaves escaped from Toulon could not have wished for a better hiding place. The two massifs were also an attraction to those who sought solitude. Before St. Honoratus finally settled in Lérins, he had stayed for a time in the Esterel, and later members of the austere Carthusian order followed his example.

After Saracen invasions on land had been stopped by Charles Martel in 732, they came by sea, terrorizing the coastline for hundreds of years. During the ninth century, a number of Saracens nestled into the Massif des Maures, where they established fortified pirate nests (*fraxinets*) from which they could pounce on trading ships between Spain and Italy. But they went too far when they kidnapped Majolus, the abbot of Cluny, while he was returning from a trip to Rome. They further enraged all of Western Christendom by demanding an immense amount of ransom for his return. Demands for a kind of crusade against them could no longer be ignored. Holy Roman Emperor Otto the Great, who had other troubles, commissioned his loyal vassal William, count of Arles, to deal with the problem. Accordingly, William the "Peacebringer" assembled his Provençal barons and knights and, in 973, captured and destroyed the Saracens' main outpost, Fraxinet—the modern La Garde-Freinet. The deadly danger from independent pirate emirates in the Massif des Maures was ended for good.

Although the coastline itself continued to be exposed to attack by pirates for centuries to come, the interior, Provence proper, was able to recover economically and to take part in the development of Western Europe. Count William was wise enough to resist butchering the resident Saracens en masse, keeping them instead as a segregated ethnic group of feudal laborers. Clearly his strict separation of the races was not maintained, for the faces of the people of this stretch of coastline still reveal a strong Arabic heritage today.

Corniche des Maures

THE CORNICHE DES MAURES, THE INCOMPARABLY picturesque shoreline road between Cap Blanc and Cap Camarat, is situated at some distance from the major highways or railroads, and so far has avoided the effects of mass tourism. There are no particularly noteworthy art treasures to be seen along the Corniche des Maures, but a series of small towns are of interest for their evidence of the civilizations at the Phocaeans, Ligurians, Greeks, and Romans. The tiny settlement of *Bregançon*, for example, preserves something of its Greek name, Per-gantion. Here, protected from the feared east wind, Massalian and Roman merchants loaded their ships with lead and granite from mines and quarries in the Massif des Maures. *Le Lavandou*, which still maintains shipping connections with the Iles d'Or, may have been the ancient Lavandula Stoechas. When the German writer Walter Hasenclever settled here in the late 1920s, he was the first foreigner to live in the then modest fishing harbor in years. The ancient Heraklea Caccabaria is presumed to have been near *Cavalaire*, the name *Kakabé* ("horse's head") possibly indicating Phoenician origins. Aristide Briand and Marie Curie were both longtime guests in Cavalaire. Legend has it that *La Croix-Valmer* was the spot where Constantine the Great, while rushing toward Rome, had the vision of a cross in the sky that said to him, "In this sign you will conquer," leading him to his historic decision to accept Christianity. And the fantastically situated *Ramatuelle*—you can enjoy a panorama of it from the Moulins (windmills) de Paillas—has preserved much of its old charm. If one continues eastward along the D 93, one soon has a view of the broad bay of St-Tropez.

ST-TROPEZ

ST-TROPEZ NOW SUFFERS FROM A POOR REPUTAtion, but before "St-Trop," as it is fondly called, became a chic hangout for starlets and would-be artists in the late 1950s and then for hippies and the yacht crowd, it was one of the select spots along the coast. It should be avoided in the summer, but in May, early June, late September, and October a visit is well worthwhile.

It is plausible, though debatable that the name St-Tropez derives from that of the local saint, St. Torpes and it is documented at least as far back as the fourth century. St. Torpes was a Roman officer who converted to Christianity and was martyred for it under Nero in Pisa in 68 A.D. According to legend, his headless corpse was placed in a boat with a rooster and a dog and set afloat. After a journey of nineteen days, the boat came aground at modern-day St-Tropez, where a Christian woman named Calisena discovered it and hid the corpse. The grave of St. Torpes was destroyed during the Saracen incursions. The saint's head remained in Pisa, where it is still highly venerated as a relic in the cathedral.

Modern archeologists tend to believe that the precursor of St-Tropez was the Massalian settlement Athenopolis Massiliensum. In 1951, thirteen gigantic stone blocks of the finest Carrara marble were discovered along the Quai de l'Epi which turn out to have been intended for part of a huge colonnade for a sanctuary of Augustus in Narbonne. The freighter that was to have taken the shipment to Narbonne had obviously been overloaded and sank here in Athenopolis Massiliensum. With the equipment available at that time, the cargo could not be salvaged.

THE HARBOR OF ST-TROPEZ APPARENTLY remained intact for centuries. Even though destroyed by the Saracens in 739 and 888, it was restored each time by the town's determined inhabitants. But when the city was destroyed at the end of the fourteenth century, outside effort was required to revive the port, which was crucial to the security of the coastline. In collaboration with King René the Good, Jean Cossa, the count of Grimaud and seneschal of Provence, commissioned Raphael de Garezzio of Genoa to reconstruct the ruined harbor of St-Tropez and ensure the city's repopulation. Garezzio was a man of action. He en-

Map from Le Sieur Tassin's Atlas *(1686).*

listed sixty Genoese families who were prepared to rebuild the harbor and take over the watch of the coastline, previously the task of the Knights Templar, under the condition that they be exempt from all taxes and feudal levies in future. King René, the count of Provence, consented to the plan, and the French kings continued to honor these privileges until the seventeenth century, when Louis XIV perceived them as a cloud over his status as Sun King and retracted them.

Until that time, St-Tropez had been governed quasi-autonomously by so-called Capitaines de Ville. The fleet constructed by the people of St-Tropez had considerable fighting strength, and it could come to the aid of the neighboring cities of Fréjus and Antibes. In 1637, it even managed to rout a fleet of twenty-two Spanish war galleys.

This victory was the occasion for one of the two *bravades* still celebrated annually. Forty years later, the city passed by marriage from the house of Grimaud to the Marquis Suffren of St-Cannat. In the late eighteenth century this family would produce one of the greatest admirals in French naval history—Pierre-André de Suffren (1726–1788). This "terror of the English" made the world's seas unsafe for two years during the American Revolution.

WHEN FRANZ LISZT VISITED HIS DAUGHTER Blandine in St-Tropez in 1861, the small fishing port had nothing of its later allure, allowing him to enjoy the healthy air in anonymity. A few years later, when Guy de Maupassant accidentally ended up here in his yacht he could describe the place as "one of those lovable daughters of the sea, one of those good, little, and modest towns that are like a shell wet by the salt water, nourished by fish and the sea air."

However, the artist who "discovered" St-Tropez was painter Paul Signac (1863–1935). In his genealogical investigations, this passionate sailor learned that one of his ancestors had been the administrator of the nearly sovereign naval republic in 1590, and his desire to become acquainted with the city of his ancestors led him here in his yacht *Olympia* in 1892. Signac was deeply impressed by the location, the light, and the atmosphere of this untouched paradise (something Gauguin was searching for at just that time in the South Seas), and he decided to stay—but not alone. Little by little, he drew to the spot virtually all of the important painters of that restless period that stretched from post-Impressionism to Cubism. If we run through the list of artists who followed Signac's call, there is scarcely anyone of importance missing: Bonnard, Braque, Camoin, Cross, Derain, Van Dongen, Dufy, Dunoyer de Segonzac, Friesz, Lebasque, Lhote, Manguin, Marquet, Matisse, van Rysselberghe, Seurat, Vlaminck, Vuillard, and so on, and their works are all collected in the *Musée de l'Annonciade* (the former Chapel of the Annunciation). Here you will find works of the Pointillists, the romantic and charming paintings of the Neo-Impressionists and the explosive colors of the Fauves. The crowding of one hundred paintings into two large galleries lends the collection not only a striking density and compactness but also a totally non-museumlike intimacy (it was once a private collection). It is difficult to single out a few works from this unique collection for mention, but doing so will give an idea of its scope and quality.

A small oil painting by Seurat, *Gravelines Channel* (1890), demonstrates Pointillism

The port of St-Tropez: Drawing by Thornton Oakley (1936).

at its peak while later works by Signac, van Rysselberghe, Cross, Person, and Luce reveal the stagnation of the concept. A very different, non-Pointillist Signac is apparent in his watercolors and drawings. *The First Toilette* (1899), by Maurice Denis, shows the influence of Gauguin on the Nabis, a group of French Symbolist painters. Valtat's view of the Esterel (1903) betrays the early influence of Cézanne. Two paintings, Vuillard's *Interior with Two Chairs* (1901) and Bonnard's *Nude before the Fireplace* (1919), are high points of Neo-Impressionist painting; the latter especially is doubtless one of the most luminous and intimate creations in this genre. The long-lasting influences of Neo-Impressionism and Fauvism are documented in late works by Marquet (*Port of Boulogne*, 1930, and *The*

A nineteenth-century view of St-Tropez.

Seine at Paris, 1934), Friesz (*The Garden at Cap Brun*, 1930, and *Dahlias*, 1939), Camoin (*The Canal at the Marseilles Customs House*, 1928, and *The Place des Lices, St-Tropez*, 1939), and Rouault (*Biblical Landscape*, 1935). Derain's declaration that "color became dynamite in our hands" seems believable when one looks at his London paintings (*Effects of Sun on Water*, and *Westminster*, both 1905) or the works by other Fauves, Vlaminck (*The Bridge at Châtou*, 1906) and Van Dongen (*In the Plaza*, ca. 1911). The tremendous effect of the Fauves is shown by their influence, however ephemeral, on a painter like Braque (*Landscape at l'Estaque*, 1906). Three paintings reveal the independent and powerful dynamism of the century's greatest magician with color, Henri Matisse: his still-searching and indecisive *Corsican Landscape* (1898), the explosive and captivating *Gypsy Girl* (1906), and the enlightened, assured use of color in *Interior in Nice* (1920). The sculpture of this period is also represented, notably especially by four bronzes by its chief master, Maillol.

This remarkable collection was assembled primarily by two men. Georges Grammont, a submarine cable manufacturer from Lyons, settled in St-Tropez and became an early champion and collector of "new" painting. The other was André Dunoyer de Segonzac, a painter himself and a friend of the St-Tropez artists. Grammont found a congenial adviser and custodian for his collection in this man. In 1937, Grammont acquired the small abandoned harbor chapel, dating from 1568, hoping to remodel it as a home for his paintings. Dunoyer de Segonzac became its curator. In 1950, the project was finally realized, and the Musée de l'Annonciade was established with the help of the city. Five years later, the collection was opened to the public and its ownership fell to the city on the

death of Grammont, in 1956. In 1961, a band of thieves with a clear knowledge of what they were choosing robbed the inadequately insured museum of sixty-five of its most valuable objects. A year later, however, they were all recovered, and after three years of restoration, the collection—now better guarded—was again made available to the viewing public.

ST-TROPEZ DID NOT ATTRACT ONLY PAINTERS, however. They were soon followed by the multitalented Jean Cocteau and the writer Colette. The latter stayed for fourteen years, living and writing in her villa. We are indebted to her for one of the most articulate descriptions of the old St-Tropez: "It was almost fourteen years ago now that I innocently arrived here in St-Tropez. As you can see, I am still here, and I only rarely go further than the edge of the sea or the edge of the woods....My chief concerns are whether to go walking or swimming, whether to have rosé or white, whether to have a long day or a long night. One's old worries peel away here. The blue that is here predominant is one of dreams, but one that bathes all of reality along the Provençal coast."

Leaving the Musée de l'Annonciade and proceeding to the harbor, the picturesque fishermen's houses seem hardly to have changed from earlier times, but in fact the whole harbor front was leveled during the fierce shelling between the Allies and the German occupation forces in World War II. Fortunately, the people of St-Tropez determined to rebuild the destroyed buildings in the style of a Ligurian fishing village. Along with those of Port-Grimaud and Port-la-Galère, this was one of the few exemplary rebuilding projects along the Côte d'Azur after the war.

In the 1950s, the town underwent a radical change. In 1950, the rising star of the

French cinema, Brigitte Bardot, settled in St-Tropez with her discoverer and husband Roger Vadim. Other film personalities and other stars followed: Charles Aznavour, Juliette Gréco, Jane Fonda, Audrey Hepburn, Jeanne Moreau, Françoise Sagan, to name just a few. Their fans, thanks in part to the incredible economic upswing of the 1950s and 1960s, began to arrive in such droves that the stars fled, no longer feeling comfortable. But crowds still mob St-Tropez every summer, even though the town is no longer exclusive in any way.

The Bravade of St-Tropez

THERE ARE TWO FESTIVALS CALLED *BRAVADES* each year in St-Tropez; one is on May 16–18, and the other, the so-called Spanish Bravade, is on June 15. The French word *bravade* designates a bold, challenging act. The Spanish Bravade commemorates the sea victory of the sailors of St-Tropez over 22 Spanish warships in 1637. Such celebrations are unique to the south of France.

The older bravade, in mid-May, coincides with the feast day of St. Tropes and goes back to 1470 when the spot was resettled by the Garezzios of Genoa. According to one explanation of the festival, the new Genoese settlers of St-Tropez were expected to guard the coast for which they were exempted from taxes. They thus had to be constantly on the lookout and required the most up-to-date firearms. What better opportunity to try out and become familiar with these weapons than the celebration in honor of St. Tropes? The young guardsmen must have itched to hear the explosions from their new guns—after all, noise is a component of every folk festival.

Whether or not this story is true, what is most delightful about a bravade in St-Tropez is the fact that one can still sense the excitement of the participants as the streets begin to be cleared at noon on May 16 and formations of guards start to parade in their eighteenth-century uniforms. At 5:00 comes the shooting and, after official speeches by the mayor and the "captain of the city" (appointed for the duration of the festival), the ear-splitting noise of cannon fills the air.

Naturally the bravade is attended by thousands of foreigners, but it continues to be a festival for the townspeople—a summertime carnival. Its participants, the residents of a city taken over by tourists for more than six months of the year, let themselves go and the piping, drumming, powder-smoke, and noise truly revive the atmosphere of old St-Tropez.

FREJUS

Ancient Forum Julii

THE TWO PRIMEVAL GRANITE SLABS OF THE MASSIF des Maures and the Esterel permit a wide and easy approach between each other to the sea. Here, an extensive plain opens out. This area is extremely fertile, thanks to the Argens and Reyran rivers, which run from the foothills of the Alps to the sea; these rivers also form natural routes into the mountainous interior. Because the land route between Italy and Spain touches the coast near here as well, present-day Fréjus became increasingly important under the Romans and was improved at great expense under Augustus.

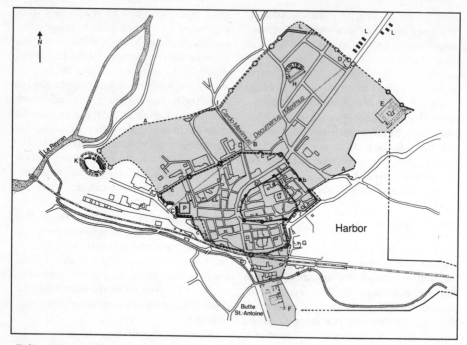

Fréjus: Map of the Roman, medieval, and modern towns. A. Roman city wall; B. Main axis of the city; C. Porte des Gaules; D. Porte de Rome; E. La Plate-form; F. Building complex on Butte St.-Antoine; G. Porte Dorée; H. Theatre; I. Porte de l'Agachon; K. Amphitheatre; L. Aqueduct; M. Lanterne d'Auguste; a. Cathedral precinct; b. Thirteenth-century city wall; b. Expansion of the wall in the sixteenth century.

The Argens and Reyran rivers, though sources of natural wealth, are also unpredictable, frequently changing their courses and flooding large areas. They both used to flow separately into the gulf of St-Raphaël, to the southwest of Fréjus, but today they share a common mouth as a result of a change in the course of the Argens in the seventeenth century and the most recent catastrophic flood in 1959. Thus, Fréjus and its plain bear no traces of their early history, unlike the surrounding hills, which are replete with finds from the past. Only at the Butte St-Antoine have recent excavations brought to light a Ligurian settlement, abandoned before the arrival of the Romans.

It is highly uncertain exactly when the Romans first established themselves in Fréjus. Their settlement, called Forum Julii, was first mentioned by Cicero in 43 B.C. (*Ad Familiares*, X15, 3), and the spot was also referred to in Pliny the Elder's *Naturalis historia*. The harbor here must have existed at the time of the Battle of Actium, in 31 B.C., since the victorious Octavian stationed here the roughly 300 galleys seized from Marc Antony.

AT PRESENT, THE ONLY CONFIRMED ARCHEOLOGI-cal detail of Forum Julii (see map, p. 92) is the course of the *Roman wall*, which dates from the third or second decade B.C. and is older than the rectangular layout of the most important streets, presumably only accomplished in the first decade B.C., whose main axis was determined by the placement of the city gates. The Roman wall describes an irregular polygon follow-ing the natural features of the spot. Some 2.2 miles long, the wall had twelve round towers. Where the most important traffic artery, the Via Aurelia, which led from Italy and on toward Gaul, intersected with the city wall, the gates (Porte de Rome in the northeast and Porte des Gaules in the southwest) are especially impressive. The Porte des Gaules, the better preserved of the two, describes a broad, concave semi-circle, some 164 feet in diameter, whose ends are surmounted by two round towers. The Porte de Rome stands a full 65 feet be-hind two round towers along the city wall. Between these towers and the actual gate is an oval wall. The most thoroughly exca-vated sections of the city are the so-called Plate-forme at its eastern tip, and another lavish structural complex at the southern end on the Butte St-Antoine. These two varied complexes, each laid out around a central courtyard, were formerly interpret-ed as military citadels because of their posi-tions above the northern and southern ends of the harbor. But since they lie with-in the city wall and reveal no additional for-tification, recent scholarship ascribes no military function to them, speculating that they were large public buildings—that they were possibly the seat of the prefect of the fleet and the residence of the provin-cial governor.

Also excavated are the foundations of the theater, in the city's northern quarter.

The 275-foot wall of the *scaenae frons*, or stage facade, had been leveled to its foun-dations. Only the ground walls of the stage, a structure 127 feet wide and 22 feet deep, still stand.

In 1974, the French government ac-quired the large area east of the Porte de l'Agachon to continue excavation that had begun in 1970 with increased intensity and thoroughness. Along with valuable individ-ual finds, all of which have been housed in the museum in the cathedral precinct, these on-going excavations have uncovered two highly important facts about the develop-ment of the city: (1) that the layout of the rectangular street grid of this section was not designed before the first decade B.C., and (2) that the city was not abandoned until the close of the fourth century A.D.

The most impressive structure from Ro-man times, despite its extremely dilapidat-ed condition, is the amphitheater, which stands at the western edge of the ancient city. This monument was excavated by the architect Texier in 1828, reburied in the catastrophic flood of 1959, and uncovered again in the 1960s. With outside dimen-sions of 373 by 270 feet, the oval theater is considerably smaller than the correspond-ing structures at Arles and Nîmes. The inte-rior of the arena, however, is only slightly smaller (223 by 128 feet). Even so, its six-teen tiers could accommodate roughly 10,000 spectators. Since it was constructed at about the same time (late first or early second century) as the amphitheaters at Arles and Nîmes, its exterior façade, which is now missing, may have resembled theirs. But the amphitheater at Fréjus boasted a gallery, consisting of a colonnade covered by a wooden roof, that completely ringed the top. The Colosseum in Rome probably shared this feature, but the Arles and Nîmes structures did not.

Fréjus: Inside the Roman amphitheatre.

An equally impressive structure is the aqueduct, which supplied the city with fresh water from the spring of Siagne near Mons, roughly 18½ miles away. The aqueduct is still standing in many places and may tempt visitors who like to hike to explore the interior on foot.

Although the interior contributed to the wealth of this Roman colony—its products included meat, leather, wool, and cheese, all from its sheep; grains, especially wheat; and minerals, particularly porphyry from the Esterel—the raison d'être of Forum Julii was its harbor, which had been selected, perhaps by Caesar, for several reasons. It was a gateway to important land routes; it lay at a favorable distance from the harbors of Antibes and St-Tropez, which had been

Fréjus: The Porte Dorée (in the southeast of the Roman city).

established by the Greeks; and the port it-self was well situated. A deep inland lake was connected with the sea, only some 1,300 yards away, by a wide, natural chan-nel that the Romans merely needed to de-velop and fortify. The northwestern shoreline of the harbor was roughly identi-cal to the southeastern course of the city wall. From the so-called Plate-forme a pro-tective wall ran due south, and a similar one ran eastward from the Butte St-An-toine. At the Lanterne d'Auguste ("Augus-tus's Lantern"; see map, p. 92), which still stands, the harbor basin opened into a nat-ural channel to the sea. Roman masonry near the base of the Lanterne d'Auguste suggests that it was a fortress built during the Middle Ages from the original Roman stone, with its counterpart on the other side of the channel.

Forum Julii continued to be, along with Misenum, one of Rome's most important naval bases in the western Mediterranean until the end of the first century A.D. As late as 1555, Henri II established a naval admi-ralty here. Finally in the eighteenth century the port was abandoned but there was talk of restoring it as recently as 1847.

The Cathedral Precinct

ALTHOUGH THE ABOVE LISTING OF ANCIENT Roman ruins is by no means complete, Fré-jus is hardly a second Pompeii. Aside from the remains of the amphitheater and the aqueduct, the lay visitor will probably find little of interest in the ruins. The main point of interest in present-day Fréjus is the magnificent cathedral precinct, with its baptistry, bishop's church, cloister, and provost's residence. The earliest known mention of a bishop of Fréjus appears in the list of bishops at the Council of Valence in 376. One of the most important bishops of Fréjus was St. Léonce (419–431), a friend of St. Honoratus. After 636, sources tell us nothing for more than 300 years. Then, after the Saracens had been driven out of Provence, Bishop Riculphe set about restoring the bishopric, and to help him, Count William presented him with half the city and its harbor. Thanks to the resources of the fertile interior and the sea, the which had also been exploited by the Romans, medieval Fréjus was soon able to flourish. Because Fréjus was a reloading point for grain shipments and because of the fairs held here and in nearby St-Raphaël, great numbers of international merchants settled in the city as early as the twelfth century. The privileged Genoese constructed a new city wall in the thirteenth century. This wall surrounded the new town that had grown up more or less immediately around the cathedral and encompassed less than a tenth of the area of the former Roman city.

THE MODERN PLACE FORMIGÉ (NAMED FOR J. Formigé, an important archeologist and ex-cavator of Fréjus who died in 1960) is dominated on the north by an impressive complex of buildings. To see important portions of the complex (the baptistry, the cloister, and the museum), one must join a guided tour (see Museums). Tickets may be purchased in the Provost's Residence (ca. 1200) on the Rue de Fleury . Only the vestibule structure and the cathedral may be seen without a guide. The official tour begins in front of the Narthex Portal, be-tween the baptistry and the cathedral. This

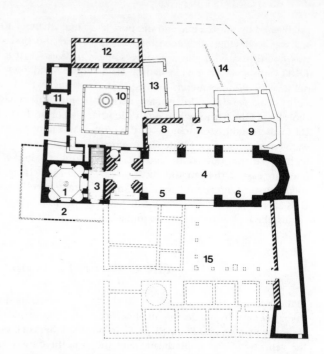

Fréjus: The Cathedral Precinct. 1. Baptistry; 2. Excavated wall surrounding the baptistry; 3. Narthex (mid-twelfth century); 4. Cathedral of Notre-Dame; 5. South wall (eleventh century); 6. Walls and vaulting (ca. 1200); 7. Church of St-Etienne; 8. Church of St-Etienne, first state (mid-eleventh century); 9. Church of St-Etienne, expansion to the east (ca. 1100); 10. Cloister; 11. West tract, so-called Provost's House; 12. Large two-storey hall (twelfth century—museum on the second floor); 13. East tract (fourteenth century or later); 14. Excavated remains of Roman cardo; 15. Map and remains of the former Bishop's Palace, now the Hôtel de Ville.

portal, facing the Place Formigé, dates from the first half of the sixteenth century. All that remains of the original portal is the lintel, which still carries the date it was set in place: April 1, 1530. Also original, but shown only on the guided tour, are the richly carved doors from the same period. Each is comprised of eight panels, the upper ones depicting figures and scenes still very much in the Late Gothic tradition: episodes from the life of Mary, depictions of

Peter and Paul, and portraits in medallions of two unknown figures (possibly donors). The frames around the panels reveal Italian Renaissance motifs. This blend of Late Gothic and Renaissance concepts is typical of the period. The Narthex Portal does not lead directly into the cathedral. Rather, a flight of eight steps leads down to the considerably lower original floor level, dating from the fifth century. The present vestibule between the cathedral and the baptistry may have been the narthex of the earlier cathedral.

The baptistry is believed to be one of the oldest in France, possibly dating back to the fourth or early fifth century. It has a square exterior and a polygonal interior on the ground floor, the customary Provençal form. The base was sheathed in regular square stonework in the twelfth century and therefore the south and west sides no longer display their original appearance. The same is true of the masonry cylinder rising from the fenestrated octagon, which is a hypothetical reconstruction as is the skull-cap cupola. Inside, semicircular conches (niches surmounted by half-domes) alternate with rectangular niches to articulate the octagon. This principle of alternation has been applied in the tambour story (the circular wall which supports the cupola) above, where blind niches of equal size intersperse with the eight window arcades transforming the octagon into a sixteen-sided polygon. The arcade arches of both floors are constructed of alternate layers of stone and brick, a practice typical of late Romanesque architecture.

While the window arcades rest on simple angular pillars, the large arcade arches of the ground floor are supported by eight slender, monolithic columns, six of which were taken from older structures. The capitals of four of these columns reveal similar stylistic features, all suggesting a dating to the fourth century.

Only the capitals of the two eastern columns flanking the doorways betray an attempt to copy ancient models, and these may well date from the time of the construction of the baptistry (possibly under St. Léonce). The extensive similarities between this baptistry and the one at Albenga, on the Ligurian coast of Italy, tend to substantiate this dating. The doorways leading to the vestibule and to the church are of unequal size. Candidates for baptism entered the baptistry through the north door as heathens. Swathed in white robes, the new Christians entered the cathedral through the larger southern portal (triumphal arch) to partake of their first Mass. The actual baptismal font was discovered sunk in the floor in the center of the rotunda. A basin (dolium), also sunk in the floor and excavated, is thought to have been used for washing the feet of candidates, but this hypothesis remains unconfirmed.

ONE ENTERS THE CATHEDRAL ITSELF THROUGH A low, unornamented portal that leads directly into a dark front bay forming a kind of narthex for the Romanesque church; a square tower rising above its powerful vaulting. The lack of ornamentation of the present-day western entrance, the interruption of the south wall in the tower bay, and the triple setback of the right-hand side chamber of this narthex lead one to assume that the original entrance to the church was also here. The cathedral consists of two unequal naves of different dates, each with its own patron. The smaller nave is consecrated to St. Stephen (Etienne), the larger one to the Holy Virgin.

The juxtaposition of two independent churches under one roof is in accord with Early Christian traditions and can be seen elsewhere in Provence at Aix and Apt. The dating of certain portions of the structure is still questionable. Major portions of the south wall of the first two nave bays, for example, as well as the north side of the tower bay and the west and north sides of the church of St. Stephen, reveal an irregular quarrystone masonry that could belong either to the period of the construction of the baptistry or to the tenth century (under Bishop Riculphe?). It is known, though, that the wall pillars and vaulting of the church of St. Stephen and the entire church of the Holy Virgin were built at the same time, at the end of the twelfth or beginning of the thirteenth century. This new, Late Romanesque structure is striking for its rigorous abandonment of any kind of sculptural decoration and its impressive, weighty cross-ribbed vaulting. Formed of perfectly plain, nearly square ribs without bosses—the ornamental projections usually found at the intersections of such ribs—this vaulting becomes increasingly monumental and is found in buildings of roughly the same period in Grasse.

The considerably lower choir apse originally had no window, and the restored choir stalls, originally commissioned by Bishop Juvenal in 1441, are particularly noteworthy. The 1551 panel painting of the Ascension, also in the choir, gives some idea of the fortified bishop's palace. The most important piece, however, is the polyptych by the Nice artist Jacques Durandi above the entrance to the sacristy in the nave of the church of St. Stephen. This well-known master, who with Louis Bréa was one of the chief representatives of the so-called School of Nice, was commissioned to execute this and various other works in 1469 by Antoine Bonnet, a benefactor of the cathedral. These painters, influenced by the Italian schools (notably Siena), created an independent, regional style of considerable strength. The retable, designed in the form of a carved gilt wood altarpiece, is dedicated to St. Margaret and her picture occupies the center of the five-panel polyptych. Above her is a small representation of the Crucifixion. Next to it, beneath Late Gothic ogee arches (ones whose reversed curves near the apex form

a point) are paired figures: on the left, St. Anthony and Mary Magdalene, the patroness of Provence; above them an Annunciation grouping; on the right, Saints Michael and Catherine; above them, Saints Raphaël and John the Baptist. Along the borders: left (from bottom to top) St. Lawrence, a bishop, and Peter of Luxembourg; right (from bottom to top) St. Stephen, a bishop, and a trio of figures. The Mannerist *Holy Family* (1561) by the Roman painter Camillo Salurno should not be overlooked. It hangs on the south wall of the nave.

A STEEP FLIGHT OF STAIRS LEADS FROM THE vestibule to the picturesque cloister, which forms a part of "Le Capitou," the tract of the cathedral's Chapter House. The original entrance to the canons' living quarters lay on the north side of the church of St. Stephen. Le Capitou and the cloister were probably constructed immediately after the completion of the cathedral, or in the first half of the thirteenth century. The light and elegant sequence of slightly pointed arcades, resting on double white marble columns, flows uninterruptedly around the perfect square of the interior courtyard. The fragility of the arcade architecture is in contrast to the weighty cross-ribbed vaulting which was never completed and is visible along the west side next to the wall of Le Capitou. However, it is unlikely that the present coffered pine ceiling was created before the fourteenth century. Although the upper gallery repeats the Romanesque form of the round arches, the stylistic features of the columns (capitals and bases) reveal that these columns were executed later than those of the lower gallery.

In the reconstructed north gallery of the upper cloister is the entrance to the small *Musée Archéologique*. The original Bishop's Palace (fourteenth century) lay to the south of the cathedral. To see the remains of this spacious complex which included a great hall, a private chapel, large and small inner courtyards, a double suite of rooms to the south, and a single one to the east, one must walk around the present Hôtel de Ville, on the Rue Sieyes.

THE CORNICHE D'ESTEREL

ONCE ONLY A MODEST FISHING VILLAGE, ST-Raphaël now boasts more than 20,000 inhabitants, nearly as many as neighboring Fréjus. Though Fréjus used to be incomparably more powerful, St-Raphaël has long since become better known. Even in Roman times, though, St-Raphaël was a favorite residence and resort for the wealthy patricians of Forum Julii. The large casino, for example, stands on the ruins of a lavishly furnished Roman villa with terraces facing the sea, mosaic floors, baths, fish-ponds, and so on. In the tenth century, the area of St-Raphaël, around whose church there was a small village, was presented to the monks of Lérins and St-Victor by Count William of Arles. When the Knights Templar were entrusted with guarding the coast in the twelfth century, they built the simple, functional fortress church that still stands.

Napoleon must have had particularly bad memories of this small fishing port, for each time he came to St-Raphaël, he came in defeat: on October 9, 1799, after his Egyptian campaign had failed, and on April 28, 1814, as a prisoner being sent to Elba. On the latter occasion, his sister Pauline secretly gave him a huge sum, amounting to several millions, that she had raised by selling her jewels in Nice, thereby providing the means for his eventual escape from Elba. The escort that brought Napoleon to St-Raphaël was led by English, Austrian, Prussian, and Russian generals who, as chivalrous victors, accorded their respected opponent with all due honors. The ship that set out for Elba, wearing the Corsican eagle, was given a twenty-one-gun salute.

One of the greatest promoters of St-Raphaël and the entire Côte d'Azur as a vacation center in the nineteenth century was Alphonse Karr (1808–1890). With his forty novels and numerous contributions to *Le Figaro* he was, along with Victor Hugo, Alexandre Dumas père, and Guy de Maupassant, one of the most widely read and best-known writers of his time. His brilliant and bitingly ironic lead articles and commentaries were feared by those they attacked but loved and devoured by *Le Figaro's* readers. His sometimes scornful and wounding comments about the Parisian bourgeoisie were not merely a fashionable pose adopted to increase his readership—he wrote what he thought and felt.

In 1851, he retired to Nice and bought a garden. Karr's pointed quill transformed itself into a rake and shovel. He grew flowers and sold and shipped his favorites. On the garden fence, a large sign read simply: "Alphonse Karr, gardener."

However, he could not lay his pen to rest altogether. Intoxicated with the beauty of Nice—the Baie des Anges, the old town, Mont Boron, and the Promenade des Anglais, which was just then being laid out—he regularly sent letters to his friends and to *Le Figaro* with enthusiastic descriptions of the landscape and people, their lives, and their festivals. These reports were read with excitement, curiosity, and envy and thus inadvertently promoted the Côte d'Azur among the cream of Parisian society and among the merely chic. And they came to visit him.

But he had selected his refuge poorly. After Nice was reunited with France in 1860 (it had belonged to Sardinia previously) and the opening of the rail line from Marseilles to Genoa, it began to turn into a metropolis itself, where the social elite of Paris felt completely at home. Again Karr fled. He wrote to Stephen Liégeard: "If I abandoned Nice it was because Nice has become a metropolis, and if I liked metro-

polises I would go back to Paris." In his search for a quiet, undisturbed spot, he found St-Raphaël, where he withdrew into his villa, the Maison Close. As the name suggests, he did not wish to be disturbed, except by his friends and closest acquaintances, who included Maupassant, Dumas, and poet Théodore de Banville. He was also able to persuade composers Charles Gounod and Hector Berlioz and writer Jean Aicard to come for extended visits. The first to come was Gounod, who wrote his opera *Roméo et Juliette* here in 1865–1866. Later, Aicard wrote his *Pere Lebonnard* in St-Raphaël.

The Esterel

THE LOW RIDGES OF THE ESTEREL RISE UP directly behind St-Raphaël. Though separated from the Massif des Maures by the Argens and Reyran rivers, the Esterel is equally as old, composed of the same minerals, and covered with identical vegetation. Mont Vinaigre, the highest elevation of the Esterel, attains a height of only 2,027 feet, and displays abrupt and bizarre outcroppings and gorges, created by the continuous erosion of 600 million years, that constitute a real barrier for traffic. Inaccessibility, along with a lack of water and topsoil, has prevented the Esterel from ever becoming inhabited. Even in the sagas of the Ligurians, it was considered to be the dwelling-place of fairies and spirits. The origin of the name Esterel is disputed to this day.

St. Honoratus and his companions were delighted with the solitude of these mountains, but in more modern times, not saints but escaped galley slaves from Toulon and fugitives from justice or the exchequer have been attracted by the region's re-

moteness, often supporting themselves by highway robbery. From one of the grottoes of Mont Vinaigre, notorious robbers like Mandrin or Gaspard de Besse used to terrorize the two main routes from Cannes to Fréjus, and travelers would breathe sighs of relief once past the way-station of the Auberge des Adrets. When the twenty-five-year-old Besse was captured in 1781, he was promptly executed with great celebration in Toulon. His head was placed atop a pike beside the road to warn his colleagues and to reassure travelers.

Aside from the indestructible thickets of maquis, the modest cork oak is the dominant tree of the region, but forest fires have destroyed large stands of it. There is so little water here and the summer sun is so merciless that the tiniest spark is enough to cause terrible blazes. When these are fanned by the mistral, there is no stopping them. To combat this devastation, the French government is sparing neither funds nor effort. Each year, large tracts are experimentally planted with all imaginable varieties of trees from Africa, the Americas, Asia, and Australia in an attempt to return topsoil to the Massif des Maures and the Esterel. The oak, native to the Esterel, seems fated to die out since its budding seed first sends a tap root down twenty to twenty-five inches before a first leaf unfolds, and the topsoil is simply not deep enough to reforest the region with oaks. Future generations will experience an Esterel covered with a completely different, highly exotic blanket of trees.

The Romans were excellent road builders, and even the Esterel presented no insurmountable obstacles to them. Their main route, the Via Aurelia (or Voie Aurélienne, the modern N 7), circled this red porphyry block to the north on its way to Fréjus, passing through Les Adrets on Mont Vinaigre. A second roadway led first along the coast, then turned inland after Cap Roux to Vallescure (north of St-Raphaël). Depopulation of this entire stretch of coastline, caused by the Saracen menace, led to the neglect of these roads.

A new coast road was developed in 1903 at the urging of the Touring Club of France. This one, the present-day Corniche d'Or, brought new life to the hopelessly run-down coastal communities. It also enabled travelers to once again visit the village of Agay (Agathonis Portus), a former Greek settlement located on a splendid bay, surrounded by flaming red porphyry cliffs of the Rastel d'Agay. Behind Agay, at the Pointe de Baumette, these cliffs plunge dramatically into the sea. The porphyry quarries of the Cap du Dramont were very profitably exploited by the Romans, but a monumental stone (menhir) at Ayre-Peyronne attests to a much earlier settlement. The hero of Jean Aicard's novel *Morin des Maures* was the droll and eccentric Parlo Soulet, alias Jacou Pouans, an Agay stone-cutter. In a grotto near Cap Roux, St. Honoratus sojourned before finally settling on the island to the east named after him, which is visible from here with the naked eye.

A few years ago the architect Jacques Couelle, the inventor of livable sculpture, constructed his ideal community near La Galère, an extensive honeycomb complex consisting of 416 dwellings. This original settlement is organically incorporated into its surroundings. Even more than the reconstructed harbor of St-Tropez or the totally new lagoon city of Port Grimaud, it represents an exemplary vacation architecture that does no violence to the landscape. In interviews with journalists, Couelle has described the secret of his work: "I am a sculptor, not an architect. I do not try to construct an organism on paper with rulers and compass; rather, I create a true skeleton on which I can study the actual movements of light and shade and the rhythms of natural life. For that reason I also detest the straight line, which does not exist in nature, and those cubes in which people are confined." Anyone who is interested in seeing alternative possibilities for modern building should definitely take a sidetrip to La Galére.

THE CASTLE OF LA NAPOULE, SITUATED picturesquely on a cliff projecting into the sea, was once the feudal castle of the younger, collateral line of the lords of Villeneuve. All that survives from the original structure are three square towers and a gateway. The rest is a romantic and audacious reconstruction by Mr. and Mrs. Harry Clews, the American sculptor who died in 1937 and his wife who bought the former ruin in 1929. Those who have an irresistible yearning for the curious and strange can admire the most unusual works by the most recent lord of the castle by paying a small entrance fee. Today, the castle houses a foundation for French-American cultural exchange.

Of more historical and architectural interest, but overlooked by most tourists, is a railway bridge across the Siagne River, some 500 yards inland. Its elegant curving arches connect the river's wooded banks and could have inspired a painting by Monet or Sisley. Built in 1890, its engineer was none other than the builder of the Viaduc de Gabarit and the tower that bears his name in Paris, Alexandre Gustave Eiffel.

*I*LES DE LERINS

NEAR LA NAPOULE, A PANORAMIC SHORELINE curves between Pointe de L'Aiguille and Cap d'Antibes, forming two splendid bays, the Golfe de la Napoule and the Golfe-Juan, which are separated by the cape of Pointe de la Croisette. Off the cape lies a group of small islands in the glittering sea, the Iles de Lérins.

Ste-Marguerite

THE GREEKS NAMED THE LARGER ISLAND LERO; the smaller one, south of it, was known as Lerina. Today, Lero is called the Ile Ste-Marguerite (about 2 miles long and 1,000 yards wide) and, except for the Domaine du Grand Jardin on its south side, belongs to the government. Light-filled forests of pines and eucalyptus, with broad *allées* running through them, help to give the island a paradisiacal calm. Its present name derives from a sister of St. Honoratus, who, according to legend, is supposed to have waited here humbly and patiently for her brother until God took note of her patience and contrived a miracle that monthly reunited the pious siblings.

Richelieu had a fortress built here that was later enlarged by Vauban. Its most prominent "guest" was the seventeenth century's most famous prisoner, the enigmatic Man in the Iron Mask—the mask was more likely black velvet—who remained here until his personal guard, M. de Saint-Mars, was promoted to Governor of the Bastille in Paris in 1698 and took his charge with him.

Ile St-Honorat: the Birth of Western Monasticism

THE SMALLER OF THE TWO MAIN ISLANDS (ONLY 16,146 square feet in area), sometimes called the Isle of the Saints, officially bears the name of St. Honoratus, one of the greatest figures in Western Christianity.

Honoratus was born in Trier in about 350. His father appears to have served as a Roman consul, and Honoratus was assured of a brilliant career, for Trier was then the capital of the Roman Empire in the West. In 375, the sixteen-year-old Flavius Gratian was chosen to be the Western Roman em-

Ile St-Honorat.

peror in Trier. About the same year, Honoratus, who was roughly the same age and had been a playmate of the future emperor, cast off his splendid worldly clothes. He had determined to become a Christian, and his older brother Venantius followed his example. Noisy, bustling Trier was not the place for Honoratus to pursue his profound yearning for God. Under the guidance of Caprasius (St. Caprais), a wise man well along in years, the two brothers set out on a pilgrimage to Greece and Rome, where thousands of believers had gone to try to satisfy this same longing through asceticism and renunciation. But the accomplishments in the deserts of the pupils of men such as Origen, Anthony, Athanasius, and Jerome impressed Honoratus without convincing him. Such a profoundly egocentric, exaggerated union with God in no way suited his more moderate temperament. It seemed to Honoratus that the proper way and the one closest to the life of Christ was the one taken by Pachomius

and his followers, whose communal life permitted not only the expression of a love of God but also a love of one's fellow men. With Venantius and Caprasius he returned to the West by land. They passed through Camenelum (Cimiez), Vintium (Vence), Vallis Aurea (Vallauris), and Neapolis (La Napoule) on their way to Forum Julii (Fréjus). Two circumstances may have moved them to remain in Provence rather than return to Trier. First, at the time they returned to Gaul, Trier had succumbed to the assaults of Germanic peoples, especially the Franks, and had been abandoned as a capital. Southeastern Gaul, however, was still essentially tranquil. Second, Leontius (St. Léonce) was then bishop in Fréjus. This energetic church leader was on the lookout for missionary spirits who led exemplary lives and had the ability to preach. The three pious pilgrims could not be talked into assuming any offices within the church, but Bishop Léonce seems to have at least succeeded in keeping them in the area, where they might serve as models of faith. They first established themselves as hermits in the grotto of Cap Roux, in the Esterel. But their reputations as holy men and the success of their sermons among local fishermen soon prevented them from attaining the peace they sought.

From Cap Roux, the unhappy trio could see the islands of Lero and Lerina, and they began to consider moving to one. The smaller of the two was reputed to be especially unlivable, even haunted. No one would follow them there, they thought.

The only residents of desolate Lerina, which had scarcely any vegetation because of its shortage of fresh water, were snakes and scorpions. Since snakes are age-old symbols of impulsive fertility and heathendom, Honoratus's first deed on Lerina was to exterminate them.

His second feat was prompted by a problem of some urgency to even the most determined ascetic. Though the hermits could keep themselves alive by eating roots, leaves, and other marginal fare, they could not do without water. Lerina, however, was barren and uninhabitable precisely because it had no fresh water. Honoratus, however, had learned not only how to handle snakes but also how to find water during his sojourn in the desert. He asked his companions to dig into the ground at a spot he found promising, and sure enough, they uncovered an abundant spring, which still provides the present-day monastery with its fresh water and was apparently able to support some 3,700 monks and their gardens and forests in the thirteenth century.

Having transformed the forbidding island into a paradise, though, Honoratus and his companions were no longer alone. He could not turn away the faithful who now descended on him in droves, so he deter-

mined to found a monastery and regulate its communal life, probably in about 410. His chief concern was to create a form of communal living that suited the Western temperament better than the isolated, at times extreme, asceticism practiced in Egypt, while still allowing the individual monk to engage in his supreme task of finding God.

The essential points of the early Western rule that developed here—isolation, acceptance into the community only under certain conditions, obedience, humility, equality of all, charity, silence, work, common celebration of the Mass and common prayer, meditation, confession and punishment of infractions, and dismissal—all make up the basic features of Western monasticism. Even though the monks still lived in separate and scattered dwellings and had a great deal of freedom of self-expression, the arrangement was revolutionary for the following reasons: (1) insulation from the outside world; (2) the assured functioning of the monastery as a result of a discipline applying to everyone; (3) communal Mass and prayer; (4) the abbot's right to name his successor; and (5) introduction of the work requirement. When later combined with the organizational spirit of Benedict of Nursia and Pope Gregory the Great, Lérins would become the standard model of Western monasticism.

Lérins prospered and became famous. Its lands were expanded by countless donations. New monasteries sprang up all over France and were soon followed by those of St-Maurice d'Agaune and Romain Motier, the oldest cloisters in Switzerland. Cities clamored to have monks from Lérins as their bishops. Thus Honoratus himself, Hilaire (his first biographer), and Cézaire became archbishops of Arles and thereby primates of Gaul, Eucher became archbishop of Lyon, and Maximin bishop of Riez. Eucher also had an influence on the early Irish church. He traveled as a companion to the papal legate St. Germain d'Auxerre on his mission to England. Their guide and translator was St. Patrick, Ireland's famous patron saint. Another monk from Lérins, St. Loup, became bishop of Troyes in 451. He so impressed Attila by standing up unarmed against the Huns that his city was spared destruction. Lérins also produced the first consistent school of theology; the writings of bishops Hilaire of Arles, Eucher of Lyon, Vincent of Lérins, Salvienus of Marseilles, Fauste of Riez, and St. Cézaire served as the foundation of later Roman Catholic orthodoxy.

Even though a strict adherence to the Benedictine rule was adopted at Lérins only after St. Aygulf was martyred in 661, the island's role in the development of that order must not be underestimated. The rule had first reached Lérins as early as 575, while St. Virgile was abbot. As archbishop of Arles (from 588) and legate to Gregory the Great, Virgile played a major role in that pope's ambitious policies. The bishop of Avignon, St. Agricola, summoned monks from his own former monastery to help reform his college of canons, which would develop into the congregation of St. Rufus, and Benedict of Aniane was greatly supported by Lérins in his drive to extend the Benedictine reform throughout the land.

The pope charged Abbot Majolus of Cluny with reforming Lérins itself. He and his successor, Odilo, served simultaneously as abbot of both Cluny and Lérins. Under them, Lérins embarked on a period of renewed vigor and prosperity. It received donations of tracts of land in Frejus, Arles, Antibes, Mouans-Sartoux, Riez, and even Ventimiglia. An especially important gift was negotiated in 1038 by the bishop of Antibes. It consisted of Vallauris, Castrum Marcellium (first built up by William of Arles, now Le Suquet), and the small fishing village of Portus Canuae. (The latter two form the historical core of present-day Cannes.)

Thanks to its wealth and influence, the monastery was now able to construct a fortified tower as protection from the Saracens, who still terrorized the sea. Meantime the Isle of the Saints had become a favorite place for pilgrimage because of its numerous relics. In 1298, the monastery provided Charles II of Anjou with some 300 pounds of silver to help him buy horses for his soldiers. He returned the favor by granting shipping rights to the island. As a result, the monastery became so affluent that it could undertake a transformation of its tower into a proper fortress

Iles de Lérins: Elevation, floor plan, and cross section of the St-Sauveur Chapel.

*Iles de Lérins: Floor plan
and cross section of La
Trinité.*

equipped with all of the most advanced comforts. Vauban would praise this structure as a masterpiece of architectural logic. Living at Lérins at this time was Raymond Ferraud, one of the greatest troubadours in the kingdom and one of the giants of the Provençal literature.

The island lost its jealously guarded autonomy in 1464, when the pope appointed Bishop Isnard of Grasse its prebendary abbot, thus making him the actual beneficiary of the wealth of Lérins. Yet even as a prebend of Grasse, Lérins continued to be the major landholder on the Côte d'Azur until the French Revolution. Then, in 1791, the island was bought by Jean Alziari de Saint-Paul. His daughter, a celebrated actress called Sanival, made the monastery her home. Bishop Jordany of Grasse bought it back in 1860 and presented it to the Cistercians of Sénanque, who took possession in 1870. Rebuilding began under Henri Revoil in 1883 and continued until the beginning of the twentieth century. Though the new structures are disappointing in terms of art history, this birthplace of Western

*Iles de Lérins: St-
Pierre Chapel with
the Monastère
Fortifié.*

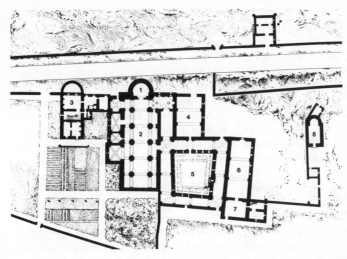

*Iles de Lérins:
Floor plan of the
monastery.*

1. Old apse
2. Main church
3. Mary Chapel
4. Chapter house
5. Cloister
6. Refectory
7. Kitchen
8. St-Porcaire Chapel

monasticism has, nevertheless, been restored to its true function, a tradition dating back more than 1500 years.

ITS FEW SURVIVING ARCHITECTURAL LANDMARKS provide only a glimpse of the former glory of the Isle of the Saints. A modest Archeological Museum has been set up for visitors. Of the seven churches and chapels once strewn across the island, only three still stand: St-Sauveur, St-Pierre, and La Trinité.

The chapel of *St-Sauveur*, on the west side of the island, is an irregular octagon. Extremely simple and only 33 feet in diameter, its regular ground plan is broken on the slightly wider east side by the inclusion of a shallow, nearly semicircular apse. Opposite the choir, there is a simple portal stepped back on the inside. The apse and portal create an east-west orientation for the otherwise symmetrical room. Set into the walls on either side are three identical, conch-type niches. The low cupola rests on a slightly irregular eight-point star resulting from the structure's slight deviation

from a perfect octagon. Prosper Mérimée was convinced that the building was a baptistry constructed during the first flowering of Lérins (fifth–sixth centuries). Modern scholarship, though, tends to date its construction to between the eighth and eleventh centuries.

THE CHAPEL OF LA TRINITÉ, AT THE OTHER END OF the island, is roughly the same age. This crude stone structure—also of an impressive simplicity—consists of two clearly separated spaces: three chapels that form a trefoil at the east end and a short nave to the west, with two broad and shallow bays roofed by stone vaults. A massive transverse arch supports the vaulting and separates the two bays; a simple cornice forms a band which marks the vault abutment. The two slender attached columns, without capitals, continue the line of the transverse arch. A choir arch, the same height as the arches in the apses, divides the choir from the nave. A primitive type of pendentive cupola adds spatial interest to the three-apse choir.

THE ISLAND'S MOST IMPRESSIVE STRUCTURE IS THE *Monastère Fortifié* ("Fortified Monastery"), whose exterior remains intact. However, only the north and west sides of the original square donjon (the tower also known as the keep)—begun under Abbot Aldebert II in 1073—remain. To finance the completion of this first tower, in 1126, Pope Honorius II granted a special indulgence to all contributors and donors to the building. The larger Monastère Fortifié, though more complicated in plan, is striking for its simple forms and solid, precisely joined masonry. The overall use of bossed, convex stones gives the structure a bristling and hostile air. This monastic fortress, also known as Château St-Honorat, was meant to be impregnable, not just to give this appearance. Since the monastery could not afford a standing force for defense against the plundering Saracens, this building had to protect the monks in the event of an attack. The structure's site reveals such an intent; it is placed on a rocky promontory surrounded by cliffs. The only entrance, on the north side (in the corner betwen the older structure and the new one) was more than 12 feet off the ground, and had no stairs. One was obliged to climb a ladder, though stairs have since been built.

Inside this functional building, you are at once struck by the generous and logical arrangement of spaces. Its five floors accommodate monks' cells, a library, refectory, chapel, and all the other facilities that monastic life requires. The expanded structure was probably begun during the twelfth century and not completed much before the close of the thirteenth century. The monastery was connected with this fortress by an underground tunnel, to permit the monks plenty of time to prepare for a move to these quarters.

Its showpiece is the cloister in the center of the complex. From the present state of the building, it is unclear whether or not a third ambulatory was present or planned for the fifth floor. The more luxurious top floor, incorporating what was perhaps a sun terrace, may not have been created before restoration work done in the fifteenth century. The south gallery of the elegant upper cloister opens into a simple Romanesque space roofed by a barrel vault. This is the Holy Cross Chapel, where the countless reliquaries of the saints of Lérins were stored for safety. To the left of the altar, one can discern the niche where the bones of the monastery's founder, St. Honoratus, were placed in 1391; they had previously lain in Arles and Ganagobie.

*P*ICASSO COUNTRY

Cannes—Golfe-Juan—Juan-les-Pins—Mougins—Antibes— Vallauris

"I then realized that this landscape was my landscape."—Pablo Picasso (speaking about Juan-les-Pins in 1920)

IT IS POSSIBLE THAT THERE HAVE BEEN GREATER painters than Picasso in the twentieth century. The name Matisse comes readily to mind. But—without wishing to anticipate the judgment of future generations—if one must name the single most gifted, universal, and influential personality in the broad spectrum of the twentieth-century arts, Picasso must receive the title.

Picasso's giant stature as figure of the century arises from the fact that he managed to accomplish brilliant and epochal work in every field of the fine arts and through a broad range of techniques. In painting, graphics, sculpture, ceramics, even stage design, his influence has been preeminent. Thanks to his remarkable talent, vitality, and inexhaustible creativity, Picasso succeeded in creating works that shocked, even when he was in advanced age. His career of over eight decades has left posterity with an oeuvre of enormous proportions: over 10,000 works. Limiting the study of Picasso to only one of his many paths will necessarily lead to the conclusion that he was a traitor, renegade, or *décadent*, for this permits the whole man to elude comprehension. However, viewed as a whole, his separate phases, works, and techniques are seen as mere facets of what was a single continuum of eighty years' duration. At the same time that he was vigorously exploring new ways, Picasso was capable of reaching back and returning to expressive possibilities that had been temporarily set aside. He would embark on fresh formal adventures in such a radical way that the art world was at times reduced to panic.

Picasso was dialectical by nature. He was blessed with a working economy—it has been compared to that of a highly diversified corporation—that could remember or forget as needed. His passionate destructiveness was countered by an equally passionate creativity. For example, he, with Braque, not only shattered the traditions of

central perspective—which had been valid for five hundred years—but by striving to penetrate closer to an object's essence, created Cubism, a means of depicting various aspects of an object simultaneously. His forward thrusts into new territory alternated with returns to traditional values. Cubism was followed by a serene neoclassicism. Hand-in-hand with his search for the new went a concern for the permanent.

The basic principle of his artistic method of repetition and variation has been compared to the technique of filmmaking, but this is inaccurate for reasons that Picasso himself forcefully pointed out on numerous occasions. They have to do with the concept of development as it is understood and employed in the sciences. A film sequence depicts similar situations in successive segments, each of which lasts only a fraction of a second. But the changes introduced take place in time and lead to a specific end; they develop toward another situation, often one already sensed and anticipated. Picasso's repetitions on a given subject don't arise from a progress toward a new situation; there is no goal anticipated by either himself or his viewers. Each segment is a different situational prognosis of one and the same initial form. In cinematography, someone standing sits down, or two isolated individuals become a couple. The standing and sitting, the separate figures and the couple, are completely different situational entities. In Picasso this is not the case. Though he might work for weeks at a time on the theme of *Las Maninas*, each situation represents a formal variation on *Las Maninas*, and nothing else. Picasso's long creative life does not permit the customary classification. One cannot speak of a "young," or unformed, Picasso as opposed to a "mature" Picasso. His work as a whole merely confirms his own brusque admission: "I do not search, I find.... There is no development in my painting."

There is another aspect of Picasso that is even more puzzling to the twentieth-century person schooled in the natural sciences and attuned to progress. Not only did this titan leave the accepted, seemingly unshakable, formal and aesthetic concepts behind him in total ruin, but—though having grown up in a deeply reactionary Catholic Spain—he jettisoned the moral notions of Christianity, finding them to be threadbare and degenerate from their two thousand years of institutionalization. He refused to accept them as conditions for his own existence in his self-chosen isolation. When Olga wished to be married in an Orthodox church, for instance, it did not upset the Spaniard in the least. Olga was worth a Mass to him if need be. His feelings about human existence correspond neither to Christianity nor to any particular modern philosophy such as existentialism, nor to Marxist materialism. They reach back much further; they are autochthonously Mediterranean, magical and mystical, concerned with life and death, sun and darkness, good and evil. The exorcising function of his most important works has been well demonstrated. In *Les Demoiselles d'Avignon*, for example, or *La Danse*, *Guernica*, and *Le Charnier*, Picasso's comments were unambiguous about this, and this function is responsible in part for the force behind their images, their cathartic, primitive power. Picasso was the only artist who truly understood both the magic significance and the aesthetic value of African art, and only he was able to reproduce its mythic force. He had become a primitive himself; all other interpretations he vigorously rejected. When a young American insisted on viewing the bull's head in *Guernica* as the symbol of Fascism,

Picasso corrected him with the suggestion that the bull is darkness and evil in general, not something specific to our own time.

This same technical power and mythical significance can be seen in the endless variations on his basic themes: isolation (his own situation), the painter vis-à-vis his model (affirmation of himself as artist), man and woman (affirmation of himself as human being) and, of course, the *corrida*, that ritualized battle with the brute (the bull symbolizing untamed nature and the realm of instinct, as well as the evil seen in *Guernica*). Just as "primitive" man employs masks to confront his demons, Picasso used his art as a weapon. Hence the aggressiveness and occasional brutality of his work. He made this perfectly clear in his public statement when he joined the Communist Party: "I am happy to be able to say that I have never considered painting a source of pleasure and comfort; since line and color are my weapons, I have always used them in my attempt to attain greater understanding of the world and of people, so that such understanding might provide all of us with greater freedom."

Matisse always understood his friend's basically magical stance well. Matisse once showed Picasso the silk robe of a Chinese mandarin that he had just bought. When Picasso asked if he could have it, Matisse responded by presenting him instead with a primitive sculpture, explaining: "No, I have something much more appropriate for you. It is from New Guinea, a life-size human figure, something utterly primitive. That is the right thing for you." Returning to Vallauris, Picasso related in a frenzy to Françoise Gilot: "People created these masks in order to conquer their fear and terror by giving form and shape to them. At that moment [in the Trocadero in 1907] I realized that this and nothing else is the meaning of

painting. Painting is not an aesthetic under-
taking, it is a form of magic. It is a way of
grasping power for ourselves by giving
form to our fears and yearnings. When I
comprehended this I knew that I had found
my way."

But art had an even more far-reaching
and profound significance for this "mythical" Picasso: by creating images that
would outlast his physical self he could
also conquer death. The noted Picasso
scholar W. Spies has confirmed that "the
unrest and fear of repetition so typical of
Picasso" were nothing more than a fear of
dying. Thus there was also magic in his dia-
logues with long-dead painters, a "subject"
he worked with increasingly through the
years. In the sequences based on works by
Delacroix, Cranach, Velázquez, or Manet
he was not concerned with the formal, aesthetic study of these masters as much as
with a simple communion with them. His
heroic struggle with death through repeating himself was a dominant factor in his
work for over fifty years.

Prior to Picasso, the Academy had received weighty blows from Realism, Impressionism, Pointillism, and Fauvism but,
with the birth of Cubism, its collapse was
total. Picasso no longer had opponents
with whom to do battle—just himself. His
real struggle with death had begun. It is appropriate that this superhuman battle with
a Hydra with seven-times-seventy heads
took place in a landscape where even today
the Greek hero Herakles is memorialized in
the names of a highway and numerous
settlments as well as in countless sagas.
Like him, Picasso ultimately prevailed, becoming, mythically speaking, a similar kind
of hero for the twentieth century.

Pablo Ruiz grew up in Andalusia and the
Basque country, but he was stamped by Catalonia and the city of Barcelona. He visited

Picasso: Still Life with Table *(ink, 1924).*

Paris on three occasions between 1900 and
1903, and it became clear to him that he
had to live there. It was in nineteenth-century Paris that the important changes in
painting had taken place, and the city was
still the melting-pot of ideas, movements,
and stimuli. Belle Epoque Paris was the
world capital of painting, filled with publi-
cists, dealers, and galleries, and teeming
with competitors and fellow rebels from all
of the countries in Europe. Pablo Ruiz de-
sired to be the salt in this bubbling stew,
and with his move to the Bâteau Lavoir in
April 1904, Pablo Picasso was born. But Picasso never fully became a Parisian. Part of
him remained planted in Catalonia, or at
least on the Mediterranean. Patrick O'Brian
has correctly noted: "When tracing Picasso's career, it is often more useful to concentrate on where he spent his summers,
for it was more often in the south that he

found the necessary peace and solitude, not in Paris, to say nothing of the sunlight; and often it was in the south that he embarked on new paths, only to explore them in detail after his return to Paris."

In 1908, Georges Braque had made great strides toward Cubism in L'Estaque, where Cézanne had occasionally worked before him. Picasso became convinced that he needed solitude to work, and, beginning in 1909, he too regularly headed south. Picasso stayed with Fernande in Horta de San Juan (in Catalonia), then, until 1913, he went to Céret (except for 1912, when he was in Sorgues with Braque). In 1914, he joined Braque and André Derain in Avignon. He remained in Paris during the first years of World War I, but by 1917, his collaboration with Diaghilev's Ballets Russes took him to Rome and Madrid.

Picasso's wife, Olga, had social pretensions and tried to steer her husband to the more fashionable French resorts on the Atlantic. She successfully got him to Biarritz on their honeymoon in 1918, but the next year he headed to St-Raphaël on the Côte d'Azur. In 1920, Olga again coaxed him to the Atlantic coast, this time to exclusive Deauville, but he continued to paint landscapes evocative of the Mediterranean and after only a few weeks he prevailed and came back here. Beginning then, excepting only the years 1928–1929 and 1932, Picasso annually came to the Côte d'Azur, generally staying near the beach at Juan-les-Pins although occasionally he chose Antibes (1923, 1926) or Cannes (1927, 1933). In

113: Menton, doorway and planters (Jon Prime).

114: Eze, angels on a door (Jon Prime).

115, top: Antibes, boy on the threshold (Susan Shapiro). Bottom: Nice, girl with yarn (Carl Purcell).

116: St. Raphael, fisherman mending his gear (John Claridge/The Image Bank). Bottom: St. Tropez, taking the waters (Peter Miller/The Image Bank).

117: Juans-Les-Pins, before the crowd (Morton Beebe/The Image Bank).

118–119: Cannes, sun and shade (Allan A. Philiba).

120, top: St. Tropez, a festive spirit (Gabe Palmer/The Image Bank). Bottom: Cannes, wall on the street (Susan Shapiro).

121: Le Vieux Antibes, the old and the new (Gilles Vauclair/The Stock Shop).

122: Vence, Château St-Martin (Tardos Camesi/The Stock Market).

123: Gourdon, terrace with umbrellas (Bullaty-Lomeo).

124–125: Nice, climbing vines (Bullaty-Lomeo).

126–127: Nice, street scene (Allan A. Philiba).

128: Nice, café (Al Assid/The Stock Market).

the 1920s and 1930s, the Côte d'Azur was still quite idyllic and granted Picasso the solitude he sought. Many people considered the summer on France's Mediterranean coast unhealthy if not downright fatal—when Picasso swam at Antibes, the fishermen were shocked. In 1925, Coco Chanel caused a sensation by exposing her sun-bronzed back to Parisian society.

Picasso liked to sleep late and to sit on the beach, swim, or receive friends until after lunch. He would then work through the afternoon until late at night. The southern sunlight was less necessary for his painting than for his spiritual well-being, his sense of himself. In 1935–1936, he underwent a creative crisis that lasted nearly two years, during which he failed to produce a single oil painting. His separation from Olga and the attendant legal complications coupled with the constant prying of newspaper reporters and the curious became too much for him, and he determined to move to the Côte d'Azur for good. The onset of the Spanish Civil War in 1936 dealt another blow to Picasso. A bright spot

that summer, though, was his meeting with Dora Maar.

An artist of Picasso's stature could not shun Paris altogether. His dealers were still there, as were the critics and galleries. But in the spring of 1937, he again headed south, this time with Dora Maar. They stayed in Golfe-Juan in the home of his long-time friend Louis Fort, the engraver and etcher. When World War II broke out he was staying in Antibes but, fearing for his pictures, he rushed back to Paris. He did not return until 1946, this time accompanied by Françoise Gilot. That year, along with poet Paul Eluard, he got to know the potteries at Vallauris. He also moved into the Grimaldi Palace in Antibes, which enabled him to work uninterruptedly and to spend two of the happiest months of his life. Matisse had moved from Cimiez to Vence, where Picasso visited him increasingly often. In the summer of 1947, he embarked on a new adventure: ceramics. For nearly a year he worked incessantly in Georges Ramié's Madoura ceramic studio in Vallauris. During this period, he bought a

Picasso: Circus Horse *(ink and pastel, 1937).*

villa, La Galloise, near Vallauris where he enjoyed a more settled existence until he separated from Françoise Gilot. When his interest in ceramics waned, he bought an abandoned perfume factory in Vallauris where he was able to revive his interest in sculpture. A junk heap near his villa gave him abundant raw material for what are known as his "ready-mades" (though this is a misuse of the term better reserved for Marcel Duchamp's work). Such well-known sculptures as *The Goat, Woman with Perambulator*, and *Girl on a Tightrope* date from this period. In 1955, Picasso moved to La Californie, near Cannes, with his last companion, Jacqueline Roque; but was still unable to find the peace he sought.

Their escape to the Château Vauvenargues proved equally futile, for that dark heap of masonry with its ancient historical associations merely depressed him; he worked there for only three months. Not until he had bought the estate of Mas Notre-Dame-de-Vie near Mougins did he finally recover his beloved solitude. When Picasso died more or less unexpectedly—on April 8, 1973—he was anything but frail and bent with age. On the contrary, he was working every day, as hard as ever, and planning an exhibition, in Avignon that autumn, of his recent work.

Cannes, Antibes, Vallauris, and other nearby towns offer many attractions, as well as those associated with Picasso.

Cannes

ALONG WITH NICE, MONTE CARLO, AND ST-Tropez, the port of Cannes always comes to mind when the Côte d'Azur is mentioned. The city's annual film festival (begun in 1946), its casinos, and its picturesque harbor—one of the largest yacht anchorages along the Riviera—combine to make Cannes a popular, cosmopolitan resort. This is confirmed by the multitudes of tourists who descend on it each summer.

The origins of modern-day Cannes are believed to be Ligurian. It was perhaps the site of the ancient city Aegitna. We know

The Bocca Wood near Cannes.

Poster for the Cannes Winter Season.

that a Marseillaise colony on the site was conquered by the Romans in 154 B.C. The Romans in turn built a fortified observation post known as Castellum Marsellinum. In the eleventh century, after the expulsion of the Saracens, the counts of Provence turned over to the monks of Lérins the hill called Le Suquet (also La Castre or Mont Chevalier) and the fishing harbor below (Portus Cannis). In 1088, Abbé Aldebert began the construction of a tower on the summit of Le Suquet which was later completed by Abbé Jean de Tournefort. The *Tour du Suquet* still commands the hill above the harbor. A climb to its top offers magnificent views of this celebrated port.

Next to the Tour du Suquet is the small Romanesque chapel of Ste-Anne. This simple church, with its unadorned façade and almost bare interior, has a rich history. Built by the monks of Lérins in the early twelfth century, it served as chapel for the adjoining priory. The church was also frequented by the inhabitants of the village that grew up around the monks' château complex until 1448 when difficulties arose and the residents demanded that a secular priest replace the monks for the parish church. This demand was finally fulfilled in 1648 when a second church, Notre-Dame-de-l'Espérance, was completed next to the small chapel. This date marks the beginning of the older chapel's fall into disrepair until it was almost totally abandoned and

A nineteenth-century view of Cannes.

during the seventeenth and eighteenth centuries the chapel of Ste-Anne and the buildings of the abbey of Lérins fell into complete decay. In 1787, the church was secularized and in 1937 extensive renovations were undertaken.

The single-nave design of the church of Ste-Anne, which is constructed of white calcaire, consists of four bays, a choir, and a semicircular apse. The extraordinary length of the chapel corresponds with the north side of the twelfth-century court of the adjacent château, also built by the monks of Lérins. The pilasters of the sparsely decorated interior are adorned with abstract grotesques typical of the Romanesque. Two altars were originally dedicated to the Madonna and to St. Anne, the first built of stone and the second of masonry. A small door in the westernmost bay of the nave leads to the monks' priory. The simplicity of the church is characteristic of the Provençal Romanesque style for a structure, geometric and sculptural in itself, which served the modest purpose of abbey church.

Beyond Ste-Anne stands the pilgrimage church of *Notre-Dame-de-l'Espérance.* This building, begun in 1521 and completed in 1648, was intended to serve as a parochial church. It is designed in a delicate and ethereal Gothic style and, like St. Maximin-la-Sainte-Baume, is an example of the late survival of the Gothic architectural tradition in Provence. A statue of the Madonna graces the high altar and has been honored by pilgrims since its creation in the seventeenth century. Of particular note among the paintings and reliquary busts which decorate the church interior is a polychrome wood statue of St. Anne dating from ca. 1500, found in the sacristy.

The remains of the château of the abbots of Lérins houses the Musée de la Castre today. This internationally-known archeological and ethnographic collection occupies nine rooms which present a variety of works: portraits from Persia and cylinder seals from the Ancient Near East; objects from Thailand, Laos, China, and Japan including precious porcelain and examples of arms and armor; a magnificent seventeenth-century Chinese Buddha. Two rooms are devoted to works from Polynesia and another room displays Pre-Columbian pieces from South America including textiles and sculptures. The outstanding Mediterranean archeological collection features finds from Egypt, Lebanon, Cyprus, Greece, and Rome.

On the east side of the harbor are slips from which boats leave several times a day for the Iles de Lérins. Just to the east begins the gentle curve of the bay belonging to the fashionable part of Cannes. Its most familiar feature is the palm-lined Boulevard de la Croisette running along the shore. It begins at the Municipal (or Winter) Casino, and at its midpoint stands the Palais des Festivals. This shaded promenade is the place to see and be seen and swarms of would-be stars wait here to be discovered—as Brigitte Bardot actually was.

Picasso first stayed in Cannes in 1927, then worked here during the winter of 1929 in the studios of the Gonzales brothers on a group of iron sculptures he intended to be placed on the Boulevard de la Croisette. The stock market crash in New York and its repercussions throughout Europe gave the stodgy citizens of Cannes a convenient excuse for rejecting the pieces which were not to their taste. The next time Picasso came here, in 1933, the city already seemed too hectic for him and he left sooner than he had planned to. He re-

Villa Brougham, à Cannes.

Cannes: Villa Brougham.

turned again in 1955, when he briefly tried living with Jacqueline Roque in a villa in the residential La Californie section.

Cannes owes its rise as a tourist center to pure coincidence. In 1834, a former British chancellor of the exchequer, Lord Brougham, was searching for a spot along the coast with a mild climate for himself and his invalid daughter Eleonore. He intended to go to Nice, but soldiers at the Var river turned him back because of an outbreak of cholera. He returned to Antibes in his coach hoping to wait out the required quarantine, but since Antibes could offer no suitable hotel he stayed in Cannes instead. The countryside so captivated him that he soon built the Villa Eléonore to the west of Le Suquet, along the road to Fréjus. In that same year France's general inspector of historic monuments, Prosper Mérimée, passed through Cannes on his way to Lérins. Twenty-five years later he returned as a convalescent and ended up staying for the rest of his life. Lord Brougham managed to entice a number of other influential and wealthy Britishers to come to the fishing village of Cannes, for Nice was rapidly growing too populous for their taste.

Stendhal stumbled on Cannes only four years after Lord Brougham and Mérimée had, announcing, "Here one could spend the last years of one's life in peace." He returned for good in 1856. The philosopher Victor Cousin was another early convert. By 1861, when Alphonse Karr wearied of Nice, Cannes had also become too noisy and crowded for his taste, and as we have seen he went to St-Raphaël. Mérimée lived to see the construction of a railway into Cannes in 1870, and he cursed it, knowing that it would spell the end of an idyll, a prediction which proved to be correct. The contingent of illustrious Englishmen was soon joined by royalty including Queen Victoria's sons the Duke of Albany and the Prince of Wales, later King Edward VII; Cannes has long since become an immensely popular seaside resort, no longer a haven for the rich and famous, though it still retains its exclusive mystique.

Antibes

ANTIPOLIS, OR "THE CITY OPPOSITE," MAY HAVE been founded by the Greeks in the late sixth century B.C. To this day, scholars disagree about just what it was "opposite" to—perhaps Nikaia (Nice), a Greek settlement at the other end of the sweeping Baie des Anges, or maybe the hostile Ligurian interior, or even the island of Corsica. The oldest inscription in Antibes is the Stone of Terpon, an oval-shaped piece of basalt some 26 inches long and 8 inches thick, weighing 73 pounds. Two hexameters have been scratched (not chiseled) into its smoothly polished surface. Oddly, though the letters themselves are Greek, they are used in a distinct local variant of that language. It is more or less agreed that the message reads: "I am Terpon, the servant of the noble Aphrodite; may Kypris therefore give grace to those who entrusted me with this task." Many interpretations of the stone's function have been offered. Some claim that it was a simple votive offering in a shrine to Aphrodite; others, citing its phallic shape, have suggested that it was the sign for a bordello. The stone had been set into the harbor wall and was not discovered until 1866. It is now privately owned, but the local *Musée Archéologique* displays a cast of it.

When the Romans took possession of Gaul in the first century B.C., they respected the sovereignty of the territories belonging to the Phocaean Massalians, including Nice and Monaco. However, at a number of strategically important spots on the Mediterranean they established settlements of their own as bases for their coastal fleet, including Antibes. It became, along with Fréjus, one of the chief bases between Italy and Arles, enjoying the extraordinary advantage of being a *civitas romana* instead of a

mere colony. Thus it was subject directly to Rome, rather than to the colonial administration. Antipolis continued to serve as a fleet base and a port city for the rich inland areas near Grasse and Vence.

Antibes is known to have had its own bishop by at least the middle of the fifth century. After the collapse of the Roman Empire in the West and centuries of Saracen attacks, Count William of Arles presented the bishopric of Antibes and portions of that of Vence to Rodoard, the founder of the ruling dynasty of Grasse. But his successors were unable to hold on to these territories. Feudal rights to Antibes passed in part to Lérins and in part to the bishop of Antibes. In 1244, the bishop's seat was moved to Grasse, and Antibes, having only recently begun to revive, was left to die slowly. The county of Nice fell to Savoy in 1388. Then, in 1482, Provence was deeded by inheritance to the royal house of France. Antibes (in France) and Nice (in Savoy) became border cities, grains of sand between two powerful millstones. Bitter struggles between France and Savoy meant that Antibes was repeatedly built up, fortified, and then destroyed. After three centuries, virtually nothing was left of either the Roman or the medieval city.

Expansion of the harbor and its fortifications was begun under Henri II. The grandiose plans included the establishment of the bastion of Fort Carré to the north of the port; accomplished between 1550 and 1578 by St-Rémy, from plans by d'Evrard and Chatillon, the predecessor of Vauban. Later, after Vauban himself had presented a detailed inspection report, Louis XIV determined to enlarge and improve the facilities constructed under Henri II, entrusting the work to Colbert and the marquis de

Antibes as seen from Fort Carré.

Louvois. The last remains of ancient buildings were swept away by these far-reaching measures. It is unclear whether or not the plans were designed by Vauban himself; the architect who actually carried them out was Niquet. In layout, this enlarged seventeenth-century Fort Carré represents the ideal Baroque fortress. Radiating outward from the circular core structure of St-Hilaire are four main bastions ending in sharp points; between these are four smaller bastions. The result is an eight-pointed star that is virtually impervious to attack.

In 1794, when Napoleon Bonaparte—a former artillery lieutenant recently promoted to general for his service at Toulon—was entrusted with the protection of France's Mediterranean coastline, he chose this fort as his base. When he returned from exile in Elba twenty-one years later, he landed in nearby Golfe-Juan. This was the prelude to an ironic anecdote: On the very same day—March 1, 1815 at 5:00 P.M.—scouts in the service of the deposed emperor seized a coach traveling eastward. In it were three women and a man who claimed to be the prince of Monaco. As it happened, Louis XVIII had just returned to the prince of Monaco his title and possessions, taken from him by the Republic. The prince, Honoré III, was rushing back to reclaim his principality and was convinced that he had fallen into the hands of highwaymen, a perfectly logical assumption in those times. He was brought to the scouts' superior, who asked where Honoré was going. He replied: "I am returning home to reclaim my throne." "I too," responded the presumed ringleader of the highwaymen: Napoleon. He ordered that the captive be allowed to continue on his way.

ANTIBES'S PARISH CHURCH STILL PRESERVES THE eastern portions of a former cathedral: its plain Romanesque choir and transept with apses. The present-day nave was built in the seventeenth century and its façade features such Baroque elements as a projecting portal with a round window above it, a niche for a statue, and a prominent cornice. The rather sterile interior houses a Rosary altarpiece in the right transept with a retable (1515) attributed to Louis Bréa. Unfortunately the middle panel has been quite clumsily restored. Around it the mysteries of the rosary are depicted in fifteen scenes. The predella (a horizontal panel appended to the base of the altarpiece) depicts three additional miracles of the rosary. A noteworthy wooden crucifix from 1447 hangs next to the apse on the north side.

Grimaldi Palace (Musée Picasso)

THE GRIMALDI PALACE, SET ON A HILL overlooking the port of Antibes, once belonged to the bishop of Grasse, who, at the time of the great schism in the Catholic Church, supported the pope in Rome rather than the one in Avignon. In 1383, Queen Jeanne punished him for this by confiscating his possessions in Antibes and presenting them to two exiled Genoese, Luca and Marco Grimaldi, who promptly moved into the pleasantly-situated bishop's palace and renamed the castle crowning the hill the Grimaldi Palace (or Château Grimaldi). The rectangular structure faces the Mediterranean and the bustling, yacht-filled port of Antibes. Its square watchtower, constructed in the twelfth century out of massive stone blocks, was once part of the building's fortifications. The city of Antibes acquired the palace in 1927, and transformed it into a museum. Unfortunately, the small collection of artifacts, pottery, and other works only filled portions of the expansive ground floor until after the Second World War.

Picasso enthusiastically returned to his beloved southern France in the summer of 1946 after a long and involuntary absence. France was recovering from the devastation of war; Picasso had recently joined the newly formed Communist Party; and he was accompanied by his new companion, Françoise Gilot. They were living on the second floor of a house at Golfe-Juan when the sculptor and photographer Sima visited and Picasso complained of his limited studio space. Sima told him of a perfect place, the upper floors of the museum at Antibes. Picasso contacted the museum's director, Jules César Romuald Dor de la Souchère, and a few days later Dor de la Souchère personally arrived to present a proposal that Picasso set up his studio at the Grimaldi Palace which Picasso happily accepted after a brief inspection of the premises.

Picasso began to paint in his new studio in July or August 1946 and continued through November when he returned to Paris after his summer "vacation." At Antibes he produced marvelous large-scale works with materials that were unusual but made necessary by postwar shortages of canvas and paint: asbestos board, plywood and boat paints the same as those on the bright fishing smacks in the harbor of Antibes. The light of the Mediterranean and the large spaces of the palace inspired the luminous, grand works. When Picasso left Antibes he also left every work he had created during his stay there.

Dor de la Souchère suggested that Picasso donate these paintings to the small museum but instead the artist agreed to establish a separate museum with the paintings on permanent loan. Picasso also added drawings and ceramics, and the collector Marie Cuttoli donated tapestries and lithographs from the same period. In 1947, Picasso presented his *Odysseus and the Sirens,* a large painting with a subject inspired by classical antiquity, the theme common to all of his Antibes paintings. Picasso himself designed the installation of the works. Its paintings, ceramics, drawings, oil paintings on paper, lithographs, wall tapestry and sculptures make the museum a unique glimpse of this late phase in the development of this artist. The works are never loaned to other institutions so that, as the artist wished, "if you want to see the Picassos of Antibes you will simply have to come to Antibes."

The collection presents joyous subjects which stem from the artist's love of life, nature and the people around him. Picasso's monumental painting from the *Antipolis* series is the famous *Joie de Vivre.* This work on fibro-cement, stretching over 98 inches in length and over 47 inches in height, expresses the pagan spirit of a bacchanalia. The horizontal arrangement, reminiscent of classical painting, depicts a centaur playing a flute as a full-breasted Maenad dances, two fauns leap about and a seated satyr plays a panpipe. The large triptych *Satyr, Faun, and Centaur* is executed in a linear style like the pictorial bands on Greek vases. Picasso also painted scenes of the everyday life around him. For example, the *Gobbler of Sea Urchins* represents a sailor in his blue-striped shirt eating a fresh shellfish.

In a conversation with Dor de la Souchère after the formation of the Musée Picasso, the artist commented:

Basically all things are original creations. When we began, none of us knew what we would actually produce. If you [Dor de la Souchère] had said to me at the time that we would create a museum I would not have come. But you said, here is a studio for you. You yourself did not know what would come of it, and something came of it precisely because you did *not* set out to imitate a museum. That is the truth of the matter.

Vallauris

NEAR VALLAURIS, ON THE NEARBY PLATEAU OF Encourdoules, the remains of a Celto-Ligurian community give evidence of one of the oldest settlements in the region. The Romans drove out the native population in about 150 A.D. and established a fortress of their own. The last inhabitants abandoned the plateau after the destruction wreaked by the Goths and Vandals, settling in the valley below. When the gorse is in bloom, this valley seems carpeted with yellow blossoms, and the settlers therefore called their new home Vallis Aurea ("golden valley").

In spite of its poetic name, Vallis Aurea suffered further devastation at the hands of the Saracens. Then, in 1038, it came into the possession of the monks of Lérins. They established an agricultural estate with a church on the site of the present-day castle. Sacked again by Raymond de Turenne in 1364 and depopulated by plague in

1480, the spot was declared uninhabitable and abandoned. In 1501, it was resettled by seventy Italian families at the instigation of Augustin of Grimaldi, the bishop of Grasse and prebendary abbot of Lérins. These settlers were all potters from Ventimiglia and Albissola. The bishop himself drew up the plans for the new city. Like most communities in the south of France, its streets would intersect at right angles, and there would be a rectangular central square.

The site's rich supply of clay and marl, its extensive forests, which provide fuel for kilns, and its proximity both to the Via Aurelia (or Voie Aurélienne) and the harbor of Antibes, had made Vallauris one of the pottery-making centers in France since Roman days. Thus its resettlement by potters in the sixteenth century was consistent with an ancient tradition. Since the local clay is relatively coarse and rich in lime, it was only possible to produce rather simple, heavy kitchenware here (called *la culinaire*). The advent of industrialization in the nineteenth century, and the resultant increase in the production of metal products, presented a stiff challenge to the craftsmen of Vallauris. But even between the two world wars, Vallauris still boasted nearly 40 ceramic workshops employing roughly 1,500 people. Only the spread of aluminum ware after World War II finally spelled the ruin of the traditional craft. The twenty-odd workshops that survived the war lost customers and faced insolvency.

This was the situation in August 1946, when the Ramiés, the owners of the Madoura pottery in Vallauris, visited Picasso at Antibes and invited him to tour the ceramic workshops. He agreed to go and produce a couple of molds on his visit. When the Ramiés showed him what he had made and promised to make expert assistants available to him, his interest grew stronger. Be-

ginning in the summer of 1947, Picasso worked for nearly two years in the Ramiés pottery. Like many other great artists, Picasso wanted to explore media other than painting on canvas. Fernand Léger, for example, turned to monumental painting on walls, Georges Rouault occupied himself with the techniques of enamel and stained glass in the abbey of Ligugé, Braque devised reliefs in precious metals, and Matisse dedicated himself to furnishing the chapel of Vence.

Picasso's first exhibition · of ceramic works, in Paris in the winter of 1948, was a sensation but did not receive notably favorable criticism. People had not expected this marvelous new world of both useful and beautiful vessels. Picasso commented on the public's reaction: "When the monster smiles they are disappointed." He had honestly sought to develop new forms, glazes, and firing techniques, but his chronic impatience only allowed him to explore this new métier for two years, after which he rarely worked in ceramics.

Despite the lukewarm reaction to the Paris exhibition and Picasso's own unenthusiastic evaluation of the pottery, one should by no means dismiss these ceramics. The works produced by this artist's restless, creative hands represent a compendium of new forms, brilliant ideas, original formulations, and boundless imagination—a unique kind of ceramics, each piece of which is a true Picasso.

Picasso's interest in ceramics was unquestionably beneficial to Vallauris and its craftsmen. Overnight the moribund town was again in the public spotlight and its ruined pottery workshops enjoyed a new upswing. Vallauris briefly became the French center of art pottery. Unfortunately, it did not sustain Picasso's example. Françoise Gilot has written: "Pablo's presence brought prosperity to the city, but his example was misunderstood. Today Vallauris is a stronghold of bad taste."

THE VISITOR TO VALLAURIS ALSO HAS THE opportunity to see two monumental works by Pablo Picasso. On the main square of the village, opposite the church, stands the *Man with a Sheep*. This bronze sculpture was originally intended to be part of the Picasso Museum collection in Antibes. Instead, Picasso decided to present the work to the village of Vallauris which had become a new home for the artist. At first the members of the Municipal Council were skeptical about the gift, but when Picasso described the work and the council realized that a valuable bronze would attract tourists to the small village, they agreed to accept Picasso's sculpture.

When set up in the Place Paul-Isnard, the local newspapers praised the artistic value of the sculpture and noted "the permanent presence of this statue in our town will draw a new influx of visitors for the great good of the economy of our city." Today, *Man with a Sheep*, a twentieth century "Good Shepherd," stands in Vallauris as a sign of hope and peace.

His gift of the sculpture brought Picasso honorary citizenship in Vallauris and the municipality also offered him a deconsecrated twelfth-century chapel to decorate as he wished. But Picasso delayed beginning work on the chapel to paint *The Massacre in Korea* in the summer of 1950. This monumental painting depicting a squad of armed figures about to fire on a group of naked women and children derives from Picasso's reaction to the news of the war in Korea, the same passionate hatred of war and love of peace that inspired his vault paintings in the Vallauris chapel. Picasso began sketches for the work in 1952 and set up his studio in a former perfume factory adjacent to the church. In the summer of 1952, he shut himself up in his studio, allowing only his son Paul to come in. When Picasso finally opened his doors in October, the two huge vault panels were completed: *War* and *Peace*.

Installed on the south side of the chapel, *War* centers on what the artist described as "the tattered, jolting procession of those provincial hearses, miserable and grimacing, that one sees passing in the streets of small towns." A naked, horned figure in a chariot drawn by three black and withered nags across the blood colored ground holds a bloody sword in one hand, and flung across his back is a net filled with skulls. Figures in the background hack at each other with axes and spears. At the far left, a second figure against the deep blue ground holds a spear and a set of scales in his right hand and in his left, a shield bearing the outline of a dove. The harsh lines and almost abstract style present war not only as ugly, but also absurd.

On the chapel's north side, the central image of *Peace* is Pegasus, the winged horse, harnessed to a plough and driven by a child. Surrounding this scene are wildly dancing figures and fanciful images (including a juggler balancing a rod with a goldfish bowl full of swallows at one end and at the other, a cage of fish. Picasso also incorporated images from the family life he loved, such as a mother nursing a child.

The west wall of the chapel is decorated with a huge composition of four men, each a different color and representing the four races. Together they hold a disk bearing the symbol of peace, a dove.

Picasso considered this room to be a "Temple of Peace." It is not only another facet in the oeuvre of this master but a representation of his personal philosophy.

GRASSE—WORLD CAPITAL OF PERFUME

SHORTLY AFTER LEAVING CANNES, ONE CROSSES the *autoroute* La Provençale and the gentle, blossoming hills of the interior lie ahead. The carpet of mimosa flowers stretching from Nice to Grasse is more than a delight to the eye. Countless thousands of these fragrant blossoms end up each year in the distilling vats of factories in and around Grasse, the world's perfume capital. The same fate awaits the sweet-smelling blooms of violets, tuberoses, jasmine, and lavender. And even though the fruit of the Seville orange and the marmalade and preserves made from it are also important to the economy of Grasse, they are derived from only that fragment of the annual crop that is permitted to ripen. These plants are used chiefly for their blossoms, which provide the raw material for perfume, one of France's most valuable exports. When you realize that, for example, 150,000 rosebuds are required to produce a mere kilogram of essence, you begin to appreciate its worth, twice that of gold.

GRASSE STANDS PICTURESQUELY AGAINST THE south flank of the Montagne de Doublier. Situated 1,092 feet above sea level and sheltered from the wind, this city of some 35,000 inhabitants enjoys a particularly moderate and pleasant climate. The climate and the beauty of the spot attracted illustrious winter guests long before coastal towns like Cannes, Nice, or Menton were "discovered." On the advice of her doctors, for example, Napoleon's eccentric and beautiful sister Pauline Borghese spent the winter of 1807–1808 here at the home of her friend Mme. Antoinette Léandre Amic (today No. 2 Boulevard du Jeu-de-Ballon). This particular guest was not warmly remembered by the townspeople. She was sickly and extremely sensitive and, so as not to disturb her rest, no bells could be rung during her stay. Even the bells worn by mules had to be silenced. In 1888, Baroness Alice de Rothschild built a luxurious villa, now the Hôtel du Parc-Palace, on the east side of town. The Grand Hotel, only 200 yards away (built in 1882, now privately owned) was visited by Queen Victoria in April 1891. Grasse ceased to be fashionable only after the upsurge of middle- and working-class tourism that followed World War I.

VIEILLES MAISONS, A GRASSE

Grasse: View in the Old Town.

The area surrounding Grasse is dotted with finds from prehistory and antiquity, dating as far back as 50,000 B.C. Countless monuments survive from the end of the Neolithic period, when the very first objects made of metal also began to appear. The vast number of tumuli (burial mounds), dolmens, and ancient settlements concentrated especially in the triangle formed by St-Vallier-de-Thiey, St-Cézaire-sur-Siagne, and Mons leads us to assume that in about 2,000 B.C., eastern Provence had become an important area through which migrating peoples passed and exchanged goods. The region retained these roles until well into our own era.

The city owes its steady economic rise not only to its favorable situation along the land route to Aix and Avignon, heavily traveled since the Middle Ages, but especially to its trading connections with Italy. Beginning in the 1170s, its closest trading part-

Grasse: City map. 1. Cathedral of Notre-Dame-du-Puy. 2. Hôtel de Ville (former Bishop's Palace). 3. Eglise de l'Oratoire. 4. Place aux Aires with fountain. 5. Hôtel de Clapiers-Cabris (Musée d'Art et d'Histoire de Provence). 6. Musée Fragonard. 7. Parking, Notre-Dame-des-Fleurs. 8. Parking du Cours. 9. Parking de la Rogue. 10. Parking for tourist buses. 11. Office de Tourisme. 12. Tour de l'Horloge. 13. Thirteenth-century townhouse. 14. Hôtel de Pontèves. 15. Hôtel de Théas-Thorenc, Hôtel Court de Fontmichel. 16. Hôtel Isnard. 17. Post office.

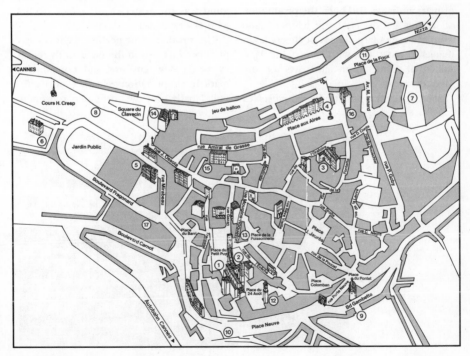

ner and ally was Genoa. This fact has given rise to the local belief that Christopher Columbus, known to have been born somewhere within the Genoese sphere of influence, first saw the light of day in Grasse.

Beginning in 1227 the city officially stood under the guardianship of an official appointed by the count of Provence or the king. The city's economic affairs, however, were governed by an oligarchy of closely interrelated families who had lived here since the eleventh century. Set well back from the Mediterranean and surrounded by a new city wall since 1305, Grasse was able to offer valuable military support to the coastal cities, such as Antibes, Fréjus, Monaco, or Nice, which were continually subject to attack by sea.

Since the High Middle Ages, the city's primary industry had been the production of leather goods. First the leather came from the area's large herds of sheep; later, thanks to close ties with Genoa and Marseilles, it came from all parts of the Mediterranean.

Soon, specialized crafts allied themselves to the tanners. One branch of Grasse's leather industry was the manufacture of gloves and during the course of the sixteenth century a sizable market developed for perfumed gloves which had become fashionable at the Spanish court and among the Medici in France. The manufacture of perfume thus arose as a sideline of the leather trade. Although the fashion of perfumed gloves did not peak until the eighteenth century, their manufacturers had attained a royal patent as early as 1614 that allowed them to call themselves not only master glovemakers but also perfumemakers. By 1724, the producers of perfumed gloves had detached themselves from the tanners' guild. They included some seventy members, a number that has remained nearly constant to the present day. One of the poorest members of the guild was the father of the famous court painter Fragonard.

The producers of perfumed gloves experienced a crisis in the eighteenth century, when new customs and tax policies made the importation of leather more difficult. Finally, only the perfumiers remained,

Grasse

filling the demand for scents in powder, salves, skin creams, and soaps. Ambitious men from Grasse—Isnard and then La Faye—began to open shops in Paris. Another, Fargeon, even succeeded in being appointed purveyor of perfumes to Marie Antoinette.

The Revolution disrupted the perfume industry for a time, but by the early nineteenth century, Grasse was again the leading supplier to Europe, thanks to technical improvements adopted in an effort to boost production, and it maintains this position today.

The first plants used for perfume were wild oranges, lavender, mimosa, and pistachios. The tuberose, imported from Italy, became native to Grasse in 1670. Today scents come from all over the world, including ambergris from whales, Tibetan musk, civet from Ethiopian cats, Persian patchouli oil, Indian ginger, and vanilla from the West Indies. Still, the majority of scents come from locally grown flowers, such as roses (an average of 500 tons annually), orange blossoms (600 tons), jasmine (600 tons), and violets, iris, lavender, mimosa, and thyme.

The three most important production methods are distillation, enfleurage, and extraction. Some essential oils can be produced only by the oldest method, repeated distillation; these are then further refined. Especially for orange blossoms, distillation is the preferred process. In enfleurage, the extract is attained by mixing the blossoms with animal fat. This procedure is required for sensitive blossoms like jasmine, tuberose, and narcissus, which do not respond to distillation. The third major process, extraction by means of hydrocarbons, is used for even more sensitive blossoms—notably the mimosa—because no heat is used at all in this process.

Today some 2,000 people are employed in the perfume industry in Grasse, which is still in the hands of the city's old families, despite the investment of a great deal of foreign capital since the mid-1960s. Most of the factories, even the largest ones, confine themselves to producing only the precious essences, which are then sent to Paris to be made into perfume. Some of the most famous factories, such as Fragonard, Gallimard, or Molinard, can be visited.

PERFUME IS NOT GRASSE'S SOLE SOURCE OF income. It has always produced a significant amount of cloth, pressed and exported a high-quality olive oil, traded in grains, manufactured soaps (in combination with the production of oil and perfume), and served as a banking center. Not only have the city's banks loaned money at high interest to debt-ridden metropolises like Paris or Lyons, but they have also influenced the trade policies of Marseilles by cleverly and unobtrusively buying up shares in ships and storage depots, thereby becoming part owners of that city's trading fleet.

The long-established oligarchy that ruled Grasse's economy, its far-flung financial connections and trading alliances, and its diversified and efficient industries, have enabled the city to survive relatively unharmed such conflicts as the struggles between Francis I and Charles V, the Wars of Religion, the Thirty Years' War, the Wars of the Spanish and Austrian Successions, and the French Revolution, as well as other trials such as plague and recession. At the close of the Ancien Régime, Grasse and Aix were the most influential and prosperous cities in Provence. Because of its socioeconomic structure, there was no bitter antagonism between the feudal aristocracy and the bourgeoisie. After the Revolution, for instance, the city promptly elected as its delegate to the Estates-General the aristocrat Jean-Joseph de Mougins-Roquefort, Grasse's first consul and mayor.

The city's political, economic, and social stability proved favorable to the expansion of the perfume industry. Moreover, it was a leader in bringing tourism to the Côte d'Azur—in 1821 during the Restoration, forty of its respected citizens circulated a tourist prospectus throughout France. Between 1890 and 1900, the so-called Opportunists (centrists and moderates) played a decisive role in developing the region, exploiting their connections with the rail companies, banking societies, and so on. Today, it might strike visitors and residents alike as a blessing that the new wave of tourism that began in the 1920s left Grasse untouched.

Before beginning a sight-seeing tour of the city, park in one of the two large lots (see map, p. 143).

The Cathedral of Notre-Dame-du-Puy

ON THE SOUTHERN EDGE OF THE ROCKY PLATEAU where medieval Grasse developed, a spot offering natural protection with its steep slopes, a strong fortress was built in the late tenth century, possibly by Rodoard, who had just been given the city in fief. A remnant of this original bastion is the square tower of brownish stone now incorporated in the Hôtel de Ville (see map, p. 143). This tower was originally twice its present height. The rest of the fortress was demolished and on its site the bishop of Antibes, who spent more time in Grasse than in his see, began the construction of a new cathedral in the twelfth century. Given the considerable thickness of its walls, ranging from 3 to 6 feet, and its few high and relatively small window openings, this church seems to have assumed some of the defensive role of the earlier structure. Its west façade, as viewed from the Place du Petit-Puy, has been considerably compromised by renovations and additions undertaken in the seventeenth and eighteenth centuries. The Romanesque cathedral of the twelfth and thirteenth centuries, with three portals and stepped-back arcaded friezes beneath the angles of the roof, resembled contemporary structures in northern Italy. By the late seventeenth century, this medieval cathedral had become far too small for the rapidly growing population. Bishop de Verjus expanded the Romanesque apse into a choir rotunda in 1689. His successor, Bishop Mesgrigny (1692–1702), continued the renovations creating a main portal with staircase in place of the medieval stepped platform, and adding a crypt beneath the western bays with access from the outside. The plans for this crypt (1714–1719) are said to have come from Vauban, but little other than the fact that Vauban was Mesgrigny's cousin supports this theory. Mesgrigny also added galleries above the side aisles.

Once visitors have adjusted to the dark of the sober interior they will discover themselves in a nave built of solid stone blocks, flanked by two side aisles. The central aisle is covered with four-part ribbed vaulting, whose strong, sharp-edged, and undecorated bands cut into the side walls without the transition of a keystone. The arcade arches rest on thick round pillars with no capitals. The arches between bays as well as the vault ribbing culminate in simple consoles (scroll-like projections) protruding from the wall. Despite the austere simplicity of this architectural system, the space achieves a certain ponderous elegance, due to the height of the central aisle which is a mere 23 feet wide. Its appearance today varies considerably due to fire damage in 1795, the installation and subsequent dismantling of Baroque decoration, and the addition of the galleries. Particularly striking is the cross-ribbed vaulting in the central aisle juxtaposed with the recessed vault supports in the side aisles. Like the church tower, the Chapel of the Holy Sacrament on the south aisle is an eighteenth-century addition.

THE CHOIR STALLS (EIGHTEENTH CENTURY) WERE moved here from the Dominican church in 1802, when the cathedral was returned to the faith after the Revolution. The great organ screen was created in 1855 by Jungh (Toulouse). A number of valuable paintings adorn the right-hand, or south, side aisle. Above the door to the sacristy hangs Jean-Honoré Fragonard's canvas of *The Washing of the Feet* which was intended for the then recently completed Chapel of the Holy Sacrament. The work, commis-

sioned by the cathedral chapter in 1755 (only shortly before the young pupil of Boucher won the Prix de Rome), is the only known religious commission of its size by this Rococo painter from Grasse. It was heavily damaged when fire swept through the cathedral in 1795 and has been repeatedly restored since that time. Another treasure is a triptych, with St. Honoratus flanked by Sts. Clement and Lambert, attributed to the chief master of the School of Nice, Louis Bréa (1443–1520). Since 1972, the same south aisle has also housed three early works by Rubens: *The Crucifixion, The Crown of Thorns,* and a depiction of St. Helen and the True Cross. These were commissioned as altar paintings for the church of Santa Croce in Gerusalemme in Rome but were refused on completion. They were willed to the hospital in Grasse in 1827 by Antoine Perolles, but in 1972 they were moved to the cathedral so that they might be seen by a larger public. To see the valuable reliquary of St. Honoratus (mid-fifteenth century) in the sacristy, you must obtain the sacristan's permission.

Hôtel de Ville (the former Bishop's Palace)

JUST NORTH OF THE CATHEDRAL ROSE THE former *Bishop's Palace* (see map, p. 143) from the twelfth century. The eastern exterior of the bishop's private chapel (visible from the Place du 24 Août) still provides some idea of that building from the High Middle Ages. The gabled front still displays its Romanesque arcades with figural consoles. The interior of the second-story chapel, now the Salle des Mariages, can be entered through the *Hôtel de Ville*, whose main portal is crowned by the city's coat of arms, an Easter lamb against an azure back-

ground. You can still make out portions of the Romanesque palace in the second courtyard of the building as well.

Directly north of the Hôtel de Ville begins the *casbah*, the old section of Grasse. Its narrow, lively alleyways remain refreshingly cool even on the hottest days, and it is well worth exploring them. In addition to its shops, workshops, and bars the *casbah* preserves a wealth of historic townhouses. This section contains the fish market (Place de la Poissonnerie) and the colorful Place Jean-Jaurès (formerly the Place aux

Grasse: Houses along the old city wall.

Herbes), where every morning housewives buy fresh foods after careful examination and much haggling. The busy Rue Droite was the main axis of the town even in the Middle Ages. Along it there is a row of houses ranging in date from the fourteenth to eighteenth centuries. Inside the house at No. 24, the Doria de Roberti, there is still a Renaissance staircase with loggias.

The Eglise de l'Oratoire, originally built in 1632, was "improved" by the addition of a neo-Gothic façade in 1851. At that time, the original portal and windows from the Church of the Mendicant Friars were transplanted here. During the Revolutionary period, the church was used for various official functions: it was the meeting place of the Sans-culottes, a polling place under the Directoire, a theater during the Consulate, and an auction-house for confiscated ecclesiastical properties. Among other things, the island of St-Honorat (Lérins) was auctioned off here to Honoré de Roquefort on August 9, 1791.

Place aux Aires

THE PLACE AUX AIRES REMAINS THE LARGEST AND loveliest square in the old town (see map, p. 143) An elongated trapezoid, it is closed on the north side by the arcades of a row of houses from the sixteenth and seventeenth centuries. At its widest point, colorful, tree-shaded flower stalls cluster around a three-tiered fountain, placed here in 1821. In the northwest corner at No. 33 is the splendid façade of the Hôtel Isnard. This elegant townhouse from the close of the Ancien Régime was built in 1781 by Maximin Isnard, a wealthy tanner and merchant of the city. The buildings around the Place aux

Aires were reserved exclusively for tanners, and other leather processors. The spaces (*aires*) between them were used to thresh grain, hence the name of the square.

Leading from the square to the west, the Rue Amiral-de-Grasse leads past the Hôtel Court de Fontmichel, at No. 18, oldest portion of which was begun in 1690. This splendid townhouse has belonged to a succession of members of the local nobility during the course of its checkered history.

Its Greek Salon is furnished with pictures supposedly commissioned by Count de Thorenc and painted in Goethe's house in Frankfurt beginning in 1759. The young Goethe (roughly age 10) is said to have suggested the subject matter—*The Sacrifice of Iphigenia, The Sacrifice of Polyxena, The Birth of Achilles*, and *Achilles Dressed as a Woman*—and they were executed by Seekatz, Schütz, Nothnagel, Hirt, and Juncker.

Musée d'Art et d'Histoire de Provence

BELOW THE PLACE DU COURS, OFF THE RUE Mirabeau, stands the Hôtel de Cabris. This magnificent townhouse was built in 1776 by Louise de Mirabeau de Cabris, who intended to use it for lavish receptions and entertainments. The house is sumptuously decorated with paintings by François Marius Granet and other Provençal artists of the period and was acquired in 1920 by the Société Fragonard to create the *Musée d'Art et d'Histoire de Provence* (see map, p. 143), which today exhibits a collection of objects from eastern Provence.

On the ground floor, the entry hall offers exhibits of Provençal ceramics from Apt and Marseilles. Fine examples of Moustiers porcelain are displayed in another ground floor room. An exquisite collection of "bergamots" (papier-mâché boxes lined with sweet-smelling bergamot peel) is also on view. Antiquities, archeological finds from the prehistoric period, and objects from Gallo-Roman Provence are housed on the basement level. The original kitchen in the basement of the Hôtel de Cabris has been restored and offers a glimpse of cooking facilities in the eighteenth century. On the first floor of the museum are examples of

Provençal furniture and ceramics along with a fine collection of eighteenth-century costumes.

Villa-Musée Fragonard

AT THE FOOT OF THE COURS H. CRESP IS THE *Villa-Musée Fragonard* (see map, p. 143). This magnificent country house surrounded by splendid gardens was constructed in the seventeenth century by Madame de Rogon. It derives its name from the fact that Jean-Honoré Fragonard, famed eighteenth-century court painter and native of Grasse, sought refuge here during the French Revolution. The house had been acquired by the perfumier and glovemaker, Maubert, a cousin and boyhood friend of Fragonard. When the painter returned to his childhood home in 1791, Maubert invited him to stay at the villa. Here, the painter whose elegant style had fallen out of favor in the democratic capital, was able to work in peace and solitude.

The villa, a recognized historic monument, was acquired by the city of Grasse in 1971 and restored to its original splendor. Today it houses several important works by Fragonard—many of which had previously hung in the Musée d'Art et d'Histoire de Provence—as well as works by the artist's son, and his sister-in-law, Marguerite Gérard. The Fragonard Room, located on the first floor, includes a rare half-length *Self Portrait* executed around 1800 in which the artist is depicted holding palette and brushes. An elegant representation of *The Three Graces* is rendered in the light, painterly style Fragonard learned from his teacher, François Boucher. A landscape, *Le Grand Paysage*, is reminiscent of the classical scenes of his seventeenth-century predecessor, Nicolas Poussin, while *Religions of the World* derives its subject matter from the philosophies of the Enlightenment and Freemasonry. Another self portrait and a portrait of Mme. Fragonard are complemented by drawings and etchings in this fascinating collection of works.

Other paintings include grisaille stairwell decorations between the first and ground floors, believed to be by Fragonard's son, Alexandre-Evariste. On the ground floor are copies of Fragonard's masterpiece, *The Progress of Love*, by the Lyonnaise painter Labrelie. The cycle, commissioned by Madame du Barry, mistress of Louis XV, was rejected and the panels were housed in the Villa Fragonard until 1898. Today they hang in New York's Frick Collection.

The Villa-Musée Fragonard also provides a lavish backdrop for municipal receptions, but for the visitor it offers a fine opportunity to become acquainted with this great master of French eighteenth-century painting.

*F*ROM GRASSE TO NICE— IN THE VALLEY OF THE LOUP

Gourdon

THE ROUTE THROUGH GOURDON IS RECOMMENDED not only because of its magnificent scenery but also because of Gourdon's castle, supposedly built on top of Saracen and medieval ruins. The four-wing, trapezoidal structure from the sixteenth century encloses a lovely Renaissance courtyard. Still privately owned, the expertly restored palace houses two valuable collections. One is the Historical Museum (Musée Historique). Any collector of antiques, especially of old weapons and armor, will delight in the objects on display on the ground floor. In addition to a secretary by Jean Dubois that belonged to Marie Antoinette, letters on parchment from Henri IV, the benefactor of the house of Gourdon, and truly fine specimens of late medieval armor, there are remarkable paintings. The most impressive of these are a *Self-Portrait* by Rembrandt, a depiction of *St. Ursula* by an artist of the Cologne School (ca. 1500), and a triptych by Bernard van Orley (ca. 1488–1541). Distinguished works by Louis Le Nain, Hyacinthe Rigaud, Nicolas de Largillière, Pieter Balten, Adam Frans van der Meulen, and others are also exhibited.

In seven rooms on the second floor is the second collection, the Museum of Naïve Painting, which includes all of the best names in this genre from the period 1925–1970: Henri Rousseau, Senlis (Séraphine Louis), Camille Bombois, André Bauchant, Le Grane, Kviatkovsky, Rabuzin, and O'Brady.

From the Terrasse des Buis, you can enjoy a view not only of the restored gardens designed by André Le Nôtre, but also a stunning panorama reaching on a clear day from the Massif des Maures to Mont Boron.

Le Bar-sur-Loup

THE SHORTER ROUTE TO VENCE RUNS THROUGH this town. Its small church of St-Jacques was built in the second half of the fifteenth century. King René facilitated its completion by freeing the town from all taxes and duties for three years. The church is unusual in that it has only one side aisle (on the

The Gorges du Loup: Drawing by Gordon Home (1908).

north side). The modest structure houses two treasures. Ornamenting the main altar is a late fifteenth-century polyptych belonging to the group of retables attributed to Louis Bréa. This *Retable of St. Jacob* consists of three registers whose two larger middle panels (Jacob the Elder, and Madonna and Child) are framed by twelve other saints. Depicted above are the Holy Trinity and the four symbols of the Evangelists. Unfortunately the predella is missing.

At the end of the nave hangs a depiction from the popular catechism, the famous *Danse Macabre of Le Bar*. The painting of the dance of death is 16 inches high and occupies only two-fifths of the 65-inch oak panel. The remaining three-fifths are taken up with a *memento mori* (reminder of human mortality) in Provençal consisting of thirty-three verses, all with the same rhyme scheme. The painting shows five couples in courtly garments performing the tambourin, a classical Provençal dance, accompanied by a flute and drum. Death stands armed with quiver and bow and aims his arrows at the dancing couples. Above the heads of the musicians and dancers is their symbolic counterpart—a small, black demon who is also dancing. One couple has just been struck; another is already dead. Three devils are busy gathering up the souls of those who have been hit. St. Michael, appointed by God to weigh mortals' souls, is powerless for this booty belongs to Hell. At the far left, the "wise" populace refrains from dancing. The picture's message is clear and the verses are even more to the point:

> O paures pecadours haias grant recordansa
> Que ves mourres tantost non hi fassa doutansa
> E vous ballas souven et menas folla dansa
> E fases autres mals ambe grand seguransa

En vous cargant forment de mortala grevansa . . .

This freely translates:

> O miserable sinner, keep well in mind
> that you yourself will die, have no doubt;
> that you often dance and weave silly steps
> and commit other sins quite assuredly,
> taking on yourself a heavy mortal burden. . . .

Tourrette-sur-Loup

THIS PICTURESQUELY SITUATED VILLAGE IS A typical *village perché*, like Mougins, Biot, Vence, St-Paul-de-Vence, and Gourdon. For reasons of defense, the Ligurians built their communities on hilltops that were difficult to attack. The Romans largely destroyed these old settlements and built their own cities on the plains, and the native populace came to follow the Roman example. But after the Roman Empire fell, barbarians and Saracens terrorized these low-lying communities. Beginning in the eleventh century, villages were once more developed on hilltops around the watchtowers of a feudal lord, much like the Ligurian settlements of centuries before. The little church on the main square of Tourrette-sur-Loup contains two works from the sixteenth century: a painted polyptych and a carved wooden retable.

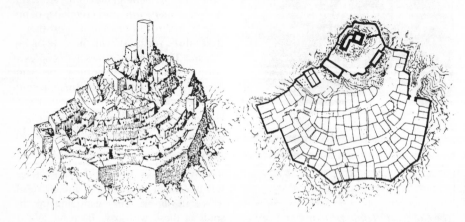

Example of a village perché.

Vence

THE LOCATION OF THIS SETTLEMENT MUST HAVE attracted a large population early on. It is protected by mountains to the north and lies open to the sun and the mild Mediterranean climate to the south. It has abundant water and is ringed by heavily forested valleys. It was also, since early historic times, surrounded by numerous hill fortresses essential to the defense of the countryside. Pliny the Elder wrote that the Ligurian tribe of the Nerusii lived in the vicinity of Vintium (Vence). Under Augustus, Vintium was elevated to the status of a *civitas romana* like many other cities in the imperial province of Alpes Maritimae, for it offered a strategically ideal base from which to conduct the conquest of the mountainous interior. Vintium also appears to have been popular as a spa during the Pax Romana due to its waters and its climate. Its name may possibly derive from a local god, Vintius, or from Vintia, the legendary beautiful but cruel priestess of Cybele. Votive inscriptions do attest to the presence of a shrine to Mars and Cybele.

The first documented bishop of the town appears to be Eusebius in 374. In 441, the Isle of the Saints dispatched the first bishop of real stature to the young Christian congregation, St. Véran. Throughout his forty-year episcopate, this former monk of Lérins and personal pupil of St. Honoratus strove not only to maintain public order and to deepen a sense of Christian morality, but also to defend the city (the fifth century was a turbulent one bringing, among other trials, the invasion by the Goths). Bishop Véran was so popular that immediately after his death in 481 the entire populace demanded and attained his sanctification according to the early Christian principle of *vox populi vox Dei* (the voice of the people is the voice of God).

The city's first cathedral doubtless dates to Véran's time. Fragments of its ornamentation appear embedded in the masonry of the present church. In the eighth century, the cathedral was burned down by plundering Saracens, and only a few decades later the entire town was destroyed. It is unclear whether Vence was rebuilt in the next century or only after the expulsion of the Saracens in the tenth century. A new and larger Early Romanesque cathedral was erected in the tenth or eleventh century, but renovations and additions made in the seventeenth and eighteenth centuries leave us only glimpses of the core structure.

Another bishop of considerable stature, St. Lambert, appeared in Vence in the twelfth century. His term was also a long one—from 1114 to 1155—and just as important to the city as St. Véran's. In fact, the two are patron saints of the city. It was also of decisive importance for Vence that the influential adviser and minister to the count of Provence, the wise and cautious Romée de Villeneuve, settled here and built himself a palace. He continually advised not only the count, Raimund Béranger IV, but also the king of France that Provence, dependent on the Holy Roman Empire, should be linked to the royal houses of France; he also brought about the politically significant marriage of Charles of Anjou and Beatrix of Provence.

In 1507, Alexander Farnese was named bishop of Vence, but never assumed office. Later, as Pope Paul III (1534–1549), he richly endowed the cathedral of Vence with reliquaries. In the seventeenth century another important man became bishop:

Antoine Godeau. Previously a writer and poet, he founded the Académie Française along with Cardinal Richelieu. In 1801, the bishopric was dissolved and the town was placed under the authority of Fréjus. After France's annexation of Nice, Vence was incorporated into that city's diocese.

The Old Cathedral

The *Old Cathedral* of Vence has preserved many aspects of its original Romanesque form, and it is considered to be an important example of Early Romanesque architecture in Provence. The first cathedral of Vence was constructed in the Merovingian period (fourth to fifth centuries) on the site of an ancient temple to Mars according to tradition. This church was destroyed (probably by the Lombards in the sixth century) and a second church was erected during the Carolingian period (ninth century). The core of the present structure—dating from the tenth–twelfth centuries—consisted of a nave with five bays flanked by side aisles. Like many churches in the region, Vence cathedral had no transept but ended simply in an apse, probably with two side chapels. This Romanesque church is basically intact despite the numerous renovations and additions that have changed the appearance of the once-modest church over the centuries. For example, in the fifteenth century the choir was reconstructed. Then in the eighteenth and nineteenth centuries side chapels were added, which promote the misapprehension that the church is five- rather than three-aisled. An entrance vestibule was created, and the original rough stonework interior was completely plastered and whitewashed. Despite these changes, Vence cathedral offers fascinating, if eclec-tic, architecture. Rich furnishings and numerous works of art are housed in the cathedral (refer to p. 155) including the tombs of St. Véran and St. Lambert.

1. The church is entered from the south side rather than the west (a usual practice for monastic churches). The elaborate Rococo *façade* was constructed in 1879. A cast iron statue of the Madonna decorates the façade of the church which is today dedicated to the birth of the Virgin. To the left and right of the entrance are Roman memorial tablets with inscriptions honoring Caesar.

2. The *Tour St-Lambert* was begun in the twelfth century, but the upper sections were rebuilt in the seventeenth century. The west façade of the tower originally faced the courtyard of the ancient bishop's palace, of which only a few arcades are preserved. Various Roman inscriptions have been incorporated into the masonry of the tower.

3. The *vestibule* was created in 1879 when the present façade was designed. Fragments of Roman inscriptions taken from a ruined aqueduct are exhibited here.

4. The sixteenth-century *crucifix*, which previously hung above the triumphal arch in front of the choir, was placed here in 1978. This expressive and rare work of sculpture was thought to have been destroyed during the French Revolution but survived and is especially venerated today.

4a. The *gallery* is furnished with magnificent Gothic choir stalls. These were executed in 1455–1459 by Jacotin Bellot from Grasse for the newly rebuilt choir but were eventually placed in the gallery. The carved wood stalls

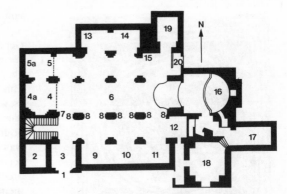

Vence: Furnishings of the Cathedral of St-Veran (numbers are explained in text).

are elaborately decorated with leaves, grotesque figures, and Gothic gables.

5. *Baptistry.* This chamber was probably constructed in the thirteenth century and was intended to be either a baptistry or possibly a funerary chapel for the bishops of Vence. Since 1979, a mosaic by Marc Chagall, *Moses among the Bullrushes*, has hung on the north wall.

5a. *Le Trésor* (the Treasury) is located in the gallery past the choir stalls. Valued objets d'art belonging to the church are kept here including lanterns and processional crosses of precious metals as well as a rare twelfth-century manuscript, *The Life of St. Lambert.* The beautiful reliquary of St. Blaise in gold-plated silver is decorated with scenes from the life of the saint. Also in the collection is an elaborate silver-plated copper bishop's wreath from the late sixteenth century.

6. The *nave* is 115 feet long by 45 feet high and dates mainly from the tenth or eleventh century. Unfortunately, alterations made in the fifteenth and seventeenth centuries have largely obscured the original Romanesque fabric.

7. *Relief fragments* from earlier Mero-

vingian and Carolingian structures at Vence are inlaid into the pillars and walls of the cathedral. These plaques display carved birds, leaves, rosettes, and interlace patterns that provide evidence of the rich ornamentation of the pre-Romanesque churches.

8. Additional *relief fragments* are found in the side aisle arcade.

9. *Chapel of the Virgin Mary.* Altarpiece.

10. *Chapel of St. Lambert.* Under the altar of the chapel is placed the sarcophagus of St. Lambert from ca. 1175 with its Latin inscription. Two silver reliquary busts, one of St. Lambert and one of St. Véran, are kept in niches and are carried in the annual procession on Easter Monday for a mass celebrated on the plateau of St-Michel. Two paintings from the seventeenth century hang in the chapel, both commissioned by another bishop of Vence, Bishop Godeau, who redecorated the chapel ca. 1666. *The Visit of St. Anthony to St. Paul the Hermit* is signed by Jean Daret, and above the altar hangs a representation of *St. Lambert in Pontifical Robes*, by an unknown artist.

11. *Chapel of St. Véran.* The tomb of St. Véran is a reused pagan sarcophagus dating from the fourth or fifth century.

Vence: Bas-relief with bird and interwoven ribbon in the former cathedral.

Fragments from other late antique sarcophagi are located near the arcade leading into the nave. A magnificent altarpiece, painted in the eighteenth century by Michel-François Dandré-Bardon, *St. Véran Blessing the People of Vence*, hangs in the chapel.

12. *Sacred Heart Chapel.* Behind the eighteenth-century painting of the Sacred Heart is a wall safe where relics of the church's patron saints were hidden during the Revolution and not rediscovered until 1914.

13. *Chapel of the Holy Family.*

14. *Chapel of the Saints and Angels.* An altarpiece from the sixteenth century by an unknown artist represents the Old Testament scene, *Tobias and the Angel.*

15. A *wooden shrine* from 1842 was created specially to hold the relics presented in 1538 by Pope Paul III.

16. The present *choir* was rebuilt in the fifteenth century with plaster decoration added in the seventeenth century. The church's main altar in polychrome marble was sculpted in 1767 by the Genoese artist Giuseppe Schiaffini.

17. *Sacristy.* A passage from the side of the choir leads to the rectangular sacristy. This room, with its Gothic ogive arches, was added to the church in the thirteenth century and still retains its original, parchment-covered door. A wall cupboard at the left conceals an access to the apse. The sacristy houses precious ecclesiastical objects, among them two lovely processional crosses of polychome wood from the 1700s.

18. *Chapel of the Evangelists.* Paintings from the seventeenth and eighteenth centuries include depictions of the Four Evangelists by Jean-Baptiste Jouvenet.

19. *Bell Tower Chapel.* The most exquisite of the Merovingian and Carolingian reliefs are exhibited in this chapel. A large relief, decorated with birds and bunches of grapes between two bands of interlace, was probably part of a choir screen from the ninth-century church. A smaller relief shows an eagle (associated with St. John the Evangelist) executed in the stiff, stylized Carolingian form. A richly carved wooden door, a splendid example of the Late Gothic style, once led into the canons' quarters of the cathedral.

20. A small *portal* opens into the Place Godeau, one of the most intimate and picturesque squares of the old town. It is surrounded by medieval houses, which continue eastward to form "l'Enfer," or the Hell quarter, with its charming, narrow streets. The Place Godeau offers a marvelous view of the cathedral, especially the east end with its fifteenth-century choir and twelfth-century bell tower.

The Boulevard Paul-André and the Avenue M. Maurel precisely trace the line of the medieval wall that formed a nearly perfect oval. In the thirteenth century, the city had only two gates, the Porte Signadour in the southeast and the Portail Levis in the northwest. To the east of the Porte Signadour, where the road from St-Paul-de-Vence now ends, the Place Anthony Mars, formerly Place Vieille, reveals something of the earliest medieval expansion of Vence at the beginning of the fifteenth century. The square was planted with trees in 1431, and in 1439 it received its own fountain to satisfy the townspeople who had settled beyond the walls.

At the other end of town, where you generally enter after parking in the Place du Grand-Jardin, the Tour Carrée dominates the Place du Frêne (*frêne* means "ash," and the enormous tree still stands in the square), formerly Place Neuve, which was constructed under King René in 1441. In order not to impede the expansion of the city, the barons of Villeneuve placed their city palace—which had stood south of the cathedral since the thirteenth century—outside the wall, between the Place du Peyra and Place du Frêne. The Tour Carrée, which was part of the palace, simultaneously guarded the new Porte du Peyra as well.

The Porte du Peyra leads to the polygonal Place du Peyra, site of the fountain, the city's most photographed landmark, and a huge chestnut tree that provides pleasant shade in summer. Here too is the beginning of the main shopping street, the Rue du Marché. The Roman forum is said to have stood on this site. To the southeast of the feudal castle attached to the Tour Carrée extended the gardens of the Villeneuve family, which were transformed into the large Place du Grand-Jardin during the nineteenth century. Though its name recalls those splendid gardens, it now functions as the city's largest parking place, ideally situated near the old city wall.

In the middle of the Place du Grand-Jardin is a column known as the Colonne Marseillaise. It is but the left half of a column presented by the Massalians to the shrine of Mars in Vintium in the third century. The other half is incorporated into the fountain on the Place Godeau, east of the cathedral.

Both of the main arteries leading west out of the city, the Avenue Henri-Isnard and the Avenue Foch–Avenue de la Résistance, are clearly posted with signs pointing the way to the city's chief point of interest today, the Chapelle du Rosaire, often called simply the Chapelle Matisse.

Chapelle du Rosaire (Rosary Chapel by Matisse)

FOR MANY TRAVELERS THE CHAPELLE DU ROSAIRE, the commonly held masterpiece of Matisse, is not only the greatest artistic attraction of Vence but of the entire Côte d'Azur.

The chapel was a great surprise to those who knew of Matisse's notorious lack of religion. Some thought that he had completely reversed his position in his last years, others that he had been converted to Catholicism as a result of illness and age—both ideas held as absurd by his closest friends like L. Aragon or Picasso. From an artistic point of view, however, the completed project engendered even more surprise, even rejection. Françoise Gilot recorded Picasso's reaction at the time:

The palette he worked with included ultramarine, a deep yellow, and green. All of the elements were to have

Vence: floor plan of the
Chapelle du Rosaire by
Matisse.

1. *Large west window*
2. *Sanctuary*
3. St. Dominic
4. *Altar*
5. *Nuns' Chapel*
6. *Lay Chapel*
7. Madonna and Child
8. Stations of the Cross

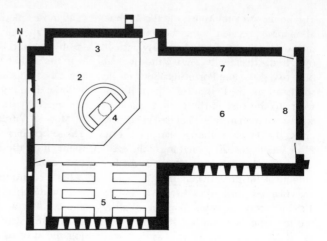

roughly the same dimensions, so that the light falling through them would be equally divided. And to that end he demanded something he had never done before: the glass had to be frosted on the outside. But when the windows were finally installed they admitted a uniform pink-violet light. And when this light fell on the forty half-matt ceramic slabs, which were in reality rather shiny, it produced a violet reflection resulting in an effect by no means favorable and certainly not one that he had intended. Pablo thought the experiment was a failure. He said that if Matisse had suspected "that the light in the interior of the chapel would have this pinkish violet tinge he would certainly have used different colors on the walls to counteract the effect. If the chapel was to be black and white there should have been no other color—at the most a spot in red or some other pure color perhaps, but not this pinkish violet. As it is, the space looks like a bathroom!"

It certainly seems to be true that most viewers who are well versed in painting are somewhat disappointed at first viewing of the Chapelle du Rosaire. But if one stays for a longer time and visits the chapel repeatedly while considering the former achievements of Matisse, his biography, and especially his explicit remarks on this project, one begins to understand why this, his last work, is not only his most important creation but is also more revolutionary than was Fauvism.

THE CREATION OF THE CHAPELLE DU ROSAIRE seems to have come about almost by accident, although the religious might credit it to divine providence. One of his nurses in Nice, herself having recovered from a serious operation, became a novice in the Dominican order and was transferred to the convent in Vence, just across from where Matisse was then living, the Villa le Rêve. Sister Jacques-Marie occasionally called on the master and one day brought some designs she had done for the stained glass to be installed in a new chapel. She hoped to get Matisse's opinion of them and, if necessary, to ask him to suggest improvements. On her next visit she brought the architecture student who had been selected to design the building, Brother Louis Rayssiguier. Rayssiguier suggested, doubtless having ulterior motives, that Matisse might like to design the windows himself.

One thing led to another and, in the course of a lengthy conversation, the idea for the chapel was born. In 1941 Matisse had been gravely ill, and when complications developed following the initial surgery, he had begged the doctors to "just give me three or four years longer so that I can finish my life's work." Despite all predictions, Matisse survived the follow-up surgery and recovered. Now, six years later, someone was giving him the opportunity to realize the desire he had expressed on his supposed deathbed. During this two-hour talk, and others over the days that followed, Matisse began to realize the implications of the chance he was being offered. For the next four years he devoted all of his artistry, skills, and experience in drawing, painting, and sculpture, as well as his hard-won wisdom to this one last work.

The technical and functional problem— that of creating a place of worship for both the laity and the sisters of the Order while at the same time keeping them separate— was easily solved. It was decided that there should be two perpendicular spaces of different depths with a diagonal altar at their intersection, which would be equally visible to both. The difficulty for him lay in finding a way to distill his whole life as an artist and then translate it into a single, total work of art. Matisse designed everything himself—walls, floors, doors, windows, the altar, the altar vessels, the vestments, the lighting.

As unusual as the building's asymmetri-cal ground plan is its orientation. The altar faces neither due east nor due west, thereby also creating an asymmetrical play of light. The south and west sides serve as the sources of light and are balanced by the north and east sides, which become basically passive, illuminated simply by the windows opposite. Matisse repeatedly stressed his purely artistic motivation, as, for example, in this letter to the Bishop of Nice on the occasion of the ceremonial dedication of the church:

> For me this is primarily a work of art. I have simply intuited the spiritual aspects of the project. I do not know whether I believe in God or not. Probably I am something more like a Buddhist. But the crucial thing is putting oneself in a spiritual state approximating that of prayer.

The rigor with which Matisse formulated and solved the aesthetic problems is probably the cause for the disappointment, or at least surprise, that the visitor feels at first. One of the few who immediately recognized the full significance of Matisse's chapel was the Belgian art collector and critic René Gaffé: "Vence? I find that it is to religious art what the year 1789 was for France, a revolution. A completely successful revolution, and of such absolute purity! Look at the light from these green and yellow windows! Never has Matisse seemed so youthful." In a public statement, Matisse clearly defined his artistic intent in designing the chapel:

> My chief interest was in balancing a surface composed of light and color against a solid white wall covered with drawings in black. This chapel has

Matisse: Early Self-Portrait *(ink drawing);*
Four Self-Portraits *(1939).*

been my ultimate goal in a lifetime full of work, the culmination of an intense, sincere, and difficult endeavor. . . . The chapel has given me an opportunity to refine my investigations and translate them into reality.

Obviously all of the artistic elements which characterized Matisse from the beginning have been brought into play in the creation of the Chapelle du Rosaire—color, drawing, chiaroscuro, and an interest in independent, but pure and active, light. The structure was created with these in mind, and it ultimately seems only coincidental whether it is used for religious or secular purposes.

Light is provided by a series of slender fifteen-foot-high windows on the south wall of the lay chapel and nine even narrower ones on the south wall of the nuns' chapel. There are also two wider panels that rise nearly the full height of the west wall of the "choir." These light sources project not only distinct bands of color, but an abundance of diffused light as well. The light from the south is harsh but neutral, while that from the west is softer and warmer. The cool morning light is reflected by both the colors in the windows themselves and the coldness of the surfaces on which it projects, the floor and the north and east walls. The color of the space changes constantly with the time of day and the height of the sun. The interior surfaces are virtually devoid of color. On the north and east it is the drawing that predominates, while the south and west sides are given over to color. A balance has been created between the artist's vision and the only partially controllable variables of light values and intensity.

A similar juggling of his artistic will and ability with articulate chance was achieved in the drawings of St. Dominic, the Madonna and Child, and the Stations of the Cross. Matisse had written in his diary in 1936: "When one's means have been so assimilated and consumed that their expressiveness is exhausted, it is necessary to return to the fundamental principles forming human speech. That is the point of departure for Fauvism: the courage to rediscover the purity of one's means." Roughly three years later he remarked about his way of drawing:

> My pen drawing is the most direct expression of my feelings. It is the simplicity of the medium that allows this. My drawings are sources of light, for when you look at them in indirect light or on a gloomy day you not only see the life's blood and feeling pulsing along their lines but also, quite clearly, a glow of light and certain values corresponding to color. ... I have always held drawing to be a medium for the expression of the subtlest movements and oscillations of the soul, a simplified means of attaining maximum simplicity, the expression from the essence of things that passes weightlessly and immediately into the spirit of the viewer.

Even the anti-Modernist must grant Matisse the distinction of master draftsman in his drawings of nudes, heads, or flowers. There are, however, many people who feel let down when they first see his drawings in the chapel at Vence—especially those who are guided solely by their religious feelings. Picasso greatly admired these drawings, particularly the Stations of the Cross on the east wall above the entrance. Doubtless he saw in them Matisse's renunciation of his own "style," something Picasso would never be capable of himself.

Matisse held drawing to be the most direct way of expressing his feelings. But feelings, no matter how trustworthy in the past, could have easily misled him in this last chance to fulfill himself. In his search for purity of means and originality of expression, only the ultimate simplification,

Vence: Matisse's Chapelle du Rosaire, Madonna and Child.

the bare symbol, or glyph, could be trusted. It was necessary for him to "return to the fundamental principles forming human speech." This meant reducing his expression to essentials, starting from that point when the child begins to recognize and name objects without further differentiation. Yet even in creating these glyphs he had to contend with his unmistakable personal style. No matter how consequential his reduction to bare symbols, that style betrayed them as personal interpretations. As soon as Matisse attempted to draw a primeval apple, for instance, it was inevitably still an apple by Matisse. Thus, at the end of a highly successful artistic career of eighty years, he found himself forced to make a most difficult leap: to renounce his own style, in a sense even himself. Matisse was striving not to intervene between his glyph of St. Dominic, or of the Flagellation, and the viewer.

His solution was brilliantly simple: he placed his brush at the end of a six-foot bamboo pole. He could still direct the brush in the creation of a head, for example, and what took shape at the other end of the pole clearly was a head, but one with none of the telltale attributes of a head "by Matisse." He had found his glyph. Picasso, who sensed this achievement, never went so far in his own work. Matisse, determined to achieve expression "from the essences," had surrendered his most intimate self: his style.

After a lifetime of painting, this man, held by many to be the greatest painter of our century, had begged for three or four years in which to complete his life's work. When given that chance, he chose not to work on one painting for three years "in a frenzy of inspiration" (he had abandoned panel painting as inadequate for his investigations of color, drawing, and light), but instead created the Chapelle du Rosaire. Perhaps not since Michelangelo destroyed everything that sculpture had counted for with his last chisel strokes on the *Pietà Rondanini* had any artist gone further.

St-Paul-de-Vence

THE MAGICAL TOWN OF ST-PAUL-DE-VENCE LIES only 3 miles south of Vence. It is known that this town was self-governing in 1241, which presupposes the existence of a well-developed and flourishing community long before that, though its ancient history is shadowy at best. In the sixteenth century, Francis I selected St-Paul over Vence as a key site in his system of defenses and had it expanded into a fortress. The job was assigned to the fortress architect St. Rémy, who razed several hundred houses in order to realize his grandiose plans. The old city walls were also torn down. The only part spared was the turreted and crenelated city gate from the fourteenth century, which was symbolically incorporated into the new system of fortifications.

Although St-Paul has become a tourist trap on weekends and especially in the summer months, it has nevertheless preserved a great deal of its quaint charm. A walk along its walls provides lovely views of the surrounding hilly countryside, the sea, and the mountains. A stroll through the town leads you through narrow, climbing, cobbled alleys that open onto picturesque squares with charming fountains. Around each corner, fragments of history await rediscovery.

Late nineteenth-century view of St-Paul-de-Vence.

THE SQUARE KEEP ON THE SMALL SQUARE NEXT to the church, its lower part consisting of convex stone blocks, is doubtless the oldest structure in St-Paul (ca. 1300) except for the church itself. The parish church, with an extremely simple exterior, was probably built in three main phases. Its present central aisle may date back to the twelfth century and displays features typical of the Romanesque in Provence. By 1300 the structure had become too small and two tall side aisles were added, creating a nearly square space. The original vaulting of what is now the central nave can still be seen in the choir, a simple pointed barrel vault of stone. After 1300 all three aisles were given Gothic cross-ribbed vaulting, which was restored at the end of the seventeenth century. In 1740 the bell tower was moved from the north side of the church to its present location south of the façade. In 1680–1681, a chapel to St. Clement was constructed to the right of the choir in the first bay of the church; its lavish plaster decoration was the work of P.-J. Bernardi.

The church treasury, housed in the sacristy, contains some notable pieces: a fourteenth-century processional cross; a *Madonna* (ca. 1300); a twelfth-century reliquary; a *St. John* on a lion base, and a *St. Sebastian* (both from the fifteenth century); and a splendid hexagonal wooden ciborium, or processional canopy (dated 1595), painted with scenes from the Old and New Testaments.

In one restaurant in St-Paul-de-Vence—the Colombe d'Or—you can dine elegantly amid paintings by Bonnard, Braque, Derain, Dufy, Léger, Matisse, Miró, Modigliani, Picasso, Rouault, Utrillo, Vlaminck, and others. M. Roux, the restaurant's owner, is a passionate collector who was able to buy the works he exhibits over a period of forty years, while they could still be had for little money. In so doing, he has assembled one of the greatest private collections of modern art in France.

A Mecca of Modern Art: The Fondation Maeght

A FEW HUNDRED YARDS FURTHER, YOU WILL FIND an iron Stabile by Alexander Calder and a large sign pointing the way to the *Fondation Maeght*. The Fondation is the home of an extraordinary collection of modern paintings and sculpture, and in addition presents concerts, dance and theatre events, and houses an experimental film studio. In the early 1950s this arts facility was planned by Aimé Maeght, one of the most notable art collectors and dealers of this century, and his wife Marguerite in a small restored chapel at St-Paul in memory of their son Paul. Their project slowly expanded to become a museum of contemporary art surrounded by extensive gardens.

The Fondation complex was designed by Spanish architect José Luis Sert, who created a series of galleries, an artists' residence and studio, a large sculpture court, and various performing arts facilities, to complement the original project, a restored chapel with decorations and stained glass windows by Georges Braque and Ubac. The unique architecture blends with its natural surroundings; buildings and courts intermingle gracefully with pine trees and sloping terraces. The various structures, while not monumental, are highlighted with near-sculptural accents such as the soaring concrete roofs of the main pavilion. This architecture fulfilled Maeght's aspirations:

I don't like museums that are closed boxes. A museum should not be shut off from life. What I wanted to make here is a museum that people can step in and out of without being conscious each time of a change of climate. I don't want them to feel *directed*. [I want to] reinstate the individual as the measure of all things.

Of significant interest in the Fondation's design is that major artists (many of whom were represented by Maeght's gallery) were commissioned for specific works of art: Braque created the design for a courtyard pool; Chagall created a wall mosaic and windows for the large, multipurpose hall; Léger produced a number of ceramic elements. The Alberto Giacometti courtyard was supervised by the artist himself and offers the rare opportunity to view his large-scale work as an ensemble. *The Women of Venice*, made for the Venice Biennale of 1956, consists of ten elongated bronze figures that vary in height from 52½ inches to 41¼ inches. The *Large Striding Man* was originally designed for the Fondation's large courtyard. Sculptures by Hans Arp, sensual and organic in form, are placed in the pine grove. Calder's *Large Stabile* is also placed in such a way as to contrast with the slender trees that hug the Fondation's buildings.

Perhaps the most fascinating work created for the Fondation is the *Labyrinth*, an elaborate sculpture garden created through the combined efforts of architect Sert, painter Joan Miró, and ceramicist José Lloréns Artigas. A huge cement arch embedded with stones—half-animal, half-architectural form—dominates the *Labyrinth*.

The painting collection includes works by almost every major artist of the twentieth century. Léger's *Country Outing* is a modern work with a traditional subject, line, and color. Vasili Kandinsky's *Red Knot* (1936) is exemplary of the artist's interest in Russian Constructivism, and the works by Miró are outstanding examples from his oeuvre. Paintings by Roberto Matta, Hans

Hartung, Pierre Soulages, Pablo Palazuelo, and Sam Francis represent more recent trends in modern art.

The Fondation Maeght also serves as a center for conferences and lectures, research and collaboration. An international festival of modern music and dance, and several special exhibitions, are organized each year. A visit to the ever-changing Fondation is always rewarding—this is a chance to see exceptional art in a unique environment.

La Colle-sur-Loup

THE ROAD FROM ST-PAUL LEADS FIRST TO La Colle-sur-Loup, where the monks of Lérins once maintained a priory that has now been transformed into a luxury hotel. On the little main square of La Colle-sur-Loup stands a bronze billy goat by the German sculptor Anna Thorwest.

Cagnes-sur-Mer

CAGNES-SUR-MER HAS THREE PARTS: THE TEEMING Cros-de-Cagnes (Lower Cagnes) around the small fishing harbor; the nineteenth-century Cagnes-Ville, which is the shopping and administrative center; and finally the upper town proudly looking down over its younger siblings, medieval Haut-de-Cagnes, which will be the focus of this section.

Haut-de-Cagnes is a world unto itself. Inside its former city walls, much of which survive, you can stroll happily through the old streets—the Rue du Pissoubran, the Rue du Dr-Michel-Provençal, Rue St-Joseph, Rue Clapier, Rue du Vallonet. These narrow thoroughfares are interrupted by small, pleasant squares, such as the Placette de l'Eglise, Placette du Murier, Placette du Platan, Placette des Acacias, and the Placette Grimaldi. When you tire of walking, a glass of dry red wine and a Provençal meal in the Auberge de la Belle Cuisse is a fine way to recuperate.

Thanks to its location slightly inland, Haut-de-Cagnes has been able to preserve its preindustrial feeling. This location was largely responsible for its being spared from the nineteenth-century population explosion of the Côte d'Azur, and the growth of the lower town on the plain closer to the sea made it unnecessary to change the structure of the historic old core. Also, Haut-de-Cagnes is still relatively undisturbed because a mile and a half separates it from Cros-de-Cagnes—too far for many beachcombers to want to walk—and due to the difficulty posed for vehicles in negotiating its streets. Buses do not venture into Haut-de-Cagnes, and even driving to it yourself will prove frustrating.

The history of Cagnes resembles that of other cities along the Côte d'Azur. It was a Ligurian settlement, then a Greek trading post. It was destroyed by Saracen pirates, then reconstructed during the Middle Ages. Its name is supposed to derive from the Ligurian word *kan*, meaning an inhabited spot on a round hill. The town first attained importance in 1309 when it was presented in fief by Robert of Anjou, the king of Naples and count of Provence, to one of his most important comrades-in-

Late nineteenth-century view of Cagnes-sur-Mer.

arms to help defend his kingdom against Aragon. This colleague was Rainier Grimaldi, the prince of Monaco and fleet admiral to Philip the Fair of France. Accordingly, Cagnes came into the possession of the house of Monaco. Rainier Grimaldi repaired the town's old walls and built himself a castle on the highest spot inside them. After his death, Cagnes fell to a collateral line of the house. At the beginning of the seventeenth century, Jean-Henri Grimaldi was living in Cagnes. Since he had persuaded his cousin, the prince of Monaco, to ally himself with France, Grimaldi stood high in Louis XIII's favor and attained considerable stature and influence. He no longer found the dark, cramped, and uncomfortable feudal castle of his ancestors adequate for his expanded household, and from 1620 to 1625, he devoted himself to giving the castle its present form. It is an imposing, princely residence providing space and a worthy backdrop for ceremonial banquets, splendid receptions, and brilliant balls.

The Castle

A DOUBLE STAIRCASE NOW LEADS TO THE CASTLE entrance. Two sides of the triangular courtyard are fitted out with three levels of elegant, soaring Renaissance arcaded galleries; the lowest level is reached by an open staircase next to the third side. Well-known artists were summoned from great distances to adorn the enlarged rooms of the castle. The justly famous ceiling fresco in the large ballroom on the second floor, the trompe-l'oeil *Fall of Phaeton*, is the result of the collaboration of two Genoese specialists, Giulio Benso and Giovanni Battista Carlone. Benso was responsible for the dizzying false architecture, with illusionist colonnades, that forms a frame for the ceiling painting by Carlone. Also of the highest quality is the stuccowork of the small adjoining court chapel and the audience chamber beyond it. The staircase in the courtyard is ornamented with a Renaissance relief showing Francis I at the Battle of Marignano.

In 1792, the Grimaldi palace was sold into private hands, but the city acquired it in 1937 for 250,000 francs and transformed it into a cultural center. In addition to rooms for municipal receptions, musical performances, and special exhibits, the rooms surrounding the courtyard on the ground floor, which still have the original Gothic vaulting from Rainier's early fourteenth-century structure, house the *Musée Ethnographique de l'Olivier*. This collection is devoted to the history and culture of the olive tree, so important to the region's economy. On the second floor, in the former boudoir of the marquise of Grimaldi, is the Suzi Solidor Bequest, a collection of forty oil portraits of this woman at various stages of her life by different artists. The collection is of interest not only because it contains works by Kees van Dongen, Foujita, Raoul Dufy, Marie Laurencin, Moïse Kisling, Othon Friesz, Francis Picabia and others, but also because you can study how forty different artists responded to the same subject. The second floor also contains the *Musée d'Art Moderne Méditérranéen*, with works by all of the artists who have worked in Cagnes (Matisse, Chagall, Kisling, and others). Since 1969, the Festival International de la Peinture has taken place annually from July 1 to September 30 in the castle. Each year the festival attempts to provide a comprehensive presentation of contemporary art from a different country.

Notre-Dame-de-Protection

SLIGHTLY BELOW THE CASTLE ON THE NORTH SIDE of the hill stands the small church of Notre-Dame-de-Protection. This structure was virtually ignored until 1936, when a fresco cycle from the sixteenth century was accidentally discovered in its choir. The painter did not sign his work, but the complete and well-preserved frescoes clearly reveal the influence of the School of Nice. Distributed over the walls of the choir apse are eight scenes from the Life of the Virgin, from her Marriage to the Slaughter of the Innocents, with inscriptions written in Provençal. The keystone of Christ as *Man of Sorrows* is surrounded by paintings—the Four Evangelists, the prophet Isaiah, and a sibyl, all with Latin inscriptions—radiating from it.

Renoir in Cagnes

IN 1895, AFTER THE FIRST SYMPTOMS OF HIS rheumatoid arthritis had appeared, Auguste Renoir took the advice of his doctors and set out to find a spot with a favorable climate where he could spend his last years. After trying out Beaulieu, Magagnosc, Nice, and Le Cannet, he moved into the post office building (now the town hall, or *mairie*) of Haut-de-Cagnes in 1903. The place offered what he had been looking for the past eight years: a pleasant climate, an idyllic landscape, and a special light.

At the advice of his friend Ferdinand Deconchy, a fellow painter and later the mayor of Cagnes, in 1907 Renoir purchased the 5½-acre property known as Les Collettes, which boasted thousand-year-old olive trees. He had a house built there and was able to move into it in the fall of 1908. The building was designed expressly for a painter and has two studios on the second floor. In addition, Renior set up a third studio with many windows in the midst of his beloved olive trees. Surrounded by his wife, his models, his three children, and a small circle of his closest friends, Renoir lived and painted in Les Collettes every day for the last twelve years of his life. A painting of him in his last year by A. André shows the old, stooped artist sitting at his easel and working with his last ounce of strength, brush tied to his crippled hand. Today this painting hangs in one of the studios, next to the empty easel and the artist's wheelchair. In 1960, the town purchased Les Collettes, left everything as it had been in Renoir's lifetime, and converted it into a museum. Thanks to gifts from Claude Renoir, A. André, Richard Guino, A. Joubert, and two loans from the Louvre,

the house vividly preserves Renoir's spirit and his art.

Among the few visitors Renoir admitted were two of the most prominent sculptors of his epoch, Auguste Rodin and Aristide Maillol. Renoir especially admired the latter and once said: "So many modern sculptors think to equal the great classics by copying them. However Maillol stands so obviously on the level of the masters that I could but think of a Greek when I saw him and watched him release his figures out of the stone." Maillol's bust of Renoir (1906) now stands in the dining room of Les Collettes. *Venus Victrix*, which stands in the garden, was completed by Renoir in 1914 in collaboration with Richard Guino, a Catalan sculptor and pupil of Maillol's; it was acquired by Cagnes-sur-Mer in 1964.

*T*HE BACK ROADS FROM GRASSE TO NICE

THE FASTEST AND EASIEST DRIVE FROM GRASSE TO Nice is the D 2085. There are two more charming alternative routes, however, if you have the time and the inclination. One,

through the valley of the Loup, goes through the towns we have just described and the other travels southward by way of Valbonne.

Notre-Dame-du-Brusc

TO FOLLOW THE LATTER ROUTE, TAKE THE D 7 after Châteauneuf. After leaving Opio behind, you will soon come within a mile of the abandoned church of *Notre-Dame-du-Brusc*. This church was destroyed in the seventeenth century, but in 1957 scholars began to study it. In 1961, systematic excavations began that have revealed a church of great archeological and historical interest.

The name *Brusc*, like the Provençal *bresc* or *brisc*, derives etymologically from *brasca*, meaning swamp or flooded terrain. As a matter of fact, Notre-Dame-du-Brusc does lie in one of the few plains of the Alpes Maritimes and once had a spring. The spot appears to have been inhabited quite early, at the latest by the third century B.C., and it lay along the Roman road from Nice to Aix via Grasse and Draguignan. The spring was reputed to have healing powers and became the site of a pre-Christian necropolis, both of which became popular pilgrimage goals in the Early Christian period.

Two unusual features of Notre-Dame-du-Brusc have led to much speculation: (1) a seven-sided spring basin in the narthex, which has been interpreted as a baptistry, and (2) the flat east wall behind the semicircular choir, which displays masonry reminiscent of late antiquity. Late antique architectural elements abound in the bases of the southwestern pillars and especially in the crypt. Moreover, beneath the easternmost bay of the nave, excavation has unearthed the foundations of an older oratory with a semicircular apse. These details support the assumption that a late antique or early medieval complex consisting of a pilgrimage church and baptismal font stood here; heretofore the only known example of a country baptismal chapel was the Collegiate Church of St-Pierre at Six-Fours-les-Plages.

Many aspects of the remains of this Early Romanesque church suggest that it was built in the eleventh century: it had a west-

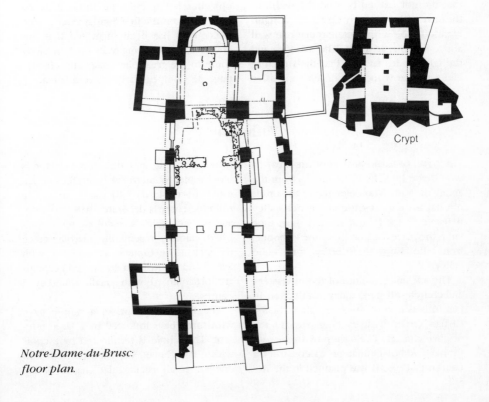

Crypt

Notre-Dame-du-Brusc:
floor plan.

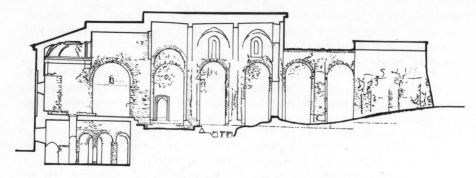

Notre-Dame-du-Brusc: Longitudinal section.

ern narthex structure with baptistry (or perhaps a font for pilgrims); a nave with two side aisles and five bays in an irregular ground plan; high side arcades; a transept that did not extend beyond the width of the nave with no eastern apses; and a slightly raised choir with a semicircular rear wall above a two-aisle crypt. The masonry and the tall arcades suggest that the structure had a simple wooden roof. Its impressive size—115 feet long by 52 feet wide, only slightly smaller than the cathedral of Vence—and complexity give Notre-Dame-du-Brusc a feeling similar to that of a bishop's church. Pilgrimages to the spot always took place on the first Sunday after Easter. Recently it has been suggested that this church was a stopping place on a southerly route to the great pilgrimage church, Santiago de Compostela in western Spain.

Valbonne

THE TOWN OF VALBONNE LIES IN THE MIDST OF woods and hills. In 1199, monks from the abbey of Prads who belonged to the order of Chalais came to settle in this rich valley irrigated by the Brague river. A short time later, the place took on the name Valbonne, from the Latin *vallisbona*, or "good valley."

The ancient buildings of the monastery and church still stand today in Valbonne. In fact, this is one of the rare abbeys of the Chalais Order with existing parts of the original cloister. The bishop of Antibes authorized Abbot Guillaume to construct a church in 1199. It was planned in the Romanesque style and thus the exterior is blocky and geometric. A beautiful Romanesque portal leads into the church. The rounded entry is decorated with moldings and on each side three colonettes, in polished calcaire resembling marble, grace the steps. The capitals are sculpted with leaves and volutes and the two end capitals are ornamented with small, round-eyed figures.

The interior comprises a simple nave with three bays followed by a large transept. The whole is terminated by a choir with a flat chevet. Off each transept arm opens a small, rectangular chapel. Today, large windows admit light into the church but originally the windows were much smaller and the interior dim and shadowy. The simplicity of the church, bare of ornamentation, is comparable to that found in Cistercian architecture and is typical of churches built for the order of Chalais.

A low door opens to the adjoining cloister from the third nave bay at the right, which is decorated simply but elegantly on the outside. Two niches beside the door once served as *armarii* closed by grilles where the monks took their prayer books before entering the church. The original cloister structure, built of wood, has long since disappeared. It measured about 55 feet in width by a length of about 64 feet and was bounded by the south side of the church and the south transept. This transept extended further to enclose the sacristy, the *salle capitulaire,* the monks' passage, which opened to the garden, and at the end, their common room, all on the ground floor. Above these rooms was the dormitory. The Valbonne abbey was never large—at its height in 1230 it was populated by only eleven monks and twelve lay brothers.

During its first years the monastery was extremely prosperous. Donations of land, as well as gifts of funds were presented to Valbonne. But in the mid-thirteenth century, financial difficulties began to plague the community, perhaps due to the enormous expense of their beautiful church, which was completed between 1230 and 1240. The abbey and church became increasing-

ly neglected and finally were annexed by the monks of Lérins. The complex was greatly restored in the seventeenth century and, in the eighteenth century, additions were made including the Chapel of the Penitents. In the nineteenth century, further changes were made including the construction of an enormous tower in one corner of the church's façade. Fortunately the abbey was declared a historic monument in 1933. It was not until 1969–1975 however, that the town of Valbonne began extensive restoration to return the church and the monastery to their previous Romanesque beauty. Today we can experience the church much as it once was, with its spare and simple yet majestic chapel.

The village of Valbonne dates from the Middle Ages but was completely rebuilt in the sixteenth century. This was accomplished in one stroke by Augustin, bishop of Grasse and abbot of Lérins, who had founded the town of Vallauris in a similar way in 1501. Unlike Vallauris, however, Valbonne has preserved its original character. The main square with its fifteenth–seventeenth-century arcades provides a charming picture of a country town from that period. With its central location, tranquility, and charm, Valbonne and its three small hotels offer a perfect location from which to explore the region. Cannes, Cagnes, Mons, Grasse, the Gorges du Loup, Vence, and St-Paul are all within a thirty-mile radius. Valbonne is peaceful and picturesque, isolated from the hubbub of the more expensive coast.

Biot

TWO AND A HALF MILES INLAND AND 260 FEET above sea level, Biot has all of the benefits

of a maritime climate without being subject to the turmoil endured by the coastal towns. Archeologists have tried to find evidence that this picturesque hilltop town is the site of the ancient city of Aegitna, but no proof of this has come to light, though the area is strewn with finds from pre-Roman and Roman times—for example, the so-called Golden Goat (*La chèvre d'or*), a massive structure whose function has not been precisely determined.

The Knights Templar were given the hill in 1207, when they were assigned the job of guarding the coast. Biot became one of the most important command posts in Provence. Then, after the Templars were dissolved, it was given over to the Order of the Knights of St. John in 1312. By the end of the fourteenth century, plague and war had left the town abandoned. King René the Good resettled Biot in 1470 with families from Oneille. Its regular street grid, carried out despite the sloping terrain, dates from this rebirth.

BIOT'S LOVELY PLACE DES ARCADES AND ITS other squares are paved with varicolored pebbles. In front of the church, for example, is laid a mosaic of two Maltese crosses, a lily, and the date 1685. The present-day church was built after 1470 (dedicated in 1479), with slight alterations made in the seventeenth century. Inside, on its west wall, hangs its most valuable furnishing, the altar retable of the *Virgin of the Rosary* by Louis Bréa, the chief painter of the School of Nice. Undated, but presumably from the close of the fifteenth century, the retable consists of a cloaked Madonna of Mercy in its central panel surrounded by seven smaller paintings of John the Baptist, Stephen, Peter, Mary Magdalene, and other Biblical figures. The Madonna's cloak, held by two angels, serves as protective canopy for all of Christendom. Typical of Bréa, the painting is dominated by red and gold, and the blue in the background was probably also mixed with gold. Unfortunately, the depiction of the Trinity at the top has been heavily reworked. Another retable in the church depicts the resurrected Christ and is attributed to Canavesio, another master of the School of Nice, whose wife was a native of Biot.

Musée Fernand Léger

IN ADDITION TO BEING A CENTER FOR STONE quarrying and the production of flowers and fruit, Biot is known for its old potteries, which still flourish. After World War II, the potters were joined by glass blowers and other craftsmen, but the town preserves a balance between artists and local people. One of Fernand Léger's pupils settled here and hit upon the idea of producing ceramics designed and signed by Léger. Thus Léger, who previously had had little interest in the south, first came to Biot in 1951. His second wife, Nadia, a Russian exile, was so delighted with the town that she stayed on after her husband's death and became the driving force behind the creation of Biot's chief tourist attraction, the Musée Fernand Léger.

Léger and Picasso were born in the same year, were "Cubists," and were members of the Communist Workers' Party, but it would be hard to find two more different men. While Picasso was complex and many-faceted and, perhaps due to his Mediterranean heritage, was deeply interested in timeless subjects, Léger was a simple, straightforward rationalist from the north of France. Both Picasso's subject matter and self-chosen isolation placed him in an elite, an "aristocracy of art." His interest in the Communist Party corresponded to his overall humanism. Léger, however, "was much too human to be a humanist," as Frank Elgar has commented. He was born and remained as one with the common man.

Léger took his themes, motifs, and solutions to aesthetic problems from the everyday stimuli that surrounded him including film, advertising, and neon lights. The three most distinctive characteristics of his art could be described as a liberation of color from the object and the drawing, the creation of new pictorial spaces by means of the equal treatment of all of the picture's subjects, forms, and techniques, and finally the principle of contrast.

Léger was profoundly affected by World War I, which demonstrated to him his bond to the common man and the sense of belonging that would define his life's work. The war also gave him a new way of seeing and new sense of form:

I had left Paris in the midst of a period of abstraction, of liberation in painting. Without any transition I found myself shoulder to shoulder with the entire French populace...at the same time was blinded by the breechplate of a 75-mm cannon lying in the open sun, the magic of the light on the polished metal. This was more than

Léger. The Team.

enough to make me forget the abstract art of 1912 and 1913....For my creative development I learned more from that 75-mm cannon than from all of the museums in the world. After the war I utilized what I had learned at the front.... In my search for luster and intensity I made use of the machine in the way others use the nude body or the still life.

When this internationally recognized artist died in 1955, his wife determined to create a museum built for his works alone. She wanted the façade to include a monumental mosaic—5,400 square feet in area—that Léger had designed. A. Svetchine from Nice was selected as the architect. Roland Brice, a ceramist and former pupil of Léger's, was asked to produce the façade mosaic. Léger himself had always been in search of large walls on which to experiment with his ideas of monumentality, convinced that they would open up new paths in his art and give added expressiveness and form to architecture. To this end, he had begun to collaborate quite early with Le Corbusier. Examples of his efforts may be seen in the churches of Audincourt (1951) and Courfaire (1954) and on the administration building of the Gaz de France factory in Alfortville (1954–1955).

Though Nadia's intentions were no doubt good—wishing to realize Léger's designs after his death—the manner in which the designs were executed reveals Nadia's misunderstanding of her husband's ideas. Between the art work and the architecture Léger had envisioned an interaction resulting in an increased excitement. This is unfortunately not in evidence in Biot. Much

of the architecture seems virtually nonexistent, and what can be seen of it is weighed down and suppressed. The façade appears to be a gigantic painting on stilts in the middle of the landscape.

On the ground floor of the museum is a fine survey of Léger's graphic work as well as Calder's remarkable portrait of Léger in wire. The staircase is dominated by a second mosaic that forms part of the architecture—a 540-square-foot posthumously executed glass mosaic. The real focus is teaching in this museum, and on the second floor you may trace the artist's development chronologically with virtually no gaps between his earliest painting and his last.

The collection begins with Léger's two earliest dated oil paintings, *My Mother's Garden* and *Portrait of the Artist's Uncle*, both from 1905, which reveal an artist still clearly under the influence of the Impressionists. His next phase, consisting of landscape paintings from Corsica (1907–1911), reveals a debt to Cézanne. Léger's style is becoming solidified, his method of contrasts more evident as seen in the flat façades and angular roofs, the smoke and trees of *Roofs of Paris*. In 1912, his rather subdued colors begin to grow stronger. Pure colors make their appearance, especially red and blue. With *Woman in Blue* (1912), Léger has found his form of Cubism. As his colors become increasingly liberated and the pictorial elements more independent, pure color begins to resonate with linear composition. There is a noticeable wealth of new approaches to space as evident in *Contrasting Forms* (1913) and *Le Juliet* (1914). The paintings *Landscape at the Front* and *La Cocarde* (both 1916) also belong to this period.

The influence of the war and the resulting aesthetic concepts introduce a phase of experimentation with machine parts and other abstract forms that lasts until 1921. Critical tongues among the "true" Cubists designated this phase as "Tubism." Although this work may seem to contradict his claim that the war had been "more than enough to make [him] forget the abstract art of 1912 and 1913," it does so only if we do not fully understand the ambiguity, even inadequacy, of the expression "abstract." When one considers that any picture is more or less abstract in the sense of its being unreal, it becomes apparent that there is a whole range of possible approaches between the photographic likeness (which permits one to recognize a given object easily) and the purely nonobjective painting. Léger's machine pipes were concrete mementoes for Léger of things that had happened: "Modern man registers a hundred times more impressions than did the artist of the eighteenth century. The concentration of the modern painting, its many levels of meaning, and its fragmentation of forms is the result of all of this." His experience of the war machine as something abstract and destructive joins his perception of the technological face of peacetime Europe. Even the people were becoming machines, robots. This new recognition dominates the so-called monumental period, which began in 1921. Léger's equation of man and machine allows him to transform man from subject to object; to treat machine parts and people in the same way artistically. The treatment of all subjects or objects as "equal" in painting was of course not an invention of Léger's; most painters since the Impressionists have basically done so. But when Léger approached pictorial subjects, like machines or people, in his "egalitarian"

way it was not for ideological reasons. Their difference is actually emphasized through their contrast. Thus we find, for example, a wheel or pulley paired with a chessboard, and in *Mona Lisa with Keys* (1930), the most universal symbol of Western painting is juxtaposed with a banal ring of keys; both are depicted as objects of equal value isolated in a vast space. The artist continued his exploration of new pictorial spaces and his striving toward the liberation of color in every picture from 1921 until his death.

Léger succeeded in completely freeing color from domination by the subject's form. His inspiration was his experience of spotlights in New York in 1942. An early work from this new phase is the painting *The Multicolored Divers* (1942); another example is *Four Bicycle Riders*, begun in 1943 and completed in 1948. The paintings *The Construction Workers* (1950) and *Construction Workers against a Blue Background* (1953) document the extent to which the predicament of man isolated in space continues to obsess the aging Léger. The artist himself commented:

When I painted the construction workers I did not make any artistic concessions at all. The idea took hold of me as I would drive along the road to Chevreuse each evening. A factory was being built out in the fields. I could see the men balancing up there on the steel beams. I saw man as a flea; he seemed to be lost in his own constructions, and above him was the sky. This is what I wanted to depict: the contrast between man and his creations, between the worker and this whole architecture of metal.

Léger: The Three Comrades.

LES ALPES MARITIMES

---

*N*ICE, CAPITAL OF THE COTE D'AZUR

NICE IS FAR MORE THAN A TOURIST ATTRACTION. Not only is it the largest and most important city on the coast between Marseilles and Genoa, but like Venice, Paris, Marseilles, or Florence, it is a highly individual historic entity, a universe unto itself.

Terra Amata—a Prehistoric Pompeii

MARSEILLES, AS WE HAVE SEEN, CAN RIGHTLY claim to be the oldest city in France, but as yet it has failed to yield the slightest trace of prehistoric settlement. Nice, on the other hand, with its rich finds from the grottoes of Terra Amata, can boast that it is the site of one of the oldest human communities in Europe.

To the east of the city, Mont Boron projects out into the sea, marking the end of the gently curving Baie des Anges. At its base, where the Paillon river once ran into the sea, there is an inlet of a few hundred yards that separates Mont Boron from the citadel of Nice. Here, in the eighteenth and nineteenth centuries, the harbor of Lympia was created. Roughly 100 feet above sea level on the western slope of Mont Boron lies the wide opening of the Grotte Lympia, which was visible up until the close of the nineteenth century. In 1873, the archeologist E. Rivière discovered some primitive tools clearly dating back to the advanced Acheulean culture (300,000–100,000 B.C.) on the floor of this grotto. But the Grotte Lympia is only the entrance into a whole network of grottoes that were inhabited in ancient times. Additional artifacts were discovered in the adjacent Grotte Lazaret, making these grottoes of Terra Amata a veritable Pompeii of human prehistory. Thanks to recent refinements in the science of stratography, it has been possible to distinguish twenty different levels of prehistoric habitation. Finds from the oldest of these point back to the Villefranchian period (1,700,000–800,000 years ago); therefore these caves, along with the grottoes of Monaco (Observatoire) and Roquebrune (Vallonet), are among the oldest known dwelling places of our ancestors. Some of the traces of Acheulean man (ca. 150,000 B.C.) are two teeth, a piece of skull, three stone axes, the core of a piece of flint, and a footprint made by a man only 5 feet tall. Near the grottoes, the city of Nice has erected the Musée de Terra Amata where these artifacts are displayed.

Cro-Magnon man (30,000–20,000 B.C.), our immediate predecessor, lived in the Grotte des Chaudronniers. This cave lies on the western slope of the more recent acropolis, right in the heart of present-day Nice. Thus, the site may well have been continuously inhabited from that very early time up to the present.

From Antiquity to the Middle Ages

THE ANCIENT WRITERS PTOLEMY, STRABO, AND Pliny the Elder disagreed about both the founding of the city and the origin of its name, questions still disputed by scholars. We do know that the Visontii, a Ligurian people, living somewhat inland, had their capital in Cemenelon (modern-day Cimiez). Their harbor, known as Nissa ("water-tip") lay on the Ponchettes bay at the base of the later citadel. It is also certain that in the fifth century or early fourth century B.C., these Visontii were driven back from the coast by the Phocaean Greeks, who then founded their own trading settlement, Nikaia ("the victorious one"). We do not know whether this colonization was instigated by Greeks in Marseilles or directly from the Phocaean homeland.

The Ligurian city of Cemenelon appears to have lived in peace with nearby Nikaia, at least until the Ligurians began to be dominated by the more warlike Celts in the fourth century B.C. Confronted with this more hostile stance on the part of the Celto-Ligurians, the Greeks called on their allies in Rome who proceeded to conquer and pacify the Celto-Ligurian territory. They then established the province of Alpes Maritimae, which would continue to be part of Italy up until the first century A.D.; its capital, Cemenelum, stood on the site of Ligurian Cemenelon. The Romans stayed in the interior, where they could secure their imperial highway, the Via Julia Augusta, later known as the Via Aurelia (today, the Voie Aurélienne). To their old ally Massalia, they left a long strip of coastline ranging in width from 2½ to 25 miles. Thus, Nikaia continued to be Greek, and Greek was spoken there until the second century A.D. For several centuries, the interior of the Alpes Maritimae was dominated by Rome, while the coastline, naturally oriented toward the sea, remained Greek. The two quite different civilizations persisted side by side.

Only with the coming of Christianity did Latin become the everyday language of Nice. Yet Nice proudly continued to assert its independence from the neighboring Roman provincial capital of Cemenelum; it had a bishop of its own as early as the fourth century. Eight centuries of competition between the two settlements ended only in the fifth century upon the collapse of the Roman Empire, when Cemenelum simply ceased to exist.

Its harbor and impregnable acropolis enabled Nice to weather the stormy period from late antiquity to the early Middle Ages. In the eleventh century it was a relatively prosperous commune determined to maintain its independence from the new feudal powers; since its founding by the Greeks, it had never been conquered or destroyed. Perched atop its citadel, the community began to construct a Romanesque cathedral in the Lombard style in the first half of the eleventh century. Ste-Marie-de-la-Place, consecrated in 1049, had a nave with two side aisles and semicircular apses to the east.

Nice was officially a part of Provence but in practice it was a sovereign city. It established self-government in the form of a consulate in 1144. The medieval town on the old acropolis grew rapidly in the twelfth and thirteenth centuries; with its imposing ring of walls, seven churches, monastic buildings, and hospital, it must

have looked something like Mont-St-Michel.

Nevertheless, medieval Nice never achieved the stature of St-Gilles, Montpellier, Marseilles, or Genoa. The surrounding area was not especially fertile and was cramped by the Alpine foothills that virtually reached the gates of the city, so it lacked the economic advantages of the rich valley of the Rhône. Second, Nice's harbor, Ponchettes, never achieved more than secondary importance and could not begin to compete with even Fréjus or Antibes, let alone the great international ports of Pisa, Genoa, or Marseilles. And third, because of its location, Nice was necessarily drawn into major international conflicts. One of these was the struggle between the Ghibelline and Guelph factions of Italy. When this fight concluded in the twelfth century, the Ghibellines were firmly in possession of Nice's citadel, which was acknowledged to be impregnable.

Meanwhile, a new town had come into being below the old acropolis, between the inlet to the east and the Paillon river to the west, and competition between the upper and lower towns became acute during the thirteenth and fourteenth centuries. The city's feudal lord, Raimund Béranger of Aragon, expanded the citadel into a true for-

A nineteenth-century view of pastoral Nice.

tress and thereafter—as Vauban would say toward the close of the seventeenth century—whoever held the fortress of Nice also controlled the province of Alpes Maritimes. This ominous new role as a coveted bastion situated between major powers became apparent only when the county of Provence fell to the house of Anjou in the middle of the thirteenth century. Then in 1388, Nice seceded from Provence and allied itself with the house of Savoy. The longstanding conflicts between Marseilles and Genoa and between the French king and the Holy Roman emperor entered a new and more menacing phase. Because this event determined the city's fate for the next 500 years, it warrants discussion in some detail.

September 28, 1388—A Turning Point

IN THE STRUGGLE BETWEEN THE HOUSES OF Anjou in southwestern France and the Spanish Aragon, the fourteenth century brought a distinct turn in favor of the latter. In 1348, Jeanne of Anjou, queen of Naples and countess of Provence, was forced to surrender Naples to Louis I of Hungary and take refuge in Provence. Though married four times, the queen had no heir, and in 1362 she adopted Charles of Durazzo, marrying him to her niece Margaret and making him legal heir to her lands. Seventeen years later, when the Great Schism began, Queen Jeanne unwisely supported Clement VII, the antipope, who had fled to Avignon. The Roman pope, Urban VI, responded by stripping her of her titles and bestowing them on Charles of Durazzo. Inflamed with rage, the increasingly unpredictable queen took a further fateful step. She disowned Charles of Durazzo and named Louis of Anjou, the French king's second son, as her new heir and governor of Provence. At the same time, the political situation within the county had altered. The Provençal cities lying west of the Var, or closer to Aix, allied themselves with Jeanne and Louis of Anjou, while those east of the Var, or closer to Italy and Rome, supported Urban VI and Charles of Durazzo. Intending to force his claims with the sword, Louis of Anjou swept through Italy with a powerful army. Louis's army was decimated by the resistance met in Naples as well as by fevers and plague. Amadeus VI, Count of Savoy, was one of the victims, but before dying he was clever enough to secure a written record of the war debts owed him by Louis amounting to 124,000 gold florins. This enormous sum owed by the French pretender to the house of Savoy would later prove crucial.

The man who actually forged the chains linking Provence east of the Var to Turin for nearly 500 years was Jean Grimaldi, baron of Beuil. His only daughter had married Andaro of Grimaldi, a brother of the prince of Monaco, thus creating the collateral line of the Grimaldis of Beuil. Jean of Beuil proved to be a true Grimaldi not only in his boundless ambition but also in his political brilliance.

In order to secure the favor of his powerful neighbor Amadeus VI of Savoy, Jean of Beuil undertook the ticklish job of setting the stage for Savoy's peaceful and legal annexation of Nice. Having been named governor of Provence by Margaret of Durazzo, who was acting as regent of Naples for her young son Ladislaus, he was in an excellent position to exert an influence on political events. He needed only to choose the right moment, which arrived in 1388, when the barons of western Provence who were pledged to the house of Anjou determined to use force to change the minds of their brothers east of the Var, who were loyal to Rome. Jean Grimaldi dispatched his brother to Naples to request military support from Margaret, knowing full well that due to political turmoil in southern Italy she would be unable to provide it. Predicting her response, Grimaldi instructed his brother to suggest to Margaret that the cities of eastern Provence loyal to her family be permitted to seek some other powerful protector. As soon as Jean Grimaldi had her approval of this alternative in his pocket, he recommended to the city fathers of Nice in his function of governor that the count of Savoy would make an ideal defender. The Niçois had no desire to find themselves once more under Angevin rule, so they willingly accepted the governor's recommendation. So masterful was Grimaldi's plotting that the day after the city fathers had agreed to this plan, the count of Savoy appeared with a considerable army. But the next scene reveals Grimaldi even more clearly as a politician par excellence. To prevent the Niçois from suspecting a

plot, Amadeus VII did not approach the city gates as the count of Savoy, but in his inherited guise of vicar for the Holy Roman emperor, to whom Provence owed feudal allegiance. Amadeus thus appeared to his unknowing new subjects not as a covetous neighbor but as the official representative of the highest feudal power of all. The wording of the contract of assistance drawn up with the city on September 28, 1388 was also a brilliant example of political cunning. The count of Savoy was to assume the role of Nice's feudal overlord for a period of only three years. At the end of this period, Nice would revert to the house of Durazzo, provided that the latter could repay its war debts to Savoy. The contract ran out on September 28, 1391. Durazzo was unable to come up with the required funds and Nice elected to remain a vassal of Savoy.

In 1416, the counts of Savoy were elevated to dukes by the emperor and the pope, and three years later, Yolande of France renounced her feudal claims to Nice and its surroundings. In return, the duke of Savoy "generously" absolved her of the large war debt of 124,000 gold florins dating back to 1383 and Nice was annexed by Savoy.

An Outpost of Turin

BEING SUBJECT TO SAVOY WAS BY NO MEANS advantageous to Nice. It was now cut off economically from both France and Genoa, and its new capital, Turin, lay beyond the Alps—whose passes were difficult to cross in winter. Nice and its territory had fallen into a deadly isolation. For Turin, the city was simply a Mediterranean outpost. Nice's fortress was again enlarged and occupied with troops from Savoy, while its income served only to enrich the Savoyard coffers.

Once the western part of Provence fell to the royal house of France for good in 1481, Nice and Antibes became the hostile bulwarks of two major powers. The ancient Greek cities of Nikaia and Antipolis were now being crushed between these growing states.

Nice, the "Maid of Provence," was repeatedly attacked by France, and the lower town was devastated each time. Francis I of France even recruited the aid of the Turk-

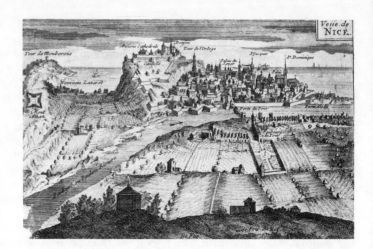

Nice, before the seventeenth-century destruction of the upper town.

ish admiral Barbarossa, thus initiating one of the bloodiest and most tragic chapters in the history of Provence. One of the players in this episode was Catherine Ségurane, a washerwoman who is now celebrated as Nice's own Joan of Arc. On August 14, 1543, after Turkish cannons had breached the fortifications and the sultan's invincible Janissaries were on the verge of storming the walls, this thirty-three-year-old woman who was said to be "like a Hun in size and strong as a bear" somehow managed to snatch the Turks' green standard. They were so startled and the Niçois so inspired by her example that the invaders abandoned their attack on the fortress and retreated to their ships. The French, fearing they would not be able to capture the citadel without the help of the Turks, plundered and set fire to the lower town, a crime that France's royal chroniclers later credited to the Turks.

For centuries, Nice suffered from its isolation and from the ravages of war. It was occupied by France for three brief periods. Louvois managed to convince Louis XIV that the control of the city was a strategic

necessity, even though its fortress was considered impregnable. But on March 30, 1691, roughly 2,000 pounds of gunpowder exploded in a tower in the citadel. To this day it is not known whether this blast was an accident or the result of sabotage, but it caused such damage that Count Frossasco of Savoy was forced to surrender to the French.

Vauban recognized Nice's importance to France and argued for holding on to it and expanding its fortifications. However, the Sun King had other plans. As a means of getting the dukes of Savoy to quit the League of Augsburg, he returned all of their possessions at the Peace of Turin in 1696.

A few years later, during the War of the Spanish Succession, the citadel of Nice, still unrepaired, again fell into French hands. The victorious English General Berwick, fighting on the side of France in 1706, ordered that Nice's walls be razed, thus sealing the fate of a citadel that was more than 2,000 years old. Once again, however, the county of Nice was restored to Savoy at the Peace of Utrecht.

Following the example of other cities in

French Provence, Nice staged a revolution of its own in 1789. The bourgeoisie gained control in 1792 after Savoyard troops had abandoned the city, and the bloody excesses that swept Paris were unknown in Nice. Inflamed by the slogan *"Liberté, Egalité, Fraternité,"* Nice voted to join the Republic, sending Paul Barras to the National Convention as its deputy. Barras would do much to advance the career of Napoleon, as did Marshal André Masséna, another native of Nice.

When the First Empire collapsed, Nice had had enough of France and the Niçois were delighted when the Congress of Vien-

na restored the city to the house of Savoy. But their pleasure was short-lived. The congress had also granted Genoa to Turin, and the dukes of Savoy and kings of Sardinia deemed Genoa all-important. The city's economic isolation was worse than ever before. Turin did not support its endeavors to open up new markets or even to undertake improvements such as building new streets, laying rail lines, or enlarging the harbor. The time was ripe for a return to France. Against the objections of Giuseppe Garibaldi and Léon Gambetta, a plebiscite was staged by Camilla Benso, count of Cavour, on April 14, 1860, when a large ma-

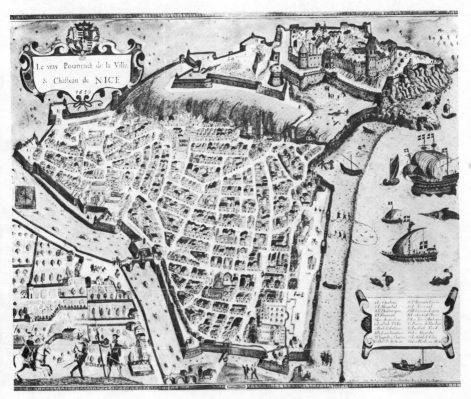

Nice before the 1706 destruction of the Citadel.

An 1874 view of Nice.

CH. BARBANT Sc.

jority voted in favor of the city's annexation by France. The official changeover was celebrated with great pomp and ceremony. Théodore Banville's play *The French City of Nice* was staged, and Napoleon III appeared on September 12 to a triumphal welcome. The emperor, true to his word at that ceremony, made sure that the city was quickly linked to France by economic bonds and new transportation lines. The years between 1860 and 1914 were unquestionably the richest phase in the city's nearly twenty-five-hundred-year history.

The Winter Capital of Europe

AFTER THE LONG-SUFFERING "MAID OF PROVENCE" had forever lost its major asset, its fortified citadel, the city had to concentrate on its second natural advantage, its harbor. Nice's development as a port seemed especially promising in 1718 when Victor-Amadeus of Savoy lost Sicily but gained in exchange Sardinia and the title of that island's king. Savoy thus became a sea empire to some extent, and its new kings required a suitable harbor linking Turin to Sardinia. With Turin's assistance, work on the Lympia Harbor, east of the citadel, began in 1749. But initial hopes were dashed when dredging revealed great unmovable blocks of stone on the harbor floor that created shallows too dangerous for larger freight vessels.

A nineteenth-century drawing of bridges across the Var.

But the eighteenth century finally provided new and unexpected possibilities. General Berwick's razing of Nice's ramparts in 1706 had made the city vulnerable to attack, but it also opened it to foreigners with more peaceful intentions. As the century progressed, a small elite began to gather here including writers, artists, aristocratic invalids and their doctors, exiled politicians, as well as travelers of means. In 1699, for example, the painter Louis Van Loo took refuge in Nice when forced to leave Amsterdam after a duel. His son Carle, who was born here in 1705, would rise to become court painter to Louis XIV.

English naval officers who had become acquainted with Nice during the War of the Austrian Succession (1740–1748) were particularly taken by its paradisiacal charms and they, along with their compatriots, came to dominate the city's foreign colony after that conflict. The Duke of York, the brother of George III, arrived in 1764. The Duke and Duchess of Gloucester soon followed; their children's tutor, the Savoyard A. Beaumont, wrote *Voyage pittoresque à travers le comté de Nice*, which contains revealing glimpses of the landscape and way of life along the Côte d'Azur at that time. The Scottish doctor and traveler Tobias Smollett wrote an even more detailed report on the surroundings, populace, customs, and conditions of Nice in his *Travels through France and Italy*, published in 1776. By the winter of 1787, 115 foreign families, not all of them British, were living in Nice.

Until the end of the nineteenth century one of the main reasons foreigners wintered or settled here was the prevalent medical belief that the mild climate of the Côte d'Azur was curative, especially in cases of lung disease. Even Voltaire apparently subscribed to this notion, for in 1777

he recommended the healing air of Nice as a cure for Trudaine, the finance minister.

The city began to change its appearance in the middle of the eighteenth century. In conjunction with work on the Lympia Harbor, an embankment promenade was laid out along the foot of the citadel, the precursor of the present-day Quai de Etats-Unis. Thanks to a royal dispensation from Turin, Nice built its first theater in 1775. With a population of 12,000, Nice had become the only major city along this coast, but its hotel accommodations were inadequate to serve the steadily growing stream of foreigners. At first these visitors took rooms with local families, but by the end of the century they were building their own villas to the west of the Paillon river in what the English referred to as "Newborough." The Savoyard coffers were continually running low and it was discovered that the sale of offices and titles could provide useful income. As a result, Tobias Smollett was able to report: "The local nobility is almost wholly false, made up of wealthy merchants—wine dealers, for example—who have purchased their titles of 'count' or 'marquis' for roughly 300 pounds sterling."

The greatest difficulty for these early tourists was getting to Nice in the first place. The journey from Paris took twelve days by coach, and then one had to cross the Var. This river, the frontier between French Provence and Savoy since 1481, was highly unpredictable, for it flowed straight down from the Alps and often proved impassable. Getting ladies across was a matter of particular delicacy: they had to be carried on the shoulders of two strong men, held tight by firm hands on their thighs. Numerous self-styled protectors of morals found this practice scandalous; however, the ladies themselves appear to have endured the grip of these strong male hands with somewhat greater equanimity. Besides, once safely landed in paradise, all such trials were forgotten. As poet Jacques Delille exclaimed: "O Nice! Joyous idyll with sweet-smelling mountains of lavender, thyme, and lemons!"

After 2,000 years of being buffeted by fate, Nice was undergoing a change for the better. All the city had to do was to make these foreigners welcome. Once they had been made to feel at home, they either stayed on or at least came back—and attracted still others by writing enthusiastic letters home. Nice played its cards wisely and the winnings began to pile up in amounts never dreamed of.

Because of the rank and temperament of its early guests, Nice came to be the second most important cultural center in France, surpassed only by Paris. Until World War I, and even for some time afterward, the Côte d'Azur was not only a haven for nature lovers and seekers after a warm climate, but also a stronghold of artistic and intellectual activity. It was frequented by aristocrats, business magnates, and political leaders from all of Europe as well as by philosophers, writers, poets, musicians, and painters.

Among the dignitaries whom Nice welcomed during this heady period were Czar Alexander II, his wife Maria Alexandrova, and other members of the Russian imperial family; King Ludwig I of Bavaria (who, after his abdication in 1848, spent his winters here and served on the Carnaval committee); the king and queen of Württemberg, Archduke Ludwig-Victor of Austria, and King Leopold II of Belgium. Baron Haussmann built himself a retirement home on Mont Boron, and in 1862, Baron von Rothschild threw a gala banquet for 600 people. Even this highly abbreviated list of Nice's prominent guests makes it clear why the city deserved its title of winter capital of Europe.

The aristocrats were driven away temporarily by the Franco-Prussian War of 1870–1871, but the British came back as soon as possible. Among the early arrivals were the Prince of Wales (later King Edward VII) and his brother-in-law Prince Henry of Battenberg. Queen Victoria herself first visited in 1894, the year she turned seventy-five; S. M. Biasini, a Nice architect, built her a truly regal residence in Cimiez, the Regina Palace, the most impressive and lavish of the winter palaces along the coast during the *fin de siècle*. Though the city had become republican after the collapse of the Second Empire, Nice continued to cater to its royal guests, and by the early 1870s the *Journal des Débats* could claim that the city had again become "the Versailles of the south of France."

Locally born residents, though not as socially glamorous, also achieved great prominence. Giuseppe Garibaldi, for example, was born in Nice in 1807. This famous Italian freedom fighter was an outspoken opponent of Cavour, who successfully arranged the transfer of the county of Nice to Napoleon III. Even though Nice is now quite content to be a part of France, it continues to revere this native son.

Léon Gambetta, an enemy of the Second Empire, a determined republican, and ultimately prime minister of the Third Republic, was born in Cahors but grew up in Nice. His ties to the city were so strong that he asked to be buried in the cemetery on the old citadel, and the Niçois rightly consider him one of their own.

The first republican mayor of Nice after the fall of the Second Empire was Borriglioni, or "Moussu Bourrioun" as his constituents fondly referred to him in Nissard,

Nice in the nineteenth century.

the local Provençal dialect. This man was a leader of genius and foresight. He not only oversaw the forging of secure links to the rest of France but managed to push through crucial programs to improve the city itself, commissioning new buildings and instigating needed public works while restoring and protecting the old town.

Creative people from all walks of cultural life also were attracted to Nice. Alphonse Karr has already been introduced in connection with St-Raphaël. A second was Stephen Liégeard, successively a lawyer, subprefect, delegate to the Assembly, and writer. In 1887 he published a historic but now almost forgotten book, *La Côte d'Azur*. This work, awarded a prize by the Académie Française and praised by *Le Figaro*, gave the coastline its modern name. Alexandre Dumas père, Frédéric Mistral, Guy de Maupassant, Eugène Scribe, Adolphe

Thiers, Stendhal, and Jean Aicard were but a few of the literati drawn to the city. Gambetta, Prévost, composer Isaac Albéniz, and others were frequent guests of Countess Ratazzi (an eccentric cousin of Napoleon III banished by him from Paris), who also frequented the soirées of Madame Germain. In the Taverne Gothique, the poet Jean Sarrasin offered not only readings of his works but also olives grown on his own trees. The young and gifted Marie Baskirtscheff, fondly known as "Moussia" and considered queen of her "season," kept a perceptive diary from 1873 until her premature death in 1884 that was posthumously published in 1887. Guillaume Apollinaire, who had gone to school here, often returned to escape Paris. Another writer drawn to Nice was the Belgian, Maurice Maeterlinck, who first occupied the Villa Les Abeilles on the elevation known as

Nice

Les Baumettes. Later, with his new wife, he settled into the somewhat unusual Villa Orlamonde, which was in fact an unfinished casino on Mont Boron.

Among the composers to frequent Nice was Hector Berlioz, who composed his overtures to *King Lear* and *The Corsair* here. Charles Gounod and Jules Massenet also visited occasionally, and in the café of the Hôtel des Etrangers one could find Jacques Offenbach composing at the piano. The Spanish composer and pianist Albéniz finally settled here for good in the Villa Château St-Laurent, just around the corner from the Maeterlincks.

Not all of the artists living in Nice were caught up in the glittering world of the salons and casinos, however. Jean Lorrain, for example, was not averse to reviling the exclusive world to which he himself was not admitted. In the Villa Bounin (today on the Boulevard de l'Impératrice), he wrote *Le Crime des Riches* in 1905, from which we learn:

All of the deranged and crazed souls of the world, all of the misfits and hysterics, tend to rendezvous here, all in dead earnest. They come from Russia, they come from America, from Tibet, from southern Africa... and on top of that what an endless stream of old ladies! The Riviera is their undeserved homeland; nowhere do you run into such an array of youthful centenarians and tarted-up ostriches....O Riviera! Riviera, the blue paradise for confidence men and deviates! False noses bloom here more abundantly than the mimosas, false noses and false names and false titles. All this is here waiting for anyone who crosses the Var, the Rubicon of the Alpes Maritimes.

Another well-known though antisocial figure, philosopher Friedrich Nietzsche, spent five winters in Nice, each time in the most modest of rooms. When he left Nice in April 1888, he had in his suitcase the completed manuscript of *The Will to Power.*

IN 1878, AUGUSTE RODIN'S TEACHER, C.-H.-J. Cordier, brought his pupil to Nice where they each created one of the caryatids for the Villa Neptune (105 Promenade des Anglais). Rodin described his stay with enthusiasm: "I am carving on my caryatid with delight. Right before me is the sea, with nothing to obscure it but laurels and rose bushes, tropical trees and cactuses. Each moment is a joy." When you consider that Nice produced a school of primitive painters in the fifteenth and sixteenth centuries (Jacques Durandi, Louis Bréa, Giovanni Canavesio included), that it was home to the Van Loos in the seventeenth century, and that it has given its name to the modern Ecole de Nice centered around Yves Klein, Arman, and César, you realize that the city's contribution to the history of painting is also impressive.

But perhaps the artists who have had the greatest effect on Nice have been its architects. Thanks to the expansion required to provide for large-scale tourism, an extremely rapid population growth, and the presence of a wealthy and free-spending foreign clientele, the working conditions for architects were virtually ideal. Two additional factors affected the creation of Nice's architecture: (1) during the first half of the nineteenth century, new building materials such as steel, cast iron, and glass became available, supplementing traditional stone and brick and enabling architects to invent new forms and practices; and (2) its patrons were not only wealthy but also of diverse tastes often tending toward the exotic and downright eccentric.

The first major projects undertaken by the city itself were modeled after neoclassical forms in Piedmont and Liguria. This influence is particularly apparent in the Place Masséna, dating from 1840–1860, Place Garibaldi, and Place de l'Ile-de-Beauté, begun in 1850. A far less uniform picture is presented wherever private patrons dictated a building's proportions and style. The city's luxurious residences of this period fall into three major groupings: the Troubadour style, the Oriental or exotic style, and the Italianate style. The first of these, named for the recollections of medieval castles inspired by the romantic novels of Sir Walter Scott, was introduced by the English and is far more common in the British outpost in Cannes, where it was championed by Sir Thomas Woolfield.

The Oriental style was launched by another Englishman, a Colonel Smith, who built the Château de l'Anglais on Mont Boron, a structure locally known as "Smith's Folly." Smith had been commander of British colonial troops in India between 1803 and 1830. He retired to England early and commissioned a first "Smith's Folly" based on Indian forms, in Paignton, Devonshire. Then, when he decided to spend his old age on the Côte d'Azur, he constructed this second one, which shows less Indian influence. Created by Italian builders, it represents an absolutely unprecedented blend of Western, medieval, and Oriental elements that astonished even the jaded Niçois.

However, the overwhelming majority of private builders favored Italianate designs. One notable example was the Rothschild family, whose Villa Vigier on Mont Boron— unfortunately, no longer standing—was a replica of the Cà d'Oro in Venice. A villa on Les Baumettes, built in 1878 by the Russian Princess Kotshoubey and furnished by an American by the name of Thompson, also shows numerous elements of Genoese Mannerism.

The hill of Cimiez was incorporated into the city by a new boulevard in 1866, thus opening up a whole new area for construction. This section was truly developed only after the Franco-Prussian War, which ushered in the phase known as the Belle Epoque and a change in the style of building in Nice. The main contingent of pensioners and winter sojourners now consisted not only of the English, but of other Frenchmen who were members of both the aristocracy and the upper middle class. The style of architecture began to be oriented more to the north, to Paris and England, where the new methods of steel and glass construction were increasingly common. A number of prominent Parisian architects were awarded major commissions along the Côte d'Azur, among them Charles Garnier and Edouard Niermans. The train station in Nice (begun by Bouchot in 1865) had heralded this nationalistic trend with its borrowings from native French architecture of the seventeenth century.

A most magnificent realization of the new possibilities of glass and cast iron was the famous Casino de la Jetée-Promenade. For no apparent reason this was torn down in 1943, as was the landmark of the old harbor in Marseilles, the Transbordeur. Other important buildings that defined the image of Nice in the Belle Epoque (1880–1914) have also recently fallen to the wrecker's ball—for example, the municipal casino on Place Masséna, which was built after plans by Omer Lazard in 1881–1884 and razed in 1979. Another is the Hôtel des Anglais, torn down in 1970, which once dominated the view from the Jardin Albert I.

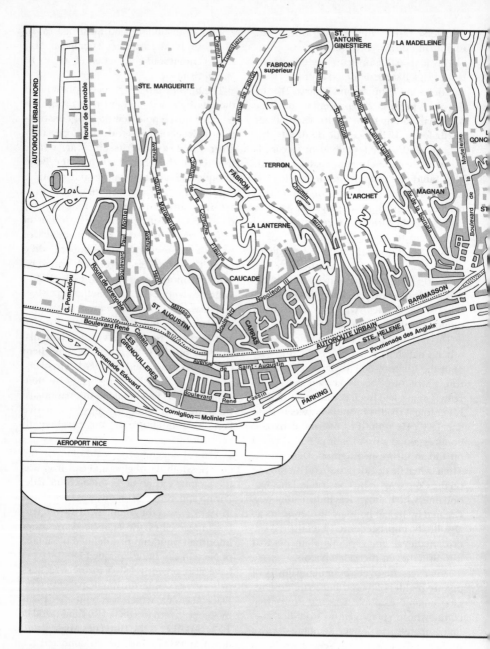

Nice: General map

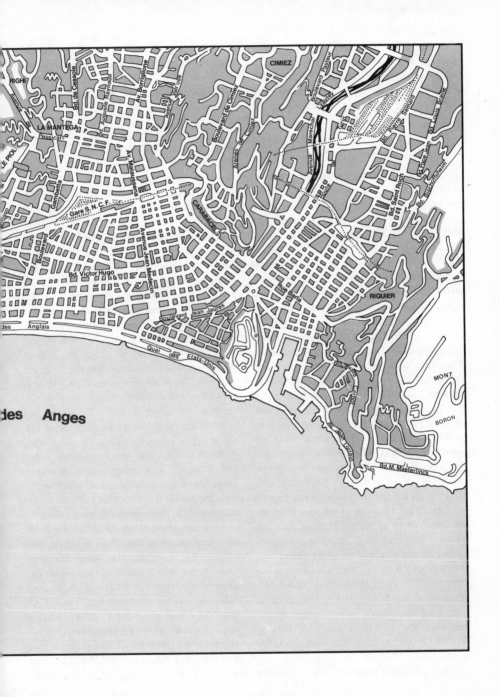

RIGHI

Bd. de Cessole

LA MANTEGA
Pessicart

Av. Auguste Raynaud

Av. Borriglione

Avenue Jan Oré

CIMIEZ

Boulevard Pasteur

Boulevard de Cimiez

Arènes de Cimiez

Av. Malausséna

Avenue Maréchal

Pierre Semard

Bd. Louis Braille

Gambetta

Gare S.N.C.F.

CARABACEL

Bd. Saint Roch

Bd. Bischoffsheim

Bd. Victor Hugo

Avenue Jean Médecin

RIQUIER

Rue Barla

Boulevard Jean Jaurès

des   Anglais

Quai   des   Etats-Unis

Boulevard Carnot

MONT

BORON

Av. Jean Lorrain

des   Anges

Bd. M. Maeterlinck

The only surviving Belle Epoque buildings on the shore are the Hôtel Negresco and the Villa Masséna (now the Musée Masséna). More of the luxurious architecture of this period still stands at the top of the Boulevard de Cimiez, where the local architects S. M. Biasini and Charles Dalmas each constructed massive projects. Most of that area's elegant residences are still preserved.

Nice Today

WORLD WAR I CHANGED THE POLITICAL MAP OF Europe and swept away for good many of the emperors, kings, princes, dukes, and magnates who had brought prosperity to Nice. The city had to adapt and find new ways to prosper. Its new mayor, the young lawyer Jean Médecin, proved to be a new Borriglioni. Under his intelligent administration, Nice began to free itself from total dependence on tourism. Médecin served as mayor for thirty-seven years until he died in 1965. During that period Nice's population grew from 200,000 to 300,000. The Promenade des Anglais was extended and given its present form, the Place Masséna was developed further, a school for hoteliers was founded, and the airport was constructed. One quite successful project was the creation of a pedestrian zone between the Jardin Albert I, the Promenade des Anglais, Place Masséna, and Rue de Magenta. Many of the city's imposing residences, no longer occupied, were turned into apartment houses or adapted for public use. Artists including Matisse, Albéniz, Maeterlinck, and Jules Romains continued to live in the city, and Serge Sandberg, the film pioneer, founded the Victorine Studios here in 1919. The Centre Universitaire Méditerrannéen was founded; its first director was poet Paul Valéry, and Valrose Palace became its administration building. By 1972, the school had some 15,000 students.

Nice is second only to Paris as France's most important museum city. The Musée Chéret occupies the Villa Thompson; the municipal museum the Palais Lascaris and the Villa Masséna; and the Musée Matisse and Musée Archéologique share the former Villa des Arènes. In addition, new structures were built for the Musée Marc Chagall and the Musée de Terra Amata.

Since the new town developed in the nineteenth century, Nice's most important city-planning problem was the gaping rift cut between the two parts of town by the Paillon river. In various stages the Paillon was simply covered over but the hole remained. The problem was brilliantly solved recently: a necessary evil of every city, a central bus terminal, was placed here beneath hanging gardens and terraces, at the same time closing the unsightly gap. Clearly, both natives and tourists alike are the beneficiaries, and behind such planning lurks the old, delightful capacity of the Niçois for *savoir vivre*—or as Jules Romains suggested, *la douceur de vivre*.

Nice has also set about attracting both light and heavy industry to the region and broadening its economic base in other ways. It has wisely offset the loss of its exclusive wintertime social stratum by developing additional drawing cards. An exhibition hall was built in 1958, creating space for a number of international fairs—since 1969 it has been the site of the annual International Book Festival, for example. And Nice has become the most popular convention center in France. By 1971 it was hosting as many as a thousand conventions annually and its development of the Palais des Expositions, a mammoth facility on the hill of St-Philippe west of the city, underscores its determination to develop this industry further. After all, what city in France is better equipped to receive guests and spoil them than Nice with its wealth of flowers, its sun, and its sea?

Points of Interest

AS WE HAVE SEEN, THE PRESENT-DAY CITY LIMITS of Nice encompass what were in antiquity two independent and culturally distinct communities: Roman Cemenelum, which died out in the sixth century, and Greek Nikaia. In the Middle Ages there were again two communities. Then, after the fortress walls were razed in 1706, only the medieval lower town survived. But beginning in the eighteenth century, two new urban centers began to take shape. The first of these was located east of the citadel, surrounding the planned Lympia Harbor and extending from Place Victor (now Place Garibaldi) to the foot of Mont Boron. Somewhat later, when the number of win-ter guests began to burgeon, the area beyond the west bank of the Paillon was built up. Lying between the hill of Les Baumettes, the Promenade des Anglais, the tracks of the Marseille–Toulon–Genoa railway, the spurs of the hill of Cimiez, and the Paillon, this latter area forms the actual core of modern Nice; the Avenue Jean-Médecin and Boulevard Victor-Hugo are its main axes. Finally, with the construction of the Boulevard de Cimiez in 1866 and the incorporation of that ancient hill into the city limits, Nice came to consist of three distinct sections, each of a different age: the old town, which developed in the thirteenth century; the new town; and Cimiez.

The Old Town

Cathédrale Ste-Réparate, Place Rosetti—Palais Lascaris—The Préfecture—Chapelle de la Miséricorde—Théâtre de l'Opéra— Cours Saleya (Flower Market)

CATHEDRALE STE-REPARATE, PLACE ROSETTI. Since the thirteenth century, the monks of St-Pons have maintained a priory and a church at the foot of the citadel consecrated to St. Reparata, Nice's patron. Reparata was a young Christian woman in Caesarea who was martyred in about 250, under Emperor Decius. Portions of the thirteenth-century building can still be seen in the lower walls on the east side of the choir. In the sixteenth century, the bishop's seat was moved into this church.

The present cathedral, constructed by Nice architect J.-A. Guibera, dates for the most part to the mid-seventeenth century. Its flat, two-story façade, with Corinthian pilasters, a high entablature, and a low pediment is clearly inspired by Italian Baroque concepts. Its spacious interior consists of a center aisle with four extremely wide perpendicular bays, two high side aisles, and adjacent chapels. The crossing appears to be constricted by the deeply projecting, massive main pillars, and it is topped by a pendentive cupola. The wall arrangement of the nave continues even into the choir bay and the rectangular choir itself. Rich stucco ornamentation, with gold and blue accents against a predominantly white background, blends harmoniously with the lavish choir stalls. The priceless seventeenth-century wood paneling of the sacristy was originally created for the Dominican monastery.

PALAIS LASCARIS (SEE MAP, BELOW). THIS residence of the ancient and influential Lascaris-Ventimiglia family is unquestionably the showpiece of the old town. In 1643–1650, Jean Baptiste, the nephew of J. P. Lascaris of Castellar and grand master of the Order of Malta, had the present palace erected in place of four adjacent buildings in the center of town. Its lavish façade contrasts with neighboring buildings and indicates that this is a noble house, even though decoration is restricted mainly to the ground floor and the *piano nobile*. On entering, you find yourself in a spacious ves-

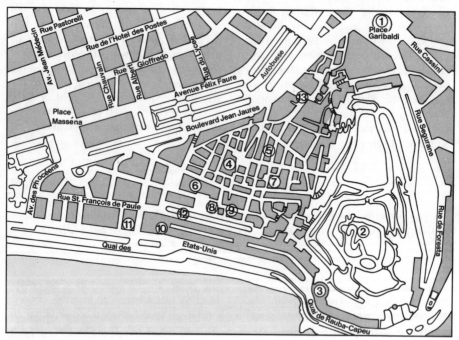

Nice: Map of the Old Town. 1. Place Garibaldi; 2. Citadel with cascade, ruins of the Old Cathedral, and Belvédère; 3. Tour Bellanda; 4. Cathedral, Place Rosetti; 5. Palais Lascaris (15, rue Droite); 6. Préfecture (former palace of the Dukes of Savoy); 7. Jesuit Church of St-Jacques; 8. St-Cajetan (Chapelle de la Miséricorde); 9. Galérie de Malacologie (3, Cours Saleya); 10. Galérie des Ponchettes; 11. Opéra; 12. Flower Market; 13. Place St-François, Fish Market.

tibule with a splendid open staircase in the style of the Genoese Baroque. The vaulting above this vestibule displays the coat of arms of the Lascaris-Ventimiglia family. Wall-painting fragments in the stairwell date back to the palace's construction. The structure was in very poor condition when it was acquired by the city in 1942, but thorough restoration began in 1963. Three rooms on the second floor have seventeenth-century ceiling frescoes on mythological subjects, including *Mercury Presenting Psyche to Olympus* and the *Fall of Phaeton*, which is ascribed, like the one in Cagnes, to the Genoese fresco painter Giovanni Battista Carlone. Gobelins tapestries on the walls were executed after drawings by Rubens and depict scenes from the life of Achilles. The more important rooms, including the stateroom (Chambre d'Apparat), are outfitted with eighteenth-century furnishings. The rooms on the fourth floor sometimes house special exhibitions.

THE PREFECTURE. NOW THE CITY'S POLICE headquarters, this edifice was once a residence of the dukes of Savoy and kings of Sardinia who long ruled Nice. Its effect has been compromised by the addition of the Palace of Justice to the west, and the only part of the structure that preserves something of its sumptuous early seventeenth-century Mannerist elegance is the south façade, facing the Place Pierre Gautier. The columned gallery that runs across the entire width of the broad building and brackets both stories gives it grace and lightness, although the strict adherence to an ordination of double Ionic columns seems somewhat repetitive.

CHAPELLE DE LA MISÉRICORDE. THIS IS NICE'S most remarkable Baroque church. Al-

though its two-story, three-bay façade, designed by Italian architect Guarino Guarini, recalls the customary elevation scheme of earlier Italian structures, it also betrays a keen and refreshing understanding of these models and a controlled virtuosity. The church's subtly convex central bay reveals the harmonious restraint of all of the rest of its parts.

The interior, open only to guided tours, also reveals a greater complexity than a first glance would suggest. The square and the oval are the basic geometric forms, and they have been combined with great sensitivity. The shallow cupola above an oval crossing appears to virtually float above the arches of adjacent chapel niches. On either side of this central oval, there are two oval chapels. The slightly concave façade and choir apse recall the shapes of these chapels. The décor and furnishings of the church have a Rococo elegance. A special rarity adorns the high altar, the *Vierge de la Miséricorde*, the only painting attributable with certainty to Jean Marailhet of Montpellier. This work, presumably created between 1430 and 1440, displays typical features of the primitive School of Nice, especially the motif of the Madonna sheltering the faithful beneath her cloak and flanked by saints—in this case, Cosmas and Damian on one side and Sebastian and Gregory on the other.

THEATRE DE L'OPÉRA. THE OPÉRA, BUILT BY F. Aune in 1882–1885, shows little influence of Garnier's love of splendor, having more in common with the Italian tradition of theater building. The façade stands on the Rue St-François-de-Paule, an extension of the *Cours Saleya*, now the *Flower Market*, a rendezvous for Nice's high society in the nineteenth century. Also facing the Cours Saleya was the famous Librairie Visconti.

The New Town

Le Paillon—Jardin Albert I (Théâtre Verdure)—Casino Ruhl—
Place Masséna—Pedestrian Zone—Promenade des Anglais—
Palais de la Méditerrannée—Hôtel Negresco—Musée
Masséna —Musée Chéret (Villa Thompson)

LE PAILLON. IN 1861 A PUNDIT WROTE: "THE PAIL- lon [river] is the cancer of Nice. It is like those *clochards* who know no moderation: either they are dry or they are full." During the Ancien Régime, a mounted guard was stationed upstream and would ride into town at a gallop to warn the washerwomen: *"Paioun ven!"* ("The Paillon is rising!"). Then, after 1860, it was decided to simply remove the problem of the river by building over it and, beginning at its mouth, the Paillon was covered in stages. The *Jardin Albert I*, built over the river, was designed by Gilly and was dominated by the Hôtel de Anglais, one of the best-known structures of its kind, which was razed in 1970, giving way to the popular but undistinguished *Casino Ruhl*. In various stages, 1893,1931, and 1972, the river was covered as far as the Palais des Expositions.

PLACE MASSENA. PLANS FOR A RECTANGULAR square at the end of the Pont Neuf across the Paillon were developed as early as 1815. This square was built in 1835 and surrounded with Italianate townhouses on the long sides. The east side was dominated by the quais and the Pont Neuf, while the west side, the present-day Avenue Jean-Médecin, was extended to form a new axis through the developing Right Bank. The arcaded façades were inspired by squares in Turin and were designed by the Savoyard architect Vernier. The overall layout of the square still represents the Baroque tradition.

THE PEDESTRIAN ZONE, BEGINNING WEST OF THE Place Masséna, now extends as far as the Rue de Congrès, but is being expanded further. It has replaced the Cours Saleya as a leading shopping center and promenade.

PROMENADE DES ANGLAIS. EARLY IN THE NINE- teenth century, a small shore promenade was developed for daytime horseback riding or a nocturnal coach ride in the section where the English aristocrats had constructed their beach residences. This dusty shore road was improved thanks to the initiative of Reverend Lewis Way, who was disturbed by the high unemployment among the local populace. He called together a crew of the poor and destitute to construct a better street and raised the necessary funds by taking up a collection among his "brothers and sisters" in the English colony. The street, at that time only a few hundred yards long, was developed before 1840. The natives referred to this new shore road between the sea and the English "Newborough" as the *"Camin dai Angles"*; translated out of dialect, this became the Promenade des Anglais. In 1900, a number of lavish palaces began to adorn the Promenade des Anglais, but only a few of them still stand—for example, No. 105, Villa Neptune (with a caryatid by Rodin), and No. 139, the 1910 Villa, with façade decoration by F. Virieux. This latter villa is

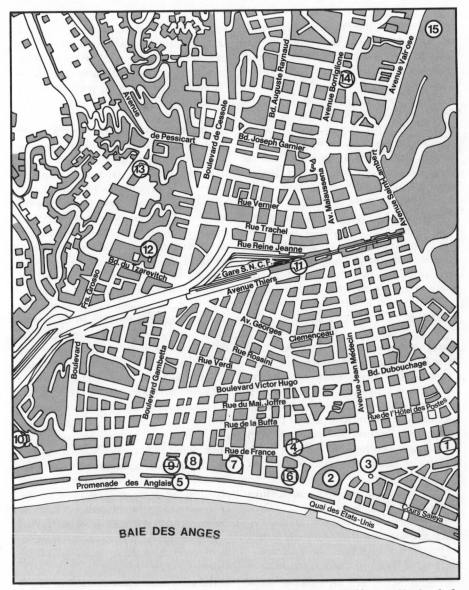

Nice: Map of the New Town. 1. Le Paillon; 2. Jardin Albert I (Théâtre de Verdure); 3. Place Masséna; 4. Pedestrian zone; 5. Promenade des Anglais; 6. Casino Rühl; 7. Palais de la Méditerranée; 8. Musée Masséna; 9. Hôtel Negresco; 10. Musée Chéret (Villa Thompson); 11. Train station; 12. Russian Orthodox Church; 13. Villa Bermond; 14. Church of Ste-Jeanne d'Arc; 15. Château Valrose.

an example of the "noodle style" *(style nouille)*, rare in Nice. The Promenade was given its present appearance during the administration of Mayor Jean Médecin in 1931.

PALAIS DE LA MEDITERRANNÉE (SEE MAP, P. 217). One of Nice's two important native architects was Charles Dalmas, who created the Winter Palace and L'Hermitage, among other monuments. His Palais de la Méditerrannée, built in 1929, reveals a new trend exemplified in Paris by Auguste Perret's Théâtre des Champs Elysées. The excessive ornamentation that was so favored until World War I has completely disappeared, even though there is still an obvious emphasis on monumentality. The Palais de la Méditerrannée is meant to be imposing, but is relatively sober and functional.

HOTEL NEGRESCO (SEE MAP, P. 217). THIS GRAND Belle Epoque hotel, constructed in 1912, exemplifies the richly ornamented, Italianate style of architecture popular during that glamorous period. The Parisian architect Edouard Niermans designed the Negresco as a symmetrical structure with façades facing both south (the Promenade des Anglais and the sea) and east (bordering the gardens of the Villa Masséna). The seaside façade is the more elaborate with a long central tract composed of nine bays, elegantly decorated with balustrades, Corinthian columns and pilasters, and rounded pavilions at each end. The six floors—the ground floor rusticated to add an air of strength and solidity—are topped by a Mansard roof. The entrance to the hotel is located in the larger east corner rotunda which echoes the design of the south façade; the attic stories are surmounted not by a Mansard roof, but a cupola. This crown on the top of the grand hotel is a landmark. The best view of the Negresco is from the southeast where the two perpendicular façades and the rotunda are all visible and the "palace by the sea" can be fully appreciated.

MUSÉE MASSENA (SEE MAP, P. 217). BETWEEN THE Palais de la Méditerrannée and the Negresco, though with considerable breathing space on either side, stands the former residence of the prince of Essling, Victor Masséna, the grandson of the famous Marshal Masséna. This villa was constructed between 1899 and 1902, and was the work of the Paris architect Thiercelin. The native architect Messiah was entrusted with its execution. The Italianate structure was modeled on Lucien Bonaparte's villa in Govone in the Piedmont. Prince André, Victor's son, donated the villa to the city in 1919 with two stipulations—it was to be turned into a museum of local history, and its gardens were to be opened to the public—to which the city has adhered.

The ground floor of this municipal museum consists of a series of salons in the Empire style that are used for special receptions. Particularly noteworthy furnishings include a bust of Marshal Masséna by Antonio Canova; chairs and divans by J. Desmalter; and a portrait of Empress Josephine by Baron Antoine-Jean Gros. A library donated by the Chevalier Victor de Cessole is housed in the former study. Two large paintings in the stairwell leading to the second floor depict members of the Masséna and Ney families.

The second floor houses exhibits dating from the Middle Ages until the time of the city's annexation by France. Among the highlights of the collection are works by the School of Nice, including their chief representatives, Louis Bréa and Jacques

Durandi, and supplemented by other early paintings from Italy, Spain, and Flanders. There are also studies of the head of the young Napoleon Bonaparte by Jacques-Louis David and a richly carved fifteenth-century wedding chest. In the stairwell leading to the third floor is a sequence of copies of late medieval frescoes whose originals lie in the mountainous interior of the county. These reproductions, executed in watercolor before 1914 by Alexis and Gustav-Adolf Mossa, testify to the style and iconography of the frescoes of that time.

The third floor houses private collections given to the city: the Porcher-Labreuil bequest, consisting of French and Italian ceramics; the Joubert bequest, including weapons and armor from the fifteenth to seventeenth centuries and various Limoges enamels, among them the reliquary casket of St. Commodus from the mid-thirteenth century; the Chapsal bequest, comprising jewelry from all over the world. Three other rooms are devoted to folk art, and one gallery commemorates the city's illustrious son Giuseppe Garibaldi.

MUSÉE CHÉRET (VILLA THOMPSON) (SEE MAP, P. 217). This splendid villa, begun on the slopes of Les Baumettes in 1875, was originally intended to be the palatial residence of the Russian Princess Kotshoubey, but construction was ultimately completed by its second owner, the American James Thompson. Designed in an Italianate style, the villa is reminiscent of a Late Renaissance country house in its spaciousness and elegance. The Villa Thompson was acquired by the city of Nice, which inaugurated the Musée Chéret in January 1928. The first director was Symbolist painter Gustav-Adolf Mossa. The collection includes the holdings of Nice's earlier Musée des Beaux-Arts, founded about 1860, plus gifts from individuals and works owned by the French government.

The ground floor houses impressive examples of seventeenth- and eighteenth-century painting. A masterpiece, *Head of an Old Man*, is a rare meditative work by Fragonard. Carle Van Loo is represented by several paintings including his *Neptune and Anymone* from 1757. Also exhibited are idyllic landscapes and scenes of classical ruins by the French painter Hubert Robert. The sculpture collection features Rodin's *Age of Bronze*, a work modeled on the artist's friend Auguste Neut. Jean-Baptiste Carpeaux, who created the elegant sculptural decoration on the Paris Opéra, is represented by his maquette, or study, for *The Three Graces*. This lighthearted and delicate polished plaster work stands 29½ inches high and shows three young girls dancing joyfully.

The Musée Chéret houses an exceptional collection of salon paintings created during the Second Empire and the Belle Epoque. Portraits, history paintings, interior scenes, still lifes, and landscapes are executed with the technical perfection demanded by the French Academy. Outstanding works include Alexandre Cabanel's *Tamar* which takes its subject from the Old Testament's second book of Samuel. The *Servant of the Harem* by Paul Desire Trouillebert, a poignant representation of a young slave girl, is an example of nineteenth-century artists' fondness for the Oriental and the exotic. Other masters of academic painting exhibited here include Eugène Carrière, Thomas Couture, J.-E. Blanche, and Georges Moreau.

The stairway joining the first and second floors is dedicated to works of Jules Chéret, creator of the modern poster. Most of the works were given by Baron Joseph Vitta and Maurice Fenaille to form the most complete collection of this artist's work in the world. The style of the master draftsman Chéret is evident in his brilliant pastel, *Portrait of Arlette Dorgère* from 1904. The sketchy style and sure line have influenced international commercial art for decades.

The second floor, with works from the nineteenth and twentieth centuries, offers a fine collection of Impressionist paintings. Renoir's voluptuous *Les Grandes Baigneuses* from 1903–1905 was painted while the artist lived at nearby Cagnes. A forest at sunset is the theme of Alfred Sisley's *Path at the Water's Edge,* a marvelous example of Impressionism at its purest.

Also on the second floor are several groups of works presented to the museum by private donors. A collection of thirteen ceramics by Picasso was given jointly by the artist and the Vallauris pottery owners, the Georges Ramiés. A group of works by Raoul Dufy was donated by the artist's wife and the twenty-eight paintings, fifty-nine watercolors, gouaches, and drawings, three ceramic pieces, and wall tapestry virtually form a "Dufy Museum" within the

Musée Chéret. Of particular interest is Dufy's bold and colorful image *The Casino at the Jetté Promenade with Two Calèches,* *Nice* (1927). Works by Kees van Dongen, Felix Ziem, Marc Chagall, Marie Laurencin, and other modern masters are also exhibited.

Of special interest is a group of watercolors by the former Musée Chéret director Gustav-Adolf Mossa. Mossa, considered one of the most interesting representatives of the Symbolist movement in painting, is known for his bizarre, evocative images. The majority of the works were created during the period the artist was twenty-one to twenty-seven years of age. His *Satiated Siren* from 1905 presents a mythological figure, both powerful and vampirelike. Another work, *David and Bathsheba,* sets this Old Testament scene in the early twentieth century.

The Musée Chéret offers a varied and sometimes uneven collection, yet among the academic paintings, the works by Jules Chéret and Gustav-Adolf Mossa are some true masterpieces.

Cimiez

Arena—Baths—Villa des Arènes—Notre-Dame-de-l'Assomption—Boulevard de Cimiez—Musée Marc Chagall

ACCORDING TO PLINY THE ELDER, THE LIGURIAN tribe of the Vediantii founded its capital on a hill above the coastal river Palo (later Paillon), and the Greeks called this settlement Kemenel(i)on. Even the most recent archeological investigations have not established the dates of these events, though they presumably occurred between the eighth and sixth centuries B.C. The elliptical-shaped city covered nearly 4 acres and lay north of the present-day Franciscan monastery, where some remains of a Cyclopean wall of large, unsquared stone blocks survive.

During the First and Second Punic Wars, the Romans became familiar with the important land route from Italy to Spain, which had been used by the Phoenicians, the Etruscans, and the Greeks. When Massalia asked the Romans for aid in 184 B.C., the Romans must surely have grasped the chance to strengthen their control over the peoples of the interior, and the massacre of the Roman legion under Loelius before the gates of Cemenelon led them to command the southern passage across the Alps. Successful military intervention under Quintus Opimius against the Oxybians and Deceates (155–153 B.C.) also pitted Rome against the Vediantii. The Romans leveled Cemenelon at about this time and established their own settlement there.

Under Augustus, while Rome was attempting to subjugate the remaining Alpine tribes (25–14 B.C.), the Vediantii were already well-trusted allies of the empire. And when Rome had successfully concluded these military actions, Augustus improved the route across the pass of La Turbie toward Rome. This new highway was soon named Via Julia Augusta for its builder and later became the Via Aurelia. It led right by Roman Cemenelum, the old Ligurian settlement of Cemenelon, which had become a garrison and an administrative center at least by this time. The conquered western Alps were divided into three administrative units, and Cemenelum was the capital of the southernmost of these—Alpes Maritimae.

Special attention was given to Cemenelum because of its strategic importance to the empire during the crisis in the third century, and the town then attained its greatest size (it had a second amphitheater,

baths, aqueduct, and so on), numbering some 20,000 inhabitants. But its brilliance soon faded following the imperial reforms of Diocletian and, because it was surrounded by a barren hinterland and cut off from the coast, this decline was relatively rapid. A brief revival after 439 A.D. when the city became a bishopric, at first dependent on Arles then on Marseilles, did little to stay this downturn. The town was deserted in the sixth century and remained so—except for a chapel consecrated to the Madonna of the Assumption on the abandoned hill—until the Boulevard de Cimiez was constructed in 1866 and the area became the favored residential quarter for Nice's upper class.

ARENA. ALONG WITH THE FRIGIDARIUM OF THE Magistrate's Baths, this amphitheater is the sole structure from Roman times that was never wholly buried. Overgrown with olive trees, it was known to the local populace as the *"Tina dei fada"* ("fairies' funnel"). Only 220 feet long and 184 feet wide, the Cimiez arena is one of the smallest in Gaul. It appears to have been constructed in three stages. A first, rather modest and primitive structure, partially dug into the slope, appears to have been built for athletic contests to entertain the troops stationed here under Augustus and probably seated only about 500 spectators. It seems to have been expanded between the reigns of Claudius and Vespasian (mid-first century A.D.) and again in the third century, when the city enjoyed its greatest prosperity. In its final form, the amphitheater could accommodate roughly 4,000 spectators.

The arena lay at the extreme western edge of the Roman city, although the precise boundaries have not yet been deter-

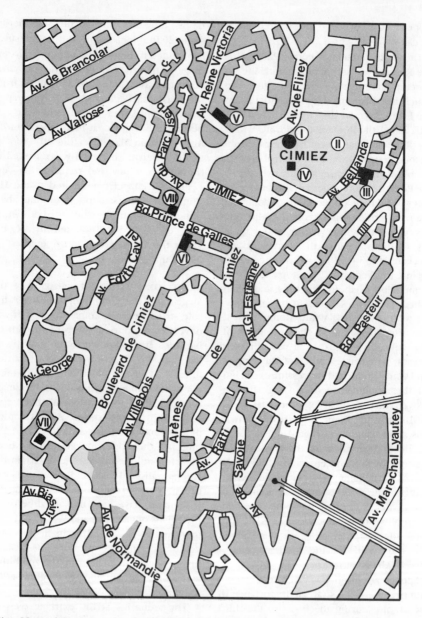

Nice: Map of Cimiez. I. Arena; II. Baths; III. Notre-Dame-de-l'Assomption; IV. Villa des Arènes (Musée Archéologique and Musée Matisse); V. Regina Palace; VI. Winter Palace; VII. Musée Marc Chagall.

mined; however, five cemeteries suggest its extent in the third and fourth centuries.

The city seems to have expanded at irregular intervals and in various phases. Our picture of it is enhanced by two aqueducts. The older Falicon aqueduct—possibly built at the time of the first Roman settlement, the first century B.C.—brought water to Cemenelum from the Torneo spring, a little more than 3 miles to the north. The Mouraille aqueduct, a much more technologically impressive structure, twists and turns for 4¼ miles along the slope of the Vallon des Fleurs, finally running past the south side of the arena and ending at the present-day Villa des Arènes museum.

BATHS. THE BATHS OF CIMIEZ ARE IN FACT AN extensive complex of three baths of different sizes. They all follow the layout of earlier baths (Pompeii, Fiesole, Glanum), but their masonry, consisting of alternating courses of brick and stone, suggests that they date from the third century A.D.

The most intact are the northern or Magistrate's Baths. To the west of the spacious palaestra (gymnasium) is the actual sequence of bath chambers. The frigidarium, or cold bath, is the best-preserved portion of the entire complex and is the most impressive Roman ruin at Cimiez. It is 52 feet long, 30 feet wide, and 33 feet high, and it still contains much evidence of its once-

Crucifix in Cimiez.

lavish furnishings. Near its south end there was a small oval basin lined with multicolored slabs of marble. Numerous niches in the walls housed priceless statues, including the one of Antonia now in the Villa des Arènes. The vaulting of this large hall consisted of a stone barrel above massive brick footings. A door led from the frigidarium, which also contained changing rooms, to the series of baths to the west: the tepidarium (warm bath), sudatorium, and the two caldaria (types of hot or "sweating" baths). The caldaria and the sudatorium each had a furnace from which warm air was channeled by means of hypocausts. South of the latrine and the swimming basin, which was surrounded by a columned portico, are the foundations of a 230-foot cogged wall from the late first century that still baffles archeologists.

A second bath complex south of the Magistrate's Baths is slightly smaller and has a virtually identical layout. Its notably less opulent furnishings indicate that these were the public Men's Baths of the city.

Southwest of the Men's Baths and separated from them by a street, there is still a third set of baths. Its isolated setting coupled with discoveries here of an earring with rubies and pearls and countless wooden hairclasps suggest that these were the Women's Baths. These contain a surprise: the remains of an early Christian cathedral and baptistry built while St. Valerian was the bishop of Cimiez. The cathedral faces east and is 89 feet long and 31 feet wide. A presbytery was placed inside the east apse, which was erected in the fifth century. The floor of this apse is at the same level as the frigidarium's, while the floor of the single-aisle nave lies somewhat lower, above the half-buried hypocausts. A door in the nave's west wall and a passageway through its north wall led to the baptistry, which was constructed over the caldarium's furnace. This baptistry is in the form of a trapezoid, and a rotunda resting on eight columns stands in the center. Four masonry columns seem to have supported a simple lean-to roof. The baptismal font itself, a little more than 5 feet in diameter, is the focus of the rotunda. Five steps led down into the hexagonal font, which was ringed by six columns.

225: Hallway in Nice (Hugh Rogers/ Monkmeyer Press).

226: St-Tropez mannequin (Mike Yamashita/The Stock Shop).

227: Antibes, sunlight in window (Hugh Rogers/Monkmeyer Press).

228–229: Vence, Matisse Chapel (Marvin E. Newman).

230–231: Monte Carlo, Oceanographic Museum (Ted Horowitz/The Stock Market).

232–233: Casino in Monaco (Al Satterwhite/The Image Bank).

234, top: The Carlton Hotel (Kim Steele/ Wheeler Pictures). Bottom: Nice, breakwater and harbor (M. Reichenthal/The Stock Market).

235: Streetlights of Villefranche (Jon Prime).

236–237: Casino in Monaco (Gabe Palmer/The Image Bank).

238–239: Cannes, carousel at night (Marvin E. Newman).

240: Marseilles, Notre-Dame-de-la-Garde (John Lewis Stage/The Image Bank).

CONCIERGE

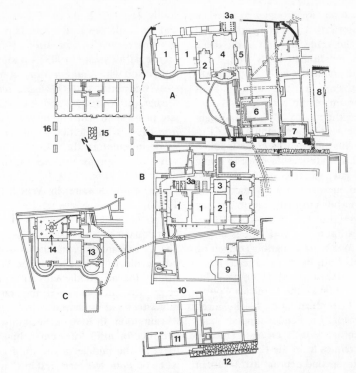

Cimiez: Excavations of the Roman bath complex. A. Magistrate's bath; B. Men's baths; C. Women's baths. 1. Caldarium (hot-water bath). 2. Tepidarium (warm bath). 3. Sudatorium (sweat-bath). 3a. Praefurnium (stove). 4. Frigidarium (cold-air room with pool). 5. Palaestra (gymnasium). 6. Piscina (swimming pool). 7. Latrine. 8. Water reservoir. 9. Scuola (assembly room). 10. Living area. 11. Shops. 12. So-called decumanus. 13. Basilica (Early Christian cathedral in the women's baths [?]. 14. Baptistry. 15. So-called cardo. 16. Steles and sarcophagi.

VILLA DES ARÉNES (SEE MAP, P. 224). THE foundations of this seventeenth-century villa rest on Roman walls, which presumably belonged to the Mouraille aqueduct. Count Garin of Coconato and his illustrious guests managed to enrich their private collections with numerous finds that were readily available in the vicinity of his villa. Thanks to Jean Médecin, systematic excavations began in 1954 under the direction of Fernand Benoît. By 1960, 424 objects had been inventoried and exhibited and thousands more awaited research and documentation.

In 1972, the antique treasures of Cimiez, Nice, and the surrounding region were arranged anew and made available to the public in the modern Musée d'Archéologie. Its contents are grouped in overlapping categories: daily life, urban and provincial life, trade, the cult of the dead, and Greek and Roman vases. The showpiece of the collection is the statue of Antonia, discovered in 1957 in the basin of the frigidarium of the Magistrate's Baths. Antonia was the niece of Augustus, daughter of Marc Antony, and mother of Claudius. Claudius apparently commissioned this splendid white marble work in Rome and it was later exported to Cemenelum. Another unique prize is a hammered and chased silver bowl from the fourth century B.C., discovered in Eze. It depicts a triumphal procession of the gods: the five quadrigas (or four-horsed chariots) driven by Nikes display attributes of Athena, Herakles, Ares, Hermes, and Dionysus. This same gallery houses the Campana Collection, with Corinthian vases, black-figured Attic *lekythoi*, or slender lipped vases (sixth century B.C.), *craters* (mixing bowls), ceramics from the Campagna dating from the second century B.C., Etruscan *bucchero nero* (black ware) ceramics from the seventh century B.C., Sardinian and Etruscan bronze statuettes, and Gallo-Roman bronzes (including a copy of the Pompeiian faun).

The second story of the Villa des Arènes is dedicated to the work of Henri Matisse. Matisse had set up his studio in the neighboring Regina Palace in 1938, and spent the last years of his life in Cimiez. Before her death in 1958, his wife made a donation to establish a museum, which was opened in 1963.

The works on display here provide an overview of the various stages in Matisse's development, from his first (unsigned) oil *Still Life with Books* (1890), his first encounter with the light and landscape of the south, *The Mill Road at Ajaccio* (1898), and his responses to the Post-Impressionists, *Interior with Harmonium* (1900) and *Figure with Parasol* (1905), up to his Fauvist period with *Madame Matisse*, his classical Nice period with *Odalisque with Red Casket* (1926–1927), and his posterlike late phase with *Still Life with Pomegranates* (1947). In addition to his complete works in sculpture, the collection includes series of preparatory studies for such key works as *La Danse* (1931–1933) and the Chapelle du Rosaire in Vence (1947–1951).

NOTRE-DAME-DE-L'ASSOMPTION (SEE MAP, P. 241). While antiquity and the modern period are nicely juxtaposed at the Villa des Arènes, the late Middle Ages are represented by two other structures: the Franciscan monastery and its church, Notre-Dame-de-l'Assomption. In Roman times one of the five necropolises of Cemenelum stood here. In the middle of the third century when St. Pons was martyred in Cimiez, he was buried here and the cemetery was named after him—Nécropole St-Pons. His remains were later taken to the Benedictine monastery of St-Pons, which was established farther up the Paillon at the end of the eighth century. Its monks continued to own a small church on the site of the former necropolis until 1546, however, when the Franciscans took over the spot. They constructed the present, rather modest church and its monastery during the sixteenth and seventeenth centuries. The Neo-Gothic façade built in 1845 dominates the Baroque portico of 1662.

The interior of the church boasts three masterpieces from the School of Nice. Most notable is the *Pietà* triptych by Louis Bréa located in the southeast chapel. Painted in

1475, this is the oldest dated work by the chief representative of this local painting tradition. The retable is 7-feet 4-inches wide and 8-feet 3-inches high. Its center panel presents a magnificent Pietà group surrounded by lamenting angels. That Italian Renaissance ideas affected the painter is apparent in the figure of St. Martin on the panel to the left.

Also by Bréa, but painted nearly three decades later, is the *Crucifixion* of 1512. Here Bréa reveals much more his Italian influence, for he has given up his usual arrangement of a center panel surrounded by smaller pictures in favor of one large and unified composition. The third painting is the less masterly *Descent from the Cross*, generally attributed to Louis's brother, Antoine Bréa.

BOULEVARD DE CIMIEZ (SEE MAP, P. 241). THE decision to link the hill of Cimiez to the city with a broad promenade laid out for coaches found immediate approval for it provided Nice's most exclusive winter guests with a new preserve where they could isolate themselves. In good weather it was customary to take a party to the beach in one's landau after a late breakfast. Then toward evening, the natives could watch the colorful spectacle, including the ringing of bells, of the gentry returning home. Cimiez can still boast the greatest concentration of truly luxurious and imposing structures from the Belle Epoque.

TO SEE THE MUSÉE CHAGALL, RETRACE YOUR STEPS down the Boulevard de Cimiez. The painter Marc Chagall, like Matisse and Picasso, lived on the Côte d'Azur and a museum of his work was created here that opened to the public in 1973. The Musée Chagall is

Chagall: Drawing for A Thousand and One Nights.

devoted exclusively to the artist's paintings on the theme of the Bible. Seventeen large canvases created between 1954 and 1966 make up Chagall's monumental cycle, *Le Message Biblique*, with scenes from Genesis, Exodus, and the Song of Songs.

These paintings have their origins in a visit Chagall made to the Holy Land in 1930, when the renowned French publisher and art dealer Ambroise Vollard offered Chagall a journey to Palestine suggesting that the artist create illustrations for a Bible. The places Chagall had so often read about from his earliest years in the Russian Jewish ghetto of Vitebsk were before him. He was influenced not only by what he saw but by the intense sunlight which seemed to heighten his experience of them. On his return to Paris, Chagall made several small gouaches of his impressions, which he preserved throughout the war years and which became the basis for the magnificent cycle now at the Chagall Museum.

In 1966, Chagall presented the entire cycle of seventeen paintings to the French state, and in return André Malraux (then minister of cultural affairs) and the Nice architect André Hermant planned a building specifically to exhibit these large, unique works. On the property of the former Villa Radziwill, amid the ethereal beauty of olive groves, the museum was constructed. Chagall added works to the collection including not only the numerous preparatory sketches and the original 1930 gouaches for the paintings but a mosaic, stained glass windows, a wall tapestry, and sculptures. This formed the largest single Chagall collection anywhere—over 450 works on a single theme.

You enter a vestibule dominated by the brilliant colors of Chagall's expansive tapestry, from which follows a long gallery devoted to preparatory sketches and gouaches for the oils. Further to the east lies the lecture and concert room with its splendid stained glass windows representing the Creation. The design, completed in 1972, is divided into three sections: one telescopes the first four days; the next, the fifth and sixth; and the series culminates in the window of the seventh day. On a field of blue are rays of the sun and the planets. A ball of fire thrown by the hand of God sets Creation in motion and flowers, animals, and man appear in turn.

The grand gallery, opening off the lobby, houses the seventeen major works that form the *Message Biblique* cycle. One work, *Abraham and the Three Angels*, was influenced by Chagall's Slavic heritage: its jewellike colors and brilliant red field bring to mind Byzantine icons. In another painting, *The Song of Songs III,* Chagall depicts pairs of opposites such as the depiction of Vitebsk countered by an image of Vence with its cathedral and château. To the west of the vestibule are exhibited works in various media also on themes from the Bible. A powerful stone sculpture in the form of a *stele,* or tomb monument, represents Moses.

Chagall himself revealed his hopes for the museum:

Perhaps younger and older people will come to this place to seek an ideal of brotherhood and love, just as my colors and my lines have envisioned it. Perhaps people will also find words here for the love I feel towards everything. Perhaps there will not be enemies anymore, and like a mother who brings forth a child in love and pain, young people and old will construct a world of love with new colors. And all, no matter what their religion, will come here and be able to speak of this desire remote from evil and hate. It is also my wish that art works and intellectual documents of all peoples be displayed here, and that people present here the music and poetry dictated by their hearts. Will it be possible to realize this desire? In art and in life anything is possible if only it is based on love.

Today, the Musée Chagall offers special exhibitions, international concerts and poetry readings, and a study center and library that are open to all who wish to use them.

*T*HE LOWER CORNICHE

Villefranche

UNLIKE NICE, WHOSE HARBOR ALWAYS PLAYED A secondary role in the city's history, neighboring Villefranche has long depended on its bay for survival. The Ligurians constructed a settlement on the hill of St-Michel from which they maintained trade with the Massalian Greeks who had settled in present-day Cap Ferrat, which they called Olivula because the olive trees they planted flourished wonderfully there. Villefranche was devastated by the Saracens and did not recover until the end of the thirteenth century: Charles II of Anjou required a protected harbor on the Provençal coast from which to pursue his policies in Sicily, and in 1295, he selected this bay

Nineteenth-century view of Villefranche.

between Mont Boron and the peninsula of Cap Ferrat. The local residents, who had moved for safety to the site of the former Ligurian hilltop community, were persuaded to resettle along the shore when promised that they would be exempted from taxes and could keep their olive trees. Thus, under the senechal Hugo of Vicinis, Cieuta-Franca or Villa-Franca came into being.

Henceforth Villefranche would remain a favored anchorage. Popes Urban V, Gregory XI, and Benedict XII disembarked here. It was from Villefranche that France and Savoy, temporarily in league, launched their campaign against Genoa. When the knights of St. John were evicted from Rhodes in 1525 they first settled in Villa-Franca. Some of the buildings in the Rue du Poilu and Rue Baron-de-Bres still bear their coat of arms. In 1538 when Emperor Charles V was moored here, his sister, the queen of France, came to see him. The royal parties advanced toward one another on the gangplank, which collapsed. The emperor, the queen, and the duke of Savoy were plunged into the sea and eventually rescued. Somewhat later, in 1557, Duke Emanuel-Philippe of Savoy had Villefranche improved as a harbor and fortress. But the development of Nice's harbor in the eighteenth and nineteenth centuries meant the closing of this 500-year-old free port.

ONE OF THE MOST FASCINATING ASPECTS OF Villefranche today is the Rue Obscure, a covered street running under rows of houses in the old town. But perhaps of greatest interest is the small chapel of St-Pierre on the waterfront once frequented

Another view of Villefranche.

by the local fishermen, which Jean Cocteau decided to decorate in 1950. Cocteau—the famed poet, novelist, playwright, film-maker, and painter—spent some time in Villefranche between the wars, and it was here that he wrote his *Orphée* among other works. It was seven years before the mayor and town officials agreed to allow Cocteau to paint the Romanesque church, but upon receiving permission in 1957, Cocteau "battled with the angel of perspective" (as he phrased it) for five months to produce a symphony of images that completely cover the thick walls and barrel vaults of the chapel.

As you enter the church, you are first struck by the movement and ease of the painted figures created by the incredible freedom of line. To the left is Cocteau's *Homage to the Women of Villefranche*, who are shown standing on a flight of twisting steps near the sea, one holding a basket of fresh fish over her arm. The right wall bears the *Homage to the Gypsies*, in which a guitarist accompanies a young girl as she joyfully dances. The remaining paintings in the nave and apse show scenes from the life of St. Peter and the whole is "crowned by a flight of angels." On the wall inside the front door are painted two flames. Cocteau, paraphrasing an Apocalyptic vision, described them: "And these flames each had a human face. And these flames each had a nose and mouth. And these flames each had an eye. And that eye had seen the lamb." These bizarre human-faced flames interject an element of surrealism and bring to mind the dreamlike, extraordinary images that Cocteau employed in his films and writing as well. All of the paintings in the chapel are almost primitive in form, rendered in simple outline. Cocteau notes that he worked with two basic styles here at the St-Pierre chapel, one figurative where the "poet tells certain stories," and the other purely decorative with geometric shapes creating a vast net of lines on the arches above.

In his *Guidebook for the Visitor to the Chapel of St-Pierre* (1957), Cocteau bid "Enter, traveler. Abandon all your aesthetic judgments." Upon entering, you find before you a poet's vision, simple and direct, painted not only for the visitor and art lover but also for the fishermen for whom the chapel was created.

Beaulieu

AT THE END OF RUE EIFFEL, ON A SMALL PENINSULA high above the sea, is Beaulieu's greatest attraction for visitors, the Villa Kérylos. This faithful recreation of an ancient Greek villa set in charming gardens on a site reminiscent of his beloved Aegean was built between 1902 and 1910 by archeologist Theodore Reinach. He lived there for twenty years. In 1928, Reinach bequeathed the property to the French Institute and today it is a museum.

The interior is decorated with rare materials such as Carrara marble, alabaster, and exotic woods. The furniture, designed after examples on classical vases and mosaics, is made of wood inlaid with bronze, ivory, and leather. Wall frescoes were reproduced from original sources and many of the vases, statuettes, lamps, and other objects are true antiquities. The Villa Kérylos offers a glimpse of one man's fascinating, if exotic, "dream house."

Cap Ferrat

IN THE SIXTH CENTURY, THE HERMIT ST. HOSPICE was leading his pious life on the peninsula of Cap Ferrat, and in the sixteenth century the Order of the Knights of St. John temporarily found refuge here. The later history of the spot is studded with illustrious names—Nietzsche, Leopold II, Isadora Duncan, and Somerset Maugham, to name but a few.

A memento of an unusual sort was left behind by Beatrice Ephrussi, the sister of Baron Edouard de Rothschild, who had fifteen architects build the Villa Ile de France in 1912. The exterior of this exclusive residence in the Venetian style envelops a complicated layout of rooms whose dimensions were in part determined by the works of art to be placed in them; for instance, original leather wall panels from the time of Louis XV required the creation of a room especially for them. On her death in 1934, the Baroness bequeathed her villa, its gardens and collections to the Institute de France, which today constitute the national museum, Musée Ile de France (or Ephrussi de Rothschild Foundation).

Magnificent paintings, furniture, and objets d'art are on view and the collection is especially rich in works from the Baroness's favorite style and period—eighteenth-century French. The covered patio, with marble columns and a mosaic floor, houses medieval and Renaissance furniture. Sumptuous tapestries from the sixteenth and seventeenth centuries adorn the walls and a rare eighteenth-century Sa-

vonnerie carpet covers the floor. Surrounding the patio is a series of rooms with Beauvais and Aubusson tapestries, and exquisite eighteenth-century French furniture, including pieces that belonged to Marie Antoinette. Paintings by Boucher, Fragonard, Nicolas Lancret and Hubert Robert exemplify the delicacy of color and design characteristic of French eighteenth-century painting.

Sculpture in the collection includes terracottas by Clodion and bronzes by Pierre Philippe Thomire. Of special interest is a marvelous collection of porcelain from Vincennes, Sèvres, and Dresden. A gallery of Far Eastern art is entered through two Chinese lacquered panels and includes rare vases, carpets, and magnificent Mandarin robes. Another gallery is devoted to the Baroness's collection of French Impressionist paintings. Outstanding canvases by Monet, Renoir, and Sisley are featured.

In addition to the collections inside the house, a series of unusual gardens surround the villa. Each garden presents a theme. The French Garden is filled with lush Mediterranean plants and includes a Temple of Love inspired by a similar structure at Versailles. The Spanish Garden includes pomegranates and papyrus; the Florentine Garden is replete with delicate marble statues; and the Stone Garden mixes fountains, columns, and sculptures from the medieval and Renaissance periods. A spare Japanese Garden and a charming English Garden complete the 17-acre showplace.

A Prince, a Casino, a Boom: Monaco—Monte Carlo

APPROACHING FROM THE LOWER CORNICHE, along the picturesque coastline from Nice via Villefranche, Cap Ferrat, Beaulieu, Eze-

Bord-de-Mer, and Cap d'Ail, you will come to Monaco, a principality that is less than 1 mile square. Monaco, a sovereign state, has

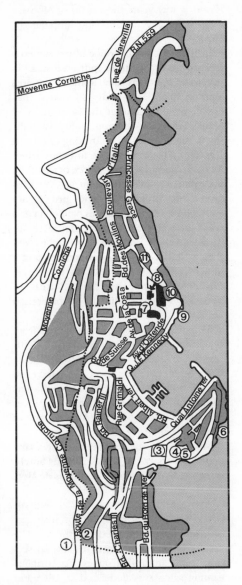

gambling as its main commercial activity but also offers the visitor fascinating museums and fine examples of nineteenth-century architecture. It consists of the old town Monaco, the new town Monte Carlo, La Condamine between the two, and Fontvieille, the industrial section. The native Monegasque population is small but thousands of tourists and temporary residents make Monaco a bustling, active city.

The venerable history of Monaco traces man from his earliest times (Acheulean) with discoveries from the *Grotte de l'Observatoire* at the foot of the *Jardin Exotique* (which is open to the public—see map). This same grotto was inhabited by our more immediate predecessor, Cro-Magnon man, as well. The ancient name of Monaco, Heraklea Monoikos, is held to be Phoenician (though no archeological proof of this has yet come to light) and Monoikos was one of the four settlements later founded by the ancient Massalians. Caesar landed in the harbor of Monoikos with his legionnaires in 59 B.C. but the city continued to be in the domain of Massalia even in Roman times. In the twelfth century, Monaco was given to the seapower Genoa by the emperor; in 1215 the Ghibelline Fulcher di Castello erected a fortress that was destined to become one of the key defenses of the coastline. The domain of Monaco was

Monaco— Monte Carlo: City map. 1. Approach from the Middle Corniche; 2. Jardin Exotique with the Musée d'Anthropologie Préhistorique; 3. Prince's Palace and Place du Palais; 4. Guard house; 5. Cathedral; 6. Musée Océanographique; 7. Hôtel de Paris; 8. Café de Paris; 9. Centre International des Congrès; 10. Casino and Theatre; 11. Musée National Collection de Galéa.

acquired from the Genoese in 1308 by Francesco Grimaldi, and his descendents have held the principality to this day, balancing politically among France, Savoy, Spain, and Genoa, although since the end of the eighteenth century Monaco has been drawn more and more into French policies and politics.

The Grimaldi princes of Monaco have experienced a dramatic history marked by intrigue, power, and innovation. In the sixteenth century, Jean II was murdered by his brother Lucien who was in turn killed by his nephew. Honoré I was tossed into the sea in 1604 by his subjects. Somewhat longer-lived, Honoré II enlarged the palace and gathered treasures of silver, furniture, and paintings between 1606 and 1662. He was the first to sign a pact of friendship with France that was repeatedly reaffirmed over the years. In 1731, Crown Princess Louise Grimaldi married into the Norman house of Malignon, causing that family to adopt the Grimaldi name. During the eighteenth century Monaco attained its brief period of wealth and power, and under Honoré III, expanded along the coast as far as Menton. But the French Revolution turned the Grimaldis out. They did not return to Monaco until the Restoration and by then the greatest sources of income, the possessions in Roquebrune and Menton, were lost forever. Monaco, without arable suburbs, isolated on its rocky cliff above the sea, was bankrupt.

The rebirth of Monaco came in 1856 with the establishment of a casino by the reigning prince. The casino business didn't get off the ground until after 1862 when it was moved to its own building, and François Blanc, former director of the casino at Bad Homburg, arrived to organize it. Gambling had been outlawed in France by Louis

Philippe and Napoleon III, and after 1873 Bismarck forbade gambling in Germany. Within a few years the casino of Monaco was the most famous and popular in Europe.

In 1910, Monaco's Prince Albert signed a treaty with France to keep from losing his sovereign rights (as Nice, Roquebrune, and Menton had). This treaty stipulated that France would guarantee the sovereignty of Monaco as long as the principality was willing to maintain laws conforming to French interests. This treaty came in handy when Monaco found a second source of wealth in tax evaders from other countries. The generous tax policies of the principality (where native Monegasques paid no taxes) were attractive to the rich. But after numerous French industrialists had moved their residences to Monaco, resulting in a loss of billions of tax dollars to France, President DeGaulle used the 1910 treaty to persuade Prince Rainier to adopt French tax laws.

The next financial boom resulted from real estate speculation. Since the 1940s skyscrapers have risen, roadways have been built, rail tunnels constructed, and the shoreline itself extended into the sea. Numerous luxury apartment complexes rise above the city, making Monaco one of the most expensive towns on earth.

Monte Carlo, the new town, is especially known for its casino, which, like its hotels, is owned by Les Sociétés des Bains de Mer.

CASINO AND THEATRE (SEE MAP, P. 249). THE Grand Casino is surrounded by lush gardens and its terrace overlooks the sea. The casino and theatre consist of several sections built at various stages. The original gaming salon was dedicated in 1865 but was rebuilt in 1878 by Charles Garnier, architect of the Paris Opéra. Garnier's structure is the oldest surviving part of the casino and is one of the architect's most elegant and sumptuous designs. The two-towered façade of the casino, set above the sea, rivals the better known Opéra but its painted stucco decoration suffers in comparison to the sculpted stone of the Paris building. The casino was expanded in 1898 and again in 1910, this time by Schmit and François Médecin.

A spacious entry hall leads into the casino with elegantly decorated gambling rooms to the left. The public rooms include the Renaissance Room, the European Grand Salon, the America Room, and the Room of the Graces. A small gallery separates the America Room from the private rooms, or Cercle Privé. Other rooms include the large and richly decorated François-Médecin Room. The Ganne Room, with its tea salon and night club, is reached by a grand staircase. Large murals abound, their elegance reminiscent of the eighteenth-century court style.

The theatre, also designed by Charles Garnier in 1878, is reached through the entry hall. The modest proportions and opulent decoration reflect the tastes of the late nineteenth century. A large, decorative painting by Gervais represents *Three Florentine Graces*. One of the most important concert halls in Europe, it has seen opera premiers by Saint-Saëns, Wagner, Massenet, Puccini, and Gounod, as well as of the ballet collaborations of Stravinsky and Diaghilev.

THE HÔTEL DE PARIS (SEE MAP, P. 249), ACROSS from the Casino, was begun in 1866 by the architect Dutrou and completed by Schmit in 1897. The building was changed extensively in 1908 by Edouard Niermans, archi-tect of the Hotel Negresco in Nice. The structure is an eclectic mix of styles from the late nineteenth century, and its pedimented front with stucco naiads and tritons is especially notable. A recent addition to the hotel's Empire Room is Gervais's *Garden of the Hesperides*, a triptych exhibited in the 1908 Paris Salon.

ON THE AVENUE PRINCESSE GRACE IS THE UNIQUE Musée National Collection de Galéa (see map, p. 249). This museum is dedicated to dolls and automata and is the largest collection of its kind in the world. Over four hundred dolls dating from the eighteenth century to the present are exhibited. The Musée Galéa is housed in an exquisite villa built by Charles Garnier for the banker A. Sauber. A rose and sculpture garden surrounds the villa. Among the several pieces on display is the *Young Faun* by Jean-Baptiste Carpeaux, the nineteenth-century sculptor best known for his Paris Opéra decorations.

Monaco also includes sites of interest including the Prince's Palace, which dominates the town. The oldest parts of the Palace date from the thirteenth century, while Italian Renaissance sections on the south side were constructed in the fifteenth and sixteenth centuries; a Moorish-style tower marks the entrance to the complex. Inside, the Court of Honor is surrounded by arcaded galleries, and the Hercules gallery on the floor above includes frescoes from the sixteenth and seventeenth centuries. The Throne Room and State Apartments are ornamented with rare carpets and furniture. Portraits by French artists Rigaud, Philippe de Champaigne, and J.-B. Van Loo grace the walls.

The cathedral, constructed between 1875 and 1903 in a neo-Romanesque style,

View of Monaco

houses the tombs of the princes of Monaco. Of special interest are the paintings that hang in the cathedral, early works of the Nice School. An exquisite altarpiece in the right transept above the sacristy door is by Louis Bréa and represents Christ's body being restored to his mother, set in a charming Monaco landscape. Also by Bréa is the eighteen-section St-Nicolas altarpiece, with scenes from the life of the saint executed in the jewellike style of the Nice School.

The Jardin Exotique overlooking the rock of Monaco is well worth a visit, even for those not interested in tropical flora. Beyond the beds of cacti, giant aloes, and Barbary figs is the entrance to the Grotte de l'Observatoire, with its caverns adorned with stalactites and stalagmites, and the

Musée d'Anthropologie Préhistorique. This museum includes examples of Grimaldi negroids, Cro-Magnon man, and other prehistoric remains. A small but exceptional collection of prehistoric figurines includes the famous *Grimaldi Venus*. Also exhibited is the treasure of La Condamine: Roman coins and medals, jewelry, vases, and lamps, which were discovered in the late nineteenth century.

The Musée Océanographique, founded in 1910 by Albert I, who was an amateur oceanographer, is a mecca for those interested in natural history. The well-stocked aquarium in the basement is one of the finest in Europe and the oceanic zoology hall features skeletons of sea animals and fascinating displays of coral, shells, and pearls.

MIDDLE AND UPPER CORNICHES

Eze

LOCATED ON THE MIDDLE CORNICHE, THE TOWN of Eze has a venerable history. Its nickname "the Eagle's Nest" comes from its situation 1,550 feet directly above the sea. Modern tourists relish it as one of the loveliest viewpoints of the entire Côte d'Azur, and it was prized as a lookout even in antiquity. There is a theory that the town's name goes back to the Phoenicians, who are supposed to have built a temple here to their goddess Isis (Astarte). In Roman times, this Isia became the guard station Visia or Avisium, but the oldest definite traces of habitation were left by the Ligurians, who in the sixth

century founded a fortified refuge here of which portions of walls survive. Local tradition has it that the Saracens also established an outpost here and, although there is no evidence of this, the conjecture is certainly a likely one. After the Saracens were driven from the Provençal coast, a succession of fortresses occupied the site where the charming cactus garden (or Jardin Exotique) now clothes the rocky summit. The last of these bastions was razed in 1706 under Louis XIV. Nietzsche stayed here in 1883 while writing *Also Sprach Zarathustra.*

The small church of Eze, rebuilt with a

Nineteenth-century view of Eze.

classical façade and two-story tower (1764–1771), once owned two early works by Jacques-Louis David, but both were sold in 1880. However, there is still the view from the Jardin Exotique to the azure coastline! George Sand described it as "the loveliest, most complete, and best composed" of panoramas.

La Turbie

THE UPPER CORNICHE FOLLOWS THE COURSE OF the Via Julia Augusta (later Via Aurelia), which was begun under Augustus. Its modern form goes back to another great emperor and conqueror, Napoleon, who had similar strategic reasons for developing it.

When you approach the pass of La Turbie along today's N 7, a single structure will catch your eye from afar. This is the victory trophy erected between July 1, 6 B.C. and June 30 of the following year. This Trophy of the Alps (*Alpium Tropaea* in Latin) rises to a height of 115 feet and can be seen from every direction. It is a unique achievement even for Roman art, so rich in commemorative monuments. What occasioned this gigantic victory monument, and why was it erected here of all places?

Near La Turbie: The Roman road repaired by Napoléon Bonaparte.

Augustus clearly recognized the importance of pacifying the various Alpine tribes and soon after the Battle of Actium he turned to this task. The founding of Augusta Praetoria (Aosta) was the first step in a bitter twelve-year campaign against forty-five Alpine peoples. In 13 B.C., or soon afterward, the Ligurians were finally subdued, leading to the possibility of a land link between Italy and Spain. The conquered Alpine regions were divided into new administrative units, some of them placed directly under the emperor. As we have seen, one of these was the Alpes Maritimae, whose capital was Cemenelum.

The high Alpine passes, including Mont Genèvre, were blocked in winter, but the coastal route was accessible year-round. In order to connect Cemenelum with northern Italy—and to make the new, all-season route faster and more comfortable—Augustus decided to build the new imperial road between Abentimilia (Ventimiglia) and the Var in 13 B.C. The coast from Monaco westward still belonged to the Phocaean Massalians, so this new Roman road had to cross a pass behind Roquebrune. This was the highest point on the Via Julia Augusta and a point where a saddle is formed between the mountainous interior and the spurs of Mont Agel that plunge steeply into the sea. This spot, named Alpis Summa, was even then considered the actual boundary between Italy and Gaul. When the Roman Senate decided in 6 B.C. to erect a monument to their emperor and to the victory over the Alpine tribes, the pass of Alpis Summa was an obvious location. Only after the imperial reform of Diocletian when Cemenelum had ceased

La Turbie: Victory trophy reconstruction drawing by Jules Formigé.

to be an administrative capital was a plaque affixed that read *"Huc usque Italia/Ab hinc Gallia"* ("Thus far Italy/from here on Gaul"). Cavour's propaganda campaigns for the peaceful annexation of the county of Nice by France in the nineteenth century often referred to this inscription.

Under the Roman Empire, this monument was honored and acknowledged. But the poem "La Vida de Sant Honorat" by Raimond Feraud records a Carolingian legend that St. Honoratus personally destroyed this pagan structure—the Christians believed that the crowning statue of Augustus represented Apollo, that the building was a heathen temple, and that the depictions of Ligurian prisoners portrayed a host of demons. The local populace also felt that the statue of Augustus had the ability to disclose the adulteries of married women. The Alpium Tropaea appears to have been robbed of the greater portion of its sculptural decoration in early medieval times. Then, in the High Middle Ages, it was the core of a succession of fortified complexes. The systematic dynamiting of these fortifications under Général La Feuillade in 1705 during the War of the Spanish Succession largely if not wholly destroyed this unique monument.

After excavations in 1905–1909, a first restoration of the Trophy of the Alps was undertaken. A reasonably faithful model was begun by Camille Formigé. Thanks to the generosity of American philanthropist Edward Tuck, Formigé's son Jules, chief architect for the Monuments Historiques, was able to rebuild its west side with surviving original materials. This partial reconstruction, accomplished with great care and fidelity, was completed in 1934. The restoration of the two reliefs on either side of the main inscription and especially the reconstruction of the original inscription itself were great achievements in the history of art. The inscription consists of two sequences of Roman capitals from the Augustan epoch—the top three lines contain the actual dedication, while the following six lines, in letters half as tall, list the forty-five conquered Alpine tribes in geographical sequence from east to west. The dedication reads:

To Caesar Augustus, emperor, the son of the divine Caesar, *pontifex maximus*, in the fourteenth year of his imperial power and in the seventeenth year of his office as tribune of the people, the senate and the people of Rome [dedicate this monument], for owing to his leadership and foresight all of the tribes of the Alps from the Adriatic to the Tyrrhenian Sea have been subjected to the authority of the Roman people.

Three roads led up to the monument; the placement of the inscription on its western face was only hypothesis on Formigé's part. Even by Roman standards, the Trophy was extremely large. Its overall height was 157 feet, and it was 126 feet wide from plinth to plinth. It is likely that the tomb of Mausolus of Halicarnassus in Asia Minor was the model for this three-tiered monument, and two older Roman victory monuments reveal the same basic structure: one in St-Bertrand-de-Comminges and one at Adam Klissi (Romania); the Julian monument of Glanum (Provence) also stands in the same tradition.

The small museum near the reconstructed monument, established thanks to Tuck, offers a wealth of information and a complete model.

Roquebrune and Cap Martin

THE PICTURESQUE VILLAGE OF ROQUEBRUNE LIES above the Upper Corniche on a spur of Mont Agel that falls steeply toward the shore. It not only offers extraordinary views—of the bay of Menton, Italy, Cap Martin, Monaco, and in clear weather as far as the Esterel—but it also boasts what might be the only surviving castle from the Carolingian period in France (although the foundation walls of the château do not date back any earlier than the thirteenth century). Nevertheless, it is historically documented that Conrad of Ventimiglia, fearing a return of the Saracens, built a castle (or at least a watchtower) on the height of Roquebrune (*rocca bruna*, from its brown conglomerate stone) in 970. But the construction of the surrounding fortified town did not take place until the thirteenth century. The settlement was divided from bottom to top according to social hierarchy, as was common, with its center the château where the feudal lord lived. The present-day village was developed in the fifteenth century from the three lowest levels.

Since the time of Charles of Anjou, Roquebrune had belonged to Provence, but it was sold to the house of Grimaldi for 1,000 florins in 1350. During the Revolution of 1789 Roquebrune, like her neighbors Nice and Menton, joined the First Republic and in 1848, Roquebrune rebelled against Monaco and became a free city. The town officially became part of France in 1861 when Napoleon III paid Monaco the sum of 4 million francs for it.

The only part of the castle complex that survives is the donjon, or keep, which is open to the public and provides an excellent example of the living conditions of a feudal lord in the thirteenth century. By taking the Rue Moncollet, with its medieval houses built close together, to the Rue du Château, you will come to the "flowered enclosure," the entrance to the keep. The walls of the donjon measure from six to twelve feet in thickness and feature defensive constructions such as battlements and cannon embrasures. On the first floor is the Hall of Ceremonies, or Great Hall, where

Roquebrune: Drawing by Gordon Home (1908).

the lord reigned over his fief; a recession in the wall marks the location of the lord's throne. The hall is lit by a mullioned window that was added in the fifteenth century, but originally only simple, easily defended slots allowed light into the hall. Below the Great Hall is a storeroom where food and other supplies were kept. The second floor of the donjon includes a guardroom, a prison, and a dormitory for the lord's archers. The third floor houses the lord's apartments including a small dining room, a primitive kitchen with an oven, and a bedroom. These rooms have been furnished to suggest the simple and Spartan living conditions in a medieval castle. The fourth floor, with its upper artillery platform, offers a magnificent view over the town to the sea.

Below Roquebrune *Cap Martin* juts out into the sea. Until the second half of the nineteenth century it was virtually uninhabited. Then Empress Elisabeth of Austria and the widowed Empress Eugénie of France, both finding the area delightfully remote and peaceful, maintained suites in the Hôtel du Cap Martin at the tip of the peninsula. The two empresses often took walks together and shared afternoon tea. When Empress Eugénie built her own Villa Kyrnos, there was a special garden gate always left open for "Sissy." The cape remains highly exclusive to this day and has avoided the crush of tourism.

*M*ENTON—THE PEARL OF FRANCE

IF THE CÔTE D'AZUR IS FRANCE'S GARDEN OF Eden, then the heart of this paradise is unquestionably Menton, where all of the Côte d'Azur's best features—its climate, its sunlight, its scenic beauty, and its subtropical vegetation—are most pronounced.

If you arrive in wintertime, you will be astonished to encounter a green and blossoming city. In addition to palms, olives, and laurels, there are luxuriant and thriving wild pepper trees, fig trees, eucalyptus, carobs, oleanders, mimosas, bananas, dates, cactuses, pines, and citrus trees. Only the barren branches of the plane trees, accustomed to changing their foliage once a year, are reminders of the actual season.

Olives grow to great heights in Menton. An important natural preserve is the Le Pian olive grove (see map, p. 262). Some of the trees here attain a height of sixty-five feet and are centuries old.

But Menton is most famous for its lemon trees. According to local legend, just before Adam and Eve left paradise, Eve could not resist picking one thing more: she snatched a lemon, which she hid in her bosom and smuggled out of the Garden of Eden. The two exiles wandered for a long time in great deprivation. Then they came to a place that was sheltered by mountains and splashed by an azure sea with the promise of ample water, lush vegetation, a radiant sky, and eternal spring. They could only think that they were back in paradise again and determined to stay. Eve drew forth the lemon she had stolen (it was still fresh) and planted it in the ground. Soon the valleys and slopes were covered with lemon trees, constantly in bloom and heavy with fruit; and thus the lemon came to Menton.

Until the beginning of our own century,

the valleys and slopes around Menton were overgrown with olive and lemon trees, and in the nineteenth century, lemons were Menton's leading export. As early as 1811, for example, one grower alone—a Monsieur Moléon—harvested nearly 610,000 lemons. Most of Menton's lemons were shipped to England, Germany, Austria–Hungary, and Russia—the very countries from which most of the wintering aristocrats happened to come.

For Menton, the lemon tree is not an abstract symbol of life, but rather a source of life itself: Menton is the only spot along the Côte d'Azur where the lemon trees bear ripened fruit year-round and the lemon is still important to the city's economy. In grateful recognition of this fact, the city has planted lemon trees on either side of the entrance to its city hall. And in February, while other cities are celebrating Mardi Gras, Menton revels in its Fête des Citrons, or Lemon Festival. This celebration is dominated by the sumptuous arrangements of citrus fruits in the Jardin Biovès. Even though lemons are the focus of the event, all sorts of other paradisiacal fruits are combined with them to produce fanciful patterns; you would think that the entire world was nothing but citrus fruit. The floats in the *corsi des fruits d'or* on Tuesday afternoon are laden with mosaics of lemons, oranges, grapefruit, and tangerines, along with other exotic products such as avocados, breadfruit, dates, and passion fruit. Some 65,000–85,000 pounds of fruit are used annually in the Lemon Festival.

When you consider that lemon trees can be killed if the temperature drops below 3° C (26° F), you can truly appreciate how favorable a climate Menton enjoys. The average temperature in winter is 10° C (50° F), and the mean annual temperature is 16° C (61° F). The sun shines 250 days out of the year, another 50 days bring beneficial rain, and the remainder are overcast. In midsummer, except for a few torrid days in early August, the climate is made bearable by a constant breeze off the sea. The reason for such favorable weather lies in Menton's geography: its bay is walled off on three sides by steep mountains, all of them rising more than 3,000 feet. Thus the spot is protected from cold and wind from the land side, and it enjoys the moderating influence of the Mediterranean.

Menton remained relatively undeveloped until the late nineteenth century. The Romans knew the area of course, and they gave it the romantic name Pacis Sinus ("gulf of peace"). They set up the garrison of Lumone on Cap Martin, but they did not establish a colony here. Since it belonged neither to Marseilles nor to Italy, the Gulf of Peace slumbered undisturbed until sometime in the thirteenth century; in the early Middle Ages the coastal population of Liguria had moved for safety to the interior.

The site first appears in documents in 1261 as *Mons Othonis*, referring to Count Otto of Ventimiglia, and the name Menton eventually developed from this earlier one. In 1269 a certain William of Vento received Roquebrune and Menton in fief from Ghibelline Genoa for his aid in the struggle against the Guelphs under Charles of Anjou. In 1346 one of William's descendants sold the feudal rights to both cities to Charles Grimaldi, the prince of Monaco, for 16,000 gold florins.

In the sixteenth century, during the wars between Francis I and Charles V, Menton briefly belonged to the Hapsburgs. In 1571 the Menton militia took part in the sea battle of Lepanto. Several weapons taken in booty on that occasion can be seen in the city; to this day, a Turkish lance is used as a processional standard in Good Friday parades, and a similar one hangs in the vestibule of the Palais Pretti (45 Rue Longue).

The growth of the fishing village of Menton slowly began after its final annexation by France in 1860. The development of the railroad from Genoa to Nice, Toulon, and Marseilles in 1868 finally freed the community from its age-old isolation. Various imperial and royal personages (such as France's Empress Eugénie and Empress Elisabeth of Austria) praised the beauty of the spot, but Menton nonetheless remained largely undisturbed. A number of artists, however, frequented the town—for example, George Sand, Gustave Flaubert, Friedrich Nietzsche, Maurice Maeterlinck, Paul Valéry, Anatole France, Charles Gounod, and Franz Liszt. Katherine Mansfield built her Villa Isola Bella in Garavan, and not far from it, also in Garavan, the Spanish novelist Vicente Blasco Ibáñez spent the last years of his life in exile in the Villa Fontana Rosa. Cocteau designated Menton as the site for the Musée Jean Cocteau.

The actual discoverer of Menton as a tourist paradise was the Englishman Dr. Henry Bennet. Bennet wrote a book praising the local climate, which sold five editions in England and was translated into German, Dutch, and French. This book may have caused the Viennese court physicians to recommend a stay on Cap Martin to their empress.

THE CÔTE D'AZUR IN GENERAL OWES A GREAT deal to emperors Napoleon Bonaparte and

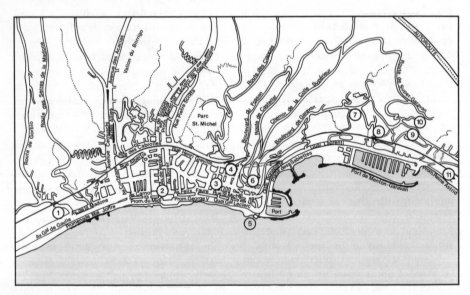

Menton: City map.
1. Palais Carnolès; 2. Jardins Biovès; 3. Hôtel de Ville; 4. Musée Municipal; 5. Musée Jean Cocteau; 6. Parvis St-Michel; 7. Le Pian olive grove; 8. Villa Blasco Ibáñez; 9. Villa Mansfield; 10. Les Colombières; 11. Baoussée Roussé, Grimaldi caves.

Napoleon III. The former constructed the Upper Corniche and the latter encouraged the construction of railroads.

As part of the design of the Grande Corniche (the present-day N 7), Napoleon Bonaparte oversaw the construction of a broad shore road bypassing the old town. This was a wise solution. Thanks to the detour around its historical core, Menton has not had the difficulty handling modern traffic experienced by other towns. And this roadway, supported by low arches and running between the town and the beach, gives Menton a distinctive appearance from the east: the city virtually appears to float above this structure—an impression featured in nearly all views from the nineteenth and twentieth centuries. The great Corsican's grandson, Napoleon III, earned the undying love of the town by constructing its first harbor, thus considerably facilitating the export of its citrus crop.

Like all the cities of the Côte d'Azur, Menton was solely a winter resort until 1936. The gradual construction of accommodations for the less well-heeled guests who began to come for brief summer vacations was hindered by the outbreak of World War II. Major changes to adapt to this new situation weren't fully instituted until 1953, under the dynamic Mayor Francis Palermo. In addition to new projects the city undertook under Palermo—for example, the creation of one of the most modern and beautiful yacht basins on the Côte d'Azur in the bay of Garavan—it has sought to preserve old and beloved sites and customs, such as Le Pian olive grove. The registry office in the Hôtel de Ville was redecorated by Jean Cocteau, a museum honoring him was established, and the Palais Carnolès was purchased to house the town's painting collection. There is now a biennial painting exhibition, or Biennale, in the Palais de l'Europe, a highly respected annual chamber music festival which originated in 1956, and a literary lecture series.

Points of Interest

Palais Carnolès—Jardin Biovès—Mairie—Musée Municipal—Musée Jean-Cocteau—Parvis St-Michel—Church of St-Michel—Les Colombières

THE PLAIN OF CARNOLÈS WAS NAMED CARNOLESIA ("place of slaughter") in ancient times. In the eleventh century a chapel was dedicated here to the Madonna and for centuries this coastal tract was owned by the monastery of Lérins until 1717, when it was purchased by Antoine I of Monaco to be the site of his summer residence. The two-storied *Palais Carnolès*, inspired by the Grand Trianon at Versailles, is composed of a long central tract with two pro-jecting side wings. The palace was designed by architects Robert de Cotte, director of the Paris Academy of Architecture, and Ange-Jacques Gabriel, who would later design the Petit Trianon for Marie Antoinette. The magnificent interior decoration included 170 paintings by J. A. and Jacques Vento, who also contributed to the façade design. The terraced gardens and tree-lined promenades that surround the palace were created by Antoine Latour.

The Pont St-Louis near Menton.

Until the French Revolution, the Palais Carnolès was the favored summer residence of the Grimaldi princes of Monaco, but during the Revolution it was confiscated and sold as state property. After having been returned to the Grimaldis in 1818, it was taken over by the free commune of Menton in 1848, and then finally restored to its original owners only to be sold privately by them. The following years saw a cavalcade of owners including the widowed queen of Prussia, Elisabeth-Louise of Bavaria. During the 1860s the property was used as a casino.

In 1896 the Palais Carnolès was acquired by an American, Dr. Edward P. Allis, who renovated the house and lived there until 1947. Unfortunately, the renovations under architect Tersling included the removal of the splendid double-curved staircase leading to the garden, although much of the eighteenth-century elegance of the mansion was retained. In 1961 the palace was purchased by the Département des Alpes-Maritime and was added to the Inventory of Historic Monuments in 1969. An extensive renovation program was begun and, in 1977, the Musée du Palais Carnolès was founded.

The core of the Palais Carnolès collection, which includes an exquisite group of both old master and modern paintings, was bequeathed to the city of Menton in 1958 by an Englishman, Wakefield-Mori. The upper floor of the palace houses Italian works from the fourteenth to sixteenth centuries as well as fine French, Dutch, and Flemish pictures. Of special interest is a *Madonna and Child with St. Francis* by Louis Bréa. A *Portrait of a Lady with a Dog* is attributed to Antonio Moro, the favorite painter of Philip II of Spain, and presents a woman in the elaborate court garb of sixteenth-century Spain. Another Spanish painting to note is a *Portrait of a Nobleman* attributed to the Flemish-trained master, Bartolomé Bermejo. In the seventeenth-century gallery, the outstanding canvas is Philippe de Champaigne's *St. Benedict Receives St. Placid and St. Maur as Children*, which was recently identified as one of fourteen paintings commissioned by Anne of Austria for the church Val de Grace. The austere and linear style characteristic of French painting of the seventeenth century is exemplified by this canvas. The last room on the second floor contains graphic work by French artists such as Jean-Baptiste Greuze, Pierre-Paul Prud'hon, and Rodin.

On the ground floor are exhibited paintings from the twentieth century. Works from the Wakefield-Mori Collection include canvases by Raoul Dufy, Charles Camoin, Marcel Gromaire, Max Jacob, and

Henri Manguin. An impressive *Nude Negress* by Suzanne Valadon is characteristic of the boldness of line and vividness of color of that artist's most successful works. The Cubist theorist Albert Gleizes is represented by a painting from 1932, *Painting for Contemplation*. The city purchased many of the contemporary works in the museum from the artists when their work was presented in the Biennale exhibitions held at the palace. The English painter Graham Sutherland, who had a summer home in Menton, is represented by several works including his surrealistic *The Fountain*. Paul Delvaux's watercolor *Maria Serena*, one of several of his works in the collection, refers to the Menton villa where the artist stayed in 1976.

LIKE THE PAILLON RIVER IN NICE, THE MOUNTAIN-fed Carei river is unpredictable and threatened to divide the new town that was developing between Carnolès and the old town. Following Nice's example, the town decided, under Mayor Biovès in 1899, to cover the stream and design a park above it. During the final week of Carnaval, the *Jardin Biovès*, Avenue de Verdun and Avenue Boyer (see map, p. 262), forms the hub of the Lemon Festival. Facing the gardens, on Avenue Boyer, stands the Palais de l'Europe. This building, begun in 1909, was originally the city's casino. Today it serves several functions. For example, it houses a number of agencies concerned with local events, sports, art exhibitions, and tourism, and every other year, most recently in 1984, it is the setting for the painting Biennale.

A FAIR NUMBER OF EXCLUSIVE WINTER residences from the Belle Epoque still stand along the Avenue Boyer and the Rue Partouneaux. These include La Malte, L'Or-ient, L'Orangeraie, Hôtel des Ambassadeurs, Résidence du Louvre, and way up on the slope beyond the railway, the Winter Palace. As in Cimiez, these splendid structures present a vivid picture of the elegant life style on the Côte d'Azur during that period.

The present-day *Mairie*, or Hôtel de Ville (see map, p. 262), was once a private residence of this type and later became a club and the municipal casino. Of its original furnishings, only the theatre survives, which is now the council chamber. Since 1957, the Mairie has also boasted a further attraction. The city's mayor at that time, Francis Palermo, was a friend of Jean Cocteau's. At the request of the gifted painter, poet, and member of the Académie Française, Palermo permitted him to redesign the registry office.

Cocteau scorned the fact that French registry offices—where countless marriages take place—serve the same function as churches but have none of their grandeur or style. A registry office ought to be bedecked in gold and purple and mirrors,

Cocteau: Young Couple *(on the back wall of the Registry Office in the Menton Hôtel de Ville).*

he thought. All of the artist's wishes were carried out. For Cocteau, even the two mirrors mounted at the entrance to the chamber bore a deep significance: as threshold between two worlds, the here and the beyond, past and future, reality and dream. (You need only recall the importance of the mirror in Cocteau's film *Orphée*.) On the far wall of the room, behind the marriage table where the actual ceremony is performed, the heads of two young people incline toward each other. She wears the broad-brimmed hat of a lemon picker, he the woolen cap of a fisherman. To the right the Oriental costumes in the wedding scene may refer to the Saracen blood in the veins of the Mentonnais. The right-hand wall depicts one of Cocteau's favorite subjects, Orpheus. The near-god has just caught sight of his beloved Eurydice, dying, surrounded by her companions. Orpheus has set down his lyre, and his song is silent. Without his poetry the figures turn into half-animals. It could be argued that his transformation of the Menton registry office is Cocteau's masterpiece as a painter.

THE NORTH END OF RUE LARCHEY IS DOMINATED by the Italianate façade of the *Musée Regional* (see map, p. 262), a structure built specifically as a museum in 1905–1907. When the city's painting collection was moved to the Palais Carnolès, space became available here for special exhibitions. The most notable object in the archeological collection on the ground floor is the famous skull of "Menton Man," a fragment of one of the countless skeletons from the Red Grottoes (Baoussé Roussé) in Menton; the most important of these finds are distributed among museums in Monaco, Paris, and Turin. Examples of Roman ceramics, as well as Gallo-Roman and Merovingian art, are also housed in the Musée Municipal.

From the Musée Municipal, you can take a direct shortcut to the old town, but the pedestrian zone provides a more pleasant and interesting route along the Rue St-Michel and the beach promenade. At the southernmost tip of Menton stands the bastion built by Prince Honoré II of Monaco to protect the city's harbor in 1619. This is where the Musée Jean-Cocteau has been set up.

FROM THE QUAI BONAPARTE, · A SPLENDID staircase with numerous switchbacks leads up to *Parvis St-Michel* (see map, p. 262). The stairs, the façade of the church of St-Michel, and the paving of the square in mosaics of uncut stone are almost all creations of the nineteenth and twentieth centuries, yet they constitute a magnificent ensemble in the Baroque manner. Lying high above

Menton: Façade of St-Michel

the noise of traffic and with an impressive view of the sea, this square is a natural setting for the chamber music festival that has been held annually since 1956.

The *Church of St-Michel* is the largest and finest Baroque church structure from the seventeenth century in the entire diocese of Monaco–Ventimiglia. Honoré II laid the cornerstone himself in 1619. This structure replaced a church from the early fourteenth century; the left-hand, smaller bell tower survives from a previous Romanesque structure. The interior reveals itself as a basilica only five bays deep with two side aisles, side chapels, and a rectangular choir. An entablature dominates the wall elevation. Italian influence is obvious; the inspiration was the Church of the Annunciation in Genoa. The most noteworthy art work inside is the altarpiece of St. Michael by A. Manchello from 1569. It represents the saint with Peter and John the Baptist. Above it is a *Pietà*. The church also boasts an altarpiece of St. Nicholas by Puppo; other works include a *Crucifixion* and an *Adoration of the Magi*. In addition, there is a seventeenth-century organ and carved choir stalls from the eighteenth century.

The west side of the church abuts the *Church of the Conception* (White Penitents), which was built in 1762 and features a magnificent Baroque façade with statues of the three theological virtues.

On the way back down to the Quai Bonaparte, you should take the Rue Longue.

This was the original main street of old Menton, and it still boasts a row of houses from the fifteenth to eighteenth centuries, including No. 4 (from 1513) and especially No. 45, behind which is hidden the house of the Pretti family (from 1649). The Palais Pretti still has its splendid staircase, similar to that of the Palais Lascaris in Nice.

IN GARAVAN, THE EXCLUSIVE DISTRICT EAST OF the old town, there is, in addition to the villas of Katherine Mansfield and Blasco Ibáñez and Le Pian olive grove, an additional treasure—the gardens and villa of *Les Colombières* (see map, p. 262). The villa was built in this century by Ferdinand Bac, the gifted grandnephew of Napoleon Bonaparte. Bac's talents as a draftsman, painter, architect, and gardener are everywhere apparent at Les Colombières. The house itself is designed in the traditional Mediterranean style with an atrium, salon, and so on. Some of the rooms, decorated with specific themes in mind (Salon of the Muses, Spanish Room, Venetian Room), are furnished with Bac's own paintings.

Bac's greatest efforts, however, were devoted to the marvelous gardens. In forty years of building, designing, and planting, Bac covered this 10-acre slope with separate gardens, each leading delightfully into the next. Its hedges, cypresses, fountains, ornamental ponds, flower beds, pine groves, balustrades, and staircases produce a wealth of views and perspectives that enchant the visitor.

A. H.

RIOULT.

EXCURSIONS INTO THE INTERIOR

ALONG THE VIA AURELIA

THE PRESENT ROUTE NATIONALE 7 (N 7) AND THE parallel Provençal Freeway still follow the approximate route of the Via Aurelia, the Roman highway developed under Augustus. As a link between Rome and southern Gaul and Spain, this road would soon become more important than the older route, known as the Road of Herakles, which followed the upper course of the Durance and crossed Mont Genèvre. Residents who still speak Provençal refer to the N 7 as "*lou camin aurélien*." Mont Aurélien, which rises some 2,950 feet, to the south of the highway in the highlands of Pourcieux (2½ miles west of St-Maximin), also commemorates the original Roman name.

Although you may take the easier and

faster B 52 from Marseilles to Toulon and the eastern section of the Côte d'Azur, you should consider the D 2 through the Massif de la Sainte Baume. This winding road up to the Col de l'Espigoulier offers magnificent views, and it leads past the Hostellerie la Ste-Baume, from which a narrow footpath leads up to the grotto. The name *La Baume* derives from the ancient Provençal world *baumo*, meaning "cave" or "grotto." This particular grotto, from which the entire massif takes its name, is the one in which, according to medieval legend, Mary Magdalene took refuge for her last thirty-three years and where she died. The surrounding oak forest was a holy spot even for the ancient Ligurians.

St-Maximin-La-Ste-Baume

IN 1831, THE MARSEILLAISE ARCHITECT PASCAL Coste described his approach to the small town of St-Maximin: "the first thing the traveler notices is the huge church, be-

neath which nestle the buildings of the town"; and the town has remained virtually unchanged for over six hundred years. The major part of the church was completed in

Basilica of St-Maximin-La-Ste-Baume, 1852.

the mid-fourteenth century when the community of St-Maximin numbered about 2,000 inhabitants, and today the population is perhaps twice that amount. The former pilgrimage church, dedicated to Mary Magdalene, still rises above the surrounding houses and shops to dominate the town. 240 feet long and 95 feet high, Sainte-Madeleine is the largest and most important Gothic church in all of Provence.

The construction of a major basilica and pilgrimage site came about in 1279 when the relics of Mary Magdalene and of St. Maximinus were "rediscovered" at St-Maximin by Charles II of Anjou. The remains of

these two venerated saints had been buried at the obscure town according to legend, but during the eighth-century Saracen invasions, the relics had been hidden. Many ecclesiastics challenged the validity of the claim that the remains were truly those of Mary Magdalene, since the bones of the Magdalene were supposedly kept at the pilgrimage church in Vézelay. But Pope Boniface VIII, after being assured by Charles that the saint herself had appeared to him in a dream commanding him to construct her church at St-Maximin, decided in favor of the new basilica. It was not until 1295, however, that Charles began to build the huge Gothic structure on the foundations of a sixth-century Merovingian church. Peter the Frenchman, an architect from the north of France, was imported but despite the abundance of soaring and elegant prototypes, the church at St-Maximin retains an austere character, its spareness associated more with the Provençal Romanesque architectural tradition, which never truly died.

Pierre d'Allamanon, former bishop of Sisteron, was put in charge of the project, which would ultimately form a Dominican monastery. The friars in fact moved into their new home as early as 1316 but it was 260 years and two major building programs (1296–1350 and 1498–1532) later when the church reached its present form. The common practice of beginning construction at the east end with the choir and continuing westward to the nave and side aisles was followed. Major financing was provided by the houses of Anjou and Savoy as well as by popes, prelates, and cardinals to the papal court in Avignon. Chapels were donated by the Limousin popes Clement VI and Gregory XI as well as by the prelates Gaillard de la Motte (1338), Guillaume de Norwich (1342), and Guillaume de Laudun. The façade portal was commissioned in 1432 but today it adorns one of the two side entrances. The bay above the crypt in the center of the church was not completed until 1508–1512, under Prior Jean Damiani. During this period the three additional western bays were also completed and a "temporary" (unfinished) west wall was constructed.

The exterior of the church of St-Maximin, with its unfinished façade, appears somewhat dark and squat. Heavy buttresses support but do not ornament the massive exterior, the simple and clear outline of which is unbroken by towers, transepts, or ambulatory chapels.

The huge, spacious interior consists of a nave and two side aisles, each lined with chapels, and is terminated with a choir flanked by two chapels at the east end. Magnificent ogive vaulting spans the wide nave and a clerestory allows light to flood the church, the once-brilliant stained glass windows having been lost. The spare decoration is highlighted by the nave vaulting bosses with their brightly painted arms of the counts of Provence and the kings of France. The style of the basilica is basically a cross between the Gothic styles of northern and western France (the Languedoc) and the traditional spirit of the simple and massive Romanesque.

THE CRYPT. THE PILGRIMAGE CHURCH WAS BUILT primarily for the veneration of the relics of Mary Magdalene and therefore its most important aspect is the crypt. This space, reached by a staircase in the middle of the nave, is a low, barrel-vaulted room measuring about 14 by 15 feet. Originally, it was probably the funerary vault of a late fourth- or early fifth-century Gallo-Roman villa. According to tradition, a monastery was founded on this site in the fifth century by the Cassianite monks from St-Victor in Marseilles. Presumably, this community was plundered by the Saracens, and in the eleventh century, a second priory was set up by the then-Benedictine monks from St-Victor, who were forced to surrender their foundation to the Dominicans in the late thirteenth century, when Charles of Anjou began his new basilica.

The four sarcophagi that are housed in the crypt are among the oldest Christian tombs in France. They were probably all carved at Arles, an important artistic center in the Early Christian period, in the late fourth or early fifth centuries. The marble Magdalene Sarcophagus is the most splendid of the four. Below the five arches on its front side are depicted three of Christ's miracles along with, at the center, the Guardians at the Tomb, and the Prophecy of Peter's Denial. The lid is sculpted with scenes of the Wedding at Cana, the Sacrifice of Abraham, Peter Receiving the Keys, and the Last Judgment. The Sarcophagus of St. Maximinus shows a continuous, narrative frieze consisting of Moses Receiving the Tablets of the Law, Peter's Denial, Christ Presenting the Law to Peter and Paul, Peter Receiving the Keys, and the Sacrifice of Abraham on the front. The lid is carved with scenes from the childhood of Christ including the Massacre of the Innocents and the Adoration of the Magi.

FURNISHINGS AND WORKS OF ART. THE BASILICA of St-Maximin is richly adorned with twenty-two altars, numerous paintings on panel and canvas, bas-reliefs, and statues. In the left chapel of the apse hangs a painted wood altarpiece with the Crucifixion and scenes from the Passion, a masterpiece by the sixteenth-century itinerant artist François Ronzen. The work was commissioned in 1520 by J. de Semblacy, superintendent of finances to Louis XII and Francis I of France. The painter's accurate depictions of topography and architecture present the Piazzetta in Venice, the Colosseum in Rome, and the Palace of the Popes at Avignon. In fact, the renderings are so exquisitely detailed that Ronzen's painting was consulted when the Monuments Historiques de France began restoring Avignon's fourteenth-century Papal Palace.

Another treasure is the pluvial of St.

Louis of Anjou. This priceless vestment of embroidered silk is ornamented with thirty medallions depicting scenes from the lives of the Virgin and Christ, painstakingly worked on a gold background. Other works include a painted altarpiece from the fifteenth century with representations of saints Lawrence, Anthony, Sebastian, and Thomas Aquinas, and a carved and gilded statue of John the Baptist from the sixteenth century. The ninety-four elaborately carved choir stalls were executed in the seventeenth century by a lay brother, Vincent Funel, and are richly decorated with medallions depicting saints of the Dominican Order.

The west wall of the nave is completely obscured by an enormous pipe organ built in 1773 by the Dominican Isnard of Tarascon. According to tradition, the organ pipes escaped confiscation and melting down during the French Revolution when Lucien Bonaparte, the young president of the local Revolutionary Committee, requested that the "Marseillaise" be played on the organ during his inspection of the basilica. The magnificent organ is considered one of the finest eighteenth-century instruments in France today.

The former monastery adjoins the basilica to the north. It too was begun in the thirteenth century but was completed in the fifteenth century before the church. In 1966 the complex became a cultural center and today concerts are held in the cloister. The chapter house is notable for its elegant, rib-vaulted ceiling and slender columns topped by foliated capitals. The old chapel and the refectory are on the north side of the cloister and the former pilgrims' hostel, constructed in the seventeenth century, is today the town hall of St-Maximin-La-Ste-Baume.

Brignoles

BRIGNOLES AND THE SURROUNDING REGION comprise France's chief center of bauxite production with an annual yield of about 2 million tons. The nearby marble quarries are also quite significant, and the annual wine fair that takes place in the first half of April makes Brignoles one of the capitals of the Provençal wine trade. Until the sixteenth century, the dried plums from Brignoles were world renowned, but during the wars of the Catholic League, all of the plum trees (an estimated 180,000 of them, all belonging to one owner) were destroyed. The *prunes de Brignoles* are still famous, but they now come from the region around Digne in Haute-Provence.

As an industrial and trading center well situated in the heart of Provence, Brignoles has enjoyed considerable stature since the thirteenth century when the Anjou dynasty established its summer residence here along one of the most important thoroughfares of the country. The Place des Comtes de Provence still commemorates their presence. Today the former palace of the counts, parts of which date from the twelfth century, houses the Musée du Pays Brignolais (see Museums). This museum's most priceless possession is the famous Sarcophagus of Gayole.

Le Gayole lies nearly six miles west of the city, and its oratory, now mostly in ruins, was presumably built in the sixth century. An inscription on the molding around the top of the sarcophagus details its reuse for the bones of a certain Syagria, presumably the patroness of the chapel at Le Gayole. The front of the sarcophagus depicts a series of figures and groupings. Beginning on the left, there is a bust on a tall pedestal, generally thought to represent Sol, the Sun. Next comes a fisherman casting with his rod(?). Then, surrounded by trees, sheep, rams, and birds, there is a standing female figure, her arms raised in an ancient gesture of prayer, possibly symbolizing paradise. The fragmentary central group consists of a seated figure in profile and a smaller figure standing opposite. There follows a shepherd with a ram across his shoulders, perhaps a depiction of the Good Shepherd. He is looking to the right where the last figure in the frieze—a half-clothed male—sits enthroned and brandishes a staff. This is possibly Pluto, god of the underworld. The central motifs—the fisherman, the praying woman, sheep, and Good Shepherd—could well be Christian, but the opposition of Sol (light, life) and Pluto (shadow, death) is clearly ancient and heathen. This probable combination of pre-Christian symbols from ancient Rome with Christian imagery poses a fascinating puzzle for iconographers. On the basis of stylistic features the sarcophagus is generally considered to date from the second or early third century, long before the rise of the sarcophagus workshops in Arles and Marseilles. Thus it would have been imported from somewhere in Italy and it may well be by far the oldest Christian monument of its kind in Gaul.

The Musée du Pays Brignolais contains another relic from the chapel in Le Gayole—the Early Christian altar table, set up to the left of the sarcophagus. It is 46 inches tall and 19 inches wide and dates from the sixth century. The front side depicts in flat relief the Chi-Rho, Alpha and Omega, and a phoenix.

The parish church of St-Sauveur, a few steps north of the museum, demonstrates the long-held aesthetic and formal conservatism of the Provençals: the nave of this simple Gothic church was built in the late fifteenth century when the style was in decline nearly everywhere else in southern Europe. The choir and transept were added in the sixteenth century and the

main altar dates from 1585. This church warrants a visit if only for its lovely fifteenth-century sacristy door—a *Descent from the Cross* by Barthélemy. Parrocel, who died here in 1660—its Late Romanesque stepped portal, and another Early Christian altar table.

Thoronet Abbey

THE THREE REMAINING CISTERCIAN ABBEYS—Sénanque, Silvacane, and Le Thoronet—are frequently referred to in the literature as the "three Provençal sisters," a florid designation that can lead to misunderstanding. In reality Provence was home to a total of eleven foundations of this order, however virtually nothing is left of the monasteries of Sauvereal, Valsainte, Châteauvieux, St-Pons, l'Almanarre Mt-Sion, or Moliges. In addition, the northernmost Cistercian abbey of Aiguebelle, though largely restored and renovated, is still in use and forbids visitors, and is therefore not accessible to those interested purely in its art.

Of the three "sisters" mentioned above, Le Thoronet is the oldest. Its founding goes back to Raimund Bérenger, count of Barcelona and marquis of Provence, who requested that the mother house of Mazan establish a community of the White Monks on his land in Provence. The brothers sent from Mazan were first given a valley in the barren mountains near Tourtour. They established a settlement there in 1136 and named it Florège, after the river flowing past it (Florieille). But for unknown reasons, the Cistercians abandoned this first settlement ten years later and relocated farther to the south, near the village of Thoronet, a move to which Raimund Bérenger agreed.

The new abbey of Thoronet was soon able to attain prosperity and high repute thanks to generous donations from other feudal lords. The most famous of Thoronet's abbots was Foulques of Marseilles, whose biography reads like a novel. Originally a wealthy merchant, then a famous troubadour, he finally joined the Order of the White Monks in 1196, and was elected abbot in 1201. As the bishop of Toulouse, this former man of the world later proved to be a motivating force behind the Albigensian Wars.

A weakening in the rigid Cistercian rule led to the decline of the abbey as early as the fourteenth century. During the Wars of Religion at the beginning of the seventeenth century, the monastery was temporarily abandoned for the first time, and even before the French Revolution, the abbey was dissolved and attached to the bishopric of Digne, its last seven monks driven away during the Revolution, and the abbey sold into private hands. The state managed to buy it back in 1854, however, and undertook some basic restoration.

Both the church and the convent buildings of Le Thoronet were begun in about 1160, and the most important structures, including the church, dormitory, chapter house, and three-fourths of the cloister, were completed by 1175—an astonishing

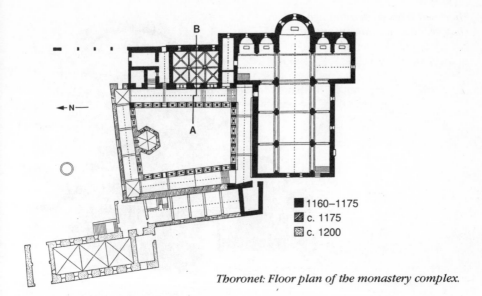

Thoronet: Floor plan of the monastery complex.

achievement. These portions still represent one of the most impressive examples of the order's early building style as set by St. Bernard himself—one gradually abandoned after his death.

Rigid centralization and the required adherence to the order's strenuous rule constituted the deeper reasons behind the striking uniformity in Cistercian monastic building. The order placed definite requirements on its structures, with clear restrictions relating to towers, ornamentation, materials, and so on. Both the austere rule and the architectural prohibitions combined to make Cistercian building—especially during the eleventh century—the only medieval architecture capable of producing an ideal plan and carrying it out, at the same time realizing a maximum blend of function and form.

Braunfels, in his *Monastic Architecture in the West*, makes clear just how this Order's building could so expertly create works of architectural significance and beauty from such asceticism and simplicity:

But just as the precept of work necessarily produced wealth out of poverty, so did a devotion to order give rise to art. All extravagance was prohibited, but clarity, purity, and durability were commanded. Thus the builders turned their attention to the stone itself, its careful shaping, its joinings, the proportions of the spaces it enclosed.... The Cistercian aesthetic which led over into the Gothic unfolded within the world of stone. Where color and ornament were forbidden, the treatment of stone attained a new perfection. Simplicity and geometric clarity of form became the ideal. Any suppressed sculptural urges only broke out in new channels. For just as poverty could not be kept, neither could un-

Thoronet: Cross section through the chapter house, dormitory, and east gallery of the cloister (see line A–B of the floor plan).

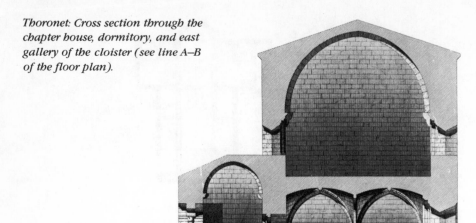

relenting plainness. Wherever work and perfection are demanded, every increase in effort in such a century of harmonious forms could only result in an increase in art.

If the puritanical austerity and practical simplicity of Cistercian architecture reflects an ascetic life of renunciation, its clarity of line a purity of thought, its economy of means the careful ordering of the working day, the durability of its stone an unshakable love of God, and its rejection of color, decoration, and figural representation the modest manner of the order, then no structure illustrates the spirit of this order better than Thoronet. No other Cistercian building has more fully realized the "unrelenting plainness" urged by St. Bernard; Thoronet is the Cistercian rule writ in stone.

The interior consists of a nave with two side aisles. The three separate spaces of the nave are clearly set apart from each other.

Access to the side aisles is provided by the simplest of doorways. The basic geometric forms of the circular oculus and the two round-arched windows are cut into the west wall with cleanliness and precision, and with no ornamentation or detailing. Even the simplest sculptural treatment of the wall would have constituted undue luxury.

Compared with Sénanque and Silvacane, Thoronet's three-aisle nave appears to be the ultimate in Cistercian simplicity. A slightly pointed stone vault runs all the way to the choir wall, resting on sharp-edged transverse arches. There is no developed crossing—certainly nothing so extravagant as a pendentive cupola—and no clerestory development. Another unornamented circular oculus above the choir wall, with the windows on the west wall, provides a minimum of light. The slightly pointed vaulting, a single-story wall elevation, and the side aisle vaulting follow regional building traditions. The relatively high wall area above the side arcades initially obscure the application of the principle of the stepped, basilica form. Half-vaults above the side aisles provide continuous support for the weight of the broad central vault, rendering flying buttresses or even simple buttressing outside each bay unnecessary, in the Provençal Romanesque tradition. Three simple windows in the choir apse are doubly stepped back, providing for an almost delicate intensification of light on the east end. Projecting half-columns end in modified square capitals. The transverse arches supporting the vaulting continue downward in the form of additional half-columns, which end in rounded consoles some 10 feet above the floor. This oddity of Cistercian churches is attributable to the desire to use a maximum amount of space for seating. The right side aisle was the only part of the monastery to which laypersons and guests

were admitted. It is set off from the central nave by a stone railing between the cruciform arcade pillars. The wide transept, typical of Cistercian structures, leads to a choir and four apsidal chapels. The chapels, which form distinct spaces when seen from within, are undistinguishable when seen from outside.

A small doorway leads from the transept to the sacristy. The adjacent staircase climbs to the monks' sleeping quarters, which are surmounted by a pointed vault 26 feet in height. From this dormitory, you can step out into the upper arcade of the cloister for the best view of the entire complex. A door at the end of the church's left side aisle leads directly into the south wing of this cloister, which describes an irregular rectangle. Its galleries lie on different levels as a result of the slope, and they have been equalized by steps. The massive stone

Thoronet: Chapter house arcades.

vaults of its corridors are braced by discreet transverse arches. Openings from the galleries to the courtyard take the form of broad, round-arched arcades whose simplicity is modified by inset twin arches on thick columns and a circular oculus. The triforium windows of the chapter house repeat the same Spartan restraint.

The only traces of a richer and less austere world of forms are in the Early Gothic chapter house itself. Its six square bays form an oblong space whose vaulting rests on two center columns. The elegant curve of the strong cross ribs with beveled undersides is cut off by an unusually broad abutment plate. Supported by a powerful column, this structure gives the sense of weight and its support. This vaulting system, otherwise so typical in Provence, actually betrays Gothic influences. The capitals of these columns stand out from all the others in the monastery because of their richness of form: a double wreath of leaves with corner volutes and, on the right-hand one, the only symbolic reliefs in the whole complex—those of a hand holding an abbot's crosier, a flower, and crossed ears of grain.

Although the north wing, the lavabo—the only one surviving in Provence—and the novices' tract were created later, between 1175 and 1200, no change in the design is visible. On the contrary, the simple, round-arched window openings of the hexagonal lavabo, with no hint of decorative molding, simply accentuate the plainness of the cloister's already reserved architecture. The novices' refectory at the northwest corner of the complex was added after 1200. Nothing remains of the monks' buildings (kitchen, refectory) that once extended from the north gallery of the cloister.

PROCEEDING NORTHWARD FROM THORONET, you reach the foothills of the Alpes Maritimes. This hilly countryside to the north of the Via Aurelia is dotted with archeological sites from the Bronze and Iron ages, before the Phocaeans arrived in Marseilles. The most impressive of the countless dolmens in the area is in Draguignan, right at the edge of town to the left of the D 955. This ancient monument, known as the *Pierre de la Fée* ("The Fairy Stone"), has been restored.

THROUGH THE MASSIF DES MAURES —FROM TOULON TO ST-TROPEZ

Solliès-Ville

THE CHURCH OF ST-MICHEL-ARCHANGE IS A structure of extreme originality built at roughly the same time as the cathedrals of Fréjus and Grasse: the end of the twelfth or beginning of the thirteenth century. The western portions show reworking from the sixteenth century. The ground plan of this two-aisle basilica describes a rectangle measuring 82 by 49 feet, with neither apses nor transept. While its masonry and architectural ornamentation are wholly consistent with local Romanesque tradition, its twin aisles are covered with primitive cross-ribbed vaulting. In addition to its highly individual architecture, St-Michel-Archange also possesses a number of noteworthy furnishings. The small organ screen at the northeast end of the left-hand nave dates from 1499; according to Viollet-le-Duc, it is the oldest of its kind in France. The wooden crucifix from the thirteenth or fourteenth century has been newly mounted but is still noteworthy. There are also two retables, one from the sixteenth century and one from the seventeenth.

Cuers

ALONG WITH CASSIS, BANDOL, AND VIDAUBAN, Cuers is one of the most important wine regions of the *Appellation Côte de Provence*. Its hearty red wine is especially popular as an accompaniment to meat and game dishes.

Chartreuse de La Verne

THE D 14 LEADS THROUGH PIERREFEU FOREST and Collobrières to the turn-off to La Verne. This is a very bad road but an excellent hiking trail. The charterhouse stands at an elevation of 1,361 feet on a plateau of the Massif des Maures and was founded as early as 1170. As it lies on the boundary between the bishoprics of Toulon and Fréjus, the bishops of both cities contributed to its construction. Three times—in 1214, 1271, and 1318—the charterhouse of La Verne was burned to its foundations.

In the eighteenth century, the charterhouse was thoroughly rebuilt and the greater part of the present complex dates from that period. Despite the ravages of the French Revolution it is still possible to make out the extent and arrangement of the monastery. Its Classicist entrance portal testifies to the elegance of its last incarnation, as do the surviving arcades of the smaller cloister, which are framed in green serpentine.

La Garde-Freinet

THE NAME OF THIS VILLAGE COMES FROM THE Provençal word *fraxinet* (from the Latin *fraxinetum*) meaning "mountain ash," which, next to the cork oak, was once the predominant tree in the Massif des Maures. The word was used to designate the mountain fortresses established by the Saracens and La Garde-Freinet was the site of the largest of these. The Saracens were entrenched here for more than a century, their rule unbroken until William the Liberator conquered this outpost in 973. La Garde-Freinet is still one of the most important towns in the interior of the Massif des Maures; its economy is based on the cork oak and chestnuts. A feudal castle, perhaps built by the Saracens, is nearby.

Grimaud

GRIMAUD WAS THE SEAT OF THE LORDS OF Grimaldi (not the same family as that of the princes of Monaco). Its small church of St-Michel dates from the late eleventh century, its first known mention made in 1096. The simple, solidly fitted stone vault rises above a cruciform ground plan. Early in the twelfth century, the Knights Templar were entrusted with guarding the coast and stationed a watch here like those at Hyères and St-Raphaël. The so-called Templars' House (thirteenth or fourteenth century) faces the church, but it is impossible to say with certainty whether the knights built this structure or not. The castle ruin provides a splendid vantage point for a view of the bay of St-Tropez.

*T*HE HINTERLAND OF NICE AND· MENTON

THE LEGENDARY BEAUTY OF THE COTE D'AZUR and the lavish abundance of its art treasures can so enchant visitors that they may look at the towering mountains behind it— such as Mont Agel (3,641 feet), Pic de Bondon (4,147 feet), and Roc d'Ormes—as merely a backdrop for the subtropical stage of the coastline. But these mountains are part of the low foothills of the Alps, and the rivers Var, Paillon, and Roya have cut deep valleys here into a world with a distinct beauty of its own. Even in earliest times, the river valleys were passageways linking the northern Italian Po valley to the Mediterranean, and the mountains here were important places of refuge for centuries.

Visitors who travel inland from the coast will notice how quickly the pleasant, subtropical lushness of the shore gives way to the austere and monumental grandeur of the mountains, and if you are going to spend any time along the Côte d'Azur, you should certainly plan to explore this Alpine hinterland, which contains many late medieval artworks, such as frescoes and panel paintings from the fifteenth and sixteenth centuries, and attracts lovers of painting and of natural beauty.

La Brigue

THE PILGRIMAGE CHURCH OF NOTRE-DAME-DES-Fontaines, 2½ miles west of the old and delightful village of La Brigue, was built on top of seven springs and dates back at least to 1375. It houses one of the largest fresco cycles in southern France, executed in 1492 by the priest-painter Giovanni Canavesio. The wall around the triumphal arch presents scenes from the life of the Virgin and the childhood of Christ. The north and south side walls depict the Passion with naïve delight. On the west wall is a large *Last Judgment.*

Châteauneuf-de-Contes

AN EARLY ROMANESQUE VILLAGE CHURCH HERE dates from the mid-eleventh century. Despite later additions—two chapels in the seventeenth century and a bell tower and sacristy in the nineteenth—the core structure is relatively intact and clearly shows northern Italian influence in its Lombard bands.

Laghet

BUILT IN 1656, NOTRE-DAME DE LAGHET IS ONE OF the most important pilgrimage churches of the former county of Nice and neighboring Italy. Well worth seeing are the hundreds of votive gifts in the covered ambulatory around the church; additional offerings are on display at a small museum in the Place du Sanctuaire.

Lucéram

THE MODEST VILLAGE CHURCH OF THIS remarkably situated medieval community boasts six painted altarpieces. All of them are from the School of Nice, and several are attributed to Louis Bréa, its chief representative. The altar of St. Anthony of Padua (ca. 1500) is a masterpiece from the School of Nice that depicts (from left to right): St. Pons, St. Bernard, St. Anthony, St. Claude, and St. Nicholas of Tolentine. Above them are half-length figures of the Madonna and Child. Each of the side panels includes a landscape, an unusual feature for this painting school's tradition. The altarpiece of St. Bernard from the same period was created by an anonymous artist. The retable of St. Margaret, representing a Madonna with Child and eight saints, also painted about the same time, is attributed to Louis Bréa. Its predella and side panels are in the Musée Masséna in Nice. A retable of the *Pietà* is heavily overpainted. The retable of Sts. Peter and Paul (ca. 1500) and the retable of St. Claude (1566) are both by an unknown master; the latter depicts an *Annunciation* and *Crucifixion* with the martyrs Lawrence and Pancras.

JUST BEFORE ENTERING LUCERAM FROM NICE, YOU pass the small chapel of St-Grat. Its rich wall paintings represent the Four Evangelists, the Virgin and Child, St. Grat, and St. Sebastian. These works were executed around 1480 by Jean Baleison, presumably as *al secco* work (tempera on plaster). This artist was closely associated with Louis Bréa and worked with him in 1483 in Taggia.

Also outside Lucéram, to the north, lies the chapel of Notre-Dame-de-Bon-Coeur. It boasts wall and ceiling paintings, also by Jean Baleison. Among the works are an *Adoration of the Magi* and scenes from the life of the Virgin.

Peille

THE ROMANESQUE CHURCH HERE, IN THE SO-called Lombard style, is impressively simple. Inside it contains two adjoining chapels from different periods: one, from the twelfth century, is still Romanesque; the other, from the thirteenth, is Gothic. The town's modern chapel of St-Martin (1951–1958) by Guzzi provides a notable contrast.

Peillon

THE SMALL CHAPEL OF THE WHITE PENITENTS (Chapelle des Pénitents Blancs) at the entrance to this striking village—its key available at the auberge—has well-preserved frescoes by Giovanni Canavesio, who also created the frescoes at La Brigue. The wall and ceiling paintings, which date from the fifteenth century, include a *Crucifixion with Sts. Anthony and Petronella*, and scenes from the Passion. They demonstrate the great artistry of the School of Nice.

St-Martin-Vésubie

IN THE SACRISTY OF ITS PARISH CHURCH (decorated in the seventeenth century) are two wings of an altar retable by Louis Bréa, depicting Sts. Peter and Martin on the left and Sts. John and Petronella on the right. The custodian will show visitors the valuable fifteenth-century processional cross with enamel ornamentation.

Saorge

THE SMALL CHURCH OF LA MADONNA DEL POGGIO outside this town still preserves the eastern portions of an eleventh-century structure. The "Romanesque" campanile with its rows of Lombard bands dates from a later time, possibly from 1511. Noteworthy wall paintings, which some scholars have attributed to Jean Baleison, have come to light beneath the whitewash of the interior.

Another church here, St-Sauveur, was built in the sixteenth century and revaulted in the eighteenth. It includes a magnificent organ designed in 1847 by Lingiardi of Pavia.

Sospel

ST-MICHEL IS A SPACIOUS BAROQUE CHURCH whose façade from 1691 greatly resembles that of St-Michel in Menton. A bell tower with Lombard arcades still survives from an earlier Romanesque church. Behind the main altar is the *Retable of the Immaculate Virgin*, attributed to François Bréa. The Baroque interior features an altar with baldachino, stucco decoration, and trompe-l'oeil painting.

The fortified bridge (eleventh century) leading across the Bévera river was destroyed during World War II. It has been partially rebuilt, however.

La Tour-sur-Tinée

THE CHAPELLE DES PENITENTS BLANCS STANDS IN the northeastern corner of this small, remote, and picturesque village. Wall paintings with twenty scenes from the Passion as well as of Virtues and Vices were executed in 1491 by Currandi Bresevi and Gerard Nadale, "*pictores de Nicia.*" Also there is a remarkable *Last Judgment*, earlier than the other paintings and painted by an anonymous artist.

Utelle

UTELLE, BETWEEN THE TINEE AND VESUBIE RIVERS, was once an important village. The lower portions of its church of St-Véran date mostly from the fourteenth century, the upper sections all from the seventeenth. Its costly furnishings include the exquisite *Retable of the Annunciation* (early sixteenth century, by an unknown master) and the richly carved doors from 1542. These doors depict in twelve panels the legend of St. Véran, bishop of Carpentras in the sixth century. Above the high altar is a carved wood altarpiece with scenes of the Passion.

Valdeblore

THE FORMER PRIORY CHURCH OF ST-DALMAS, from the eleventh century, is built on top of an older double crypt (possibly ninth century) and reveals simple but impressive stonework. This Early Romanesque structure became a parish church in the fifteenth century and was outfitted with valuable furnishings in the sixteenth. In addition to the wall paintings in the choir depicting the story of John the Baptist— possibly the oldest of this type in the *département*—you can also admire two painted altarpieces, a fifteenth-century enameled chalice, and a fourteenth-century processional cross. A retable of St. Francis dates from 1520 and is attributed to André de Cella. The *Holy Cross* altarpiece by Guillaume Planeta was executed as early as 1484. It features side panels depicting St. Dalmas, the Four Evangelists, and the Annunciation, and a predella with the *Nativity* and the *Adoration of the Magi*. A carved crucifix is in the center panel.

Venanson

THE VAULTS AND WALLS OF THE CHAPELLE ST-Sebastien are covered with frescoes depicting the legend of the church's patron saint, the Passion, and other saints. They were done in 1481 by Jean Baleison and are similar in style to his frescoes at Notre-Dame-de-Bon-Coeur in Lucéram.

N O T E S

N O T E S

N O T E S

NOTES

PRACTICAL TRAVEL SUGGESTIONS

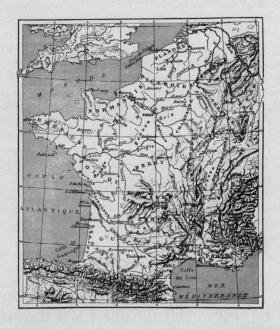

This section of the book offers vacationers a brief overview of all major aspects of traveling in France. In addition to presenting general information about the country, it contains tips about getting to France and getting around in France, about important documents and regulations, and about sources of more detailed information. It also covers local weather, accommodations, entertainment, the addresses and hours of local museums, regional gastronomic specialties, festivals, and so on. Much of this information—addresses and telephone numbers for example—is notoriously impermanent, so visitors should always try to check local listings upon arrival. Because sudden price changes in France and fluctuations in international exchange rates are inevitable, this guide does not include French prices or their equivalents in dollars or pounds; readers are advised to consult the most up-to-date sources available for such data.

Introduction to France

GETTING TO FRANCE

Many airlines provide direct service from the United States and Canada to France. Check with a travel agent for details on schedules, fares, and points of departure and arrival.

People planning to travel to France from the British Isles have many options. Many airlines—British Airways and Air France are only two—connect major cities in both countries. Aer Lingus offers service from Dublin and Cork to Paris and Lourdes.

It is also possible to travel by rail from Britain to France. Most of these services connect with cross-Channel ferries, but through railway carriages between London and Paris also operate overnight. Reservations are advisable, particularly in summer. Contact British Rail or a travel agent for particulars.

Several coach (bus) services offer transportation between major cities throughout Britain and France. Contact a travel agent for details.

Visitors who want to drive to France can use one of many car ferries that connect England and Ireland with France. Reservations on the Sealink services (Dover to Boulogne or Calais, Folkestone to Boulogne or Calais, Newhaven to Dieppe, and Weymouth to Cherbourg) may be made through British Rail (see pages 460–461), but other companies offer car ferries on other routes. The Hovercraft, which crosses the English Channel from Dover to Calais or Boulogne in 30 to 40 minutes, also accommodates cars. There are no customs restrictions on bringing a car into France, assuming one enters as a tourist and for under six months.

GETTING AROUND IN FRANCE

By Air

Air Inter is France's domestic airline, serving thirty major business and holiday centers throughout the country, including Paris (Orly and Charles-de-Gaulle airports), Nice, Marseille, Toulouse, Lyon, Strasbourg, Montpellier, and Nantes. Its central information and reservations number (in Paris) is 1/539-25-25. Information about Air Inter is also available from Air France offices in the United States, Canada, and the United Kingdom. Other domestic airlines include Touraine Air Transport, Air Littoral (serving the South of France, Spain, and Italy), and Compagnie Aérienne du Languedoc. Air France flies key domestic routes as well.

By Rail

The French National Railroads, or SNCF

(Société Nationale des Chemins de Fer Français), offers perhaps the best way to see France. SNCF is a dense network of railways connecting major cities and small towns; it has gained an enviable reputation for speed, safety, punctuality, and passenger comfort. The newest star in this system is the TGV (*train à grande vitesse*, which means simply, "high-speed train"), a train that runs between Paris and Lyon at more than 130 miles per hour and cuts travel time to a mere 2 hours—thereby placing relatively distant parts of France within day-trip distance of the capital.

On most long-distance night trains, a traveler can book either a sleeper or a *couchette* berth in either first or second class. For information about routes, reservations, and up-to-date fares, contact SNCF (in France) or French National Railroads (in the United States, the United Kingdom, and Canada). See page 460 for a listing of French National Railroads offices in these countries.

Passengers must validate their rail tickets (except those bought outside France), using the orange stamping machine, before boarding the train. Failure to do so results in an additional fee.

Americans and Canadians can take advantage of three special packages offered by French National Railroads. The Eurailpass entitles the bearer to unlimited first-class rail travel in sixteen Western European countries, including France, for 15 days, 21 days, or 1, 2, or 3 months. The Eurail Youthpass guarantees unlimited second-class rail travel in these same countries for either 1 or 2 months to anyone under 26 years old. The Frances Vacances pass is issued for 7 days, 15 days, or 1 month of first- or second-class travel. This ticket entitles the holder not only to unlimited travel on all SNCF trains (including the TGV) during the period of validity, but also to:

2, 4, or 7 days of unlimited travel on the Paris Métro, RER, and bus system

a free round-trip rail journey to Paris from Charles-de-Gaulle or Orly airport

a free admission to the Centre National d'Art et de Culture Georges-Pompidou (Centre Beaubourg)

a free one-way trip on the privately owned scenic railroad Chemin de Fer de Provence, which runs between Nice and Digne

a 10 percent discount on SNCF bus excursions

a discount on car rentals through the Budget Train + Auto service

All three passes must be purchased at one of the French National Railroads offices in the United States or Canada; see page 460 for a listing of these addresses.

British travelers should consult a travel agent or the local British Rail booking office for comprehensive packages available to them in France.

By Car

France has about 930,000 miles of roads. This extensive network includes the *autoroutes* (motorways or superhighways, with an A prefix), the *routes nationales* (major national roads, with an N prefix), and the *routes départementales* (relatively minor roads, with a D prefix). The entire system is kept in excellent condition.

In France, as in the United States, Canada, and continental Europe, driving is done on the right-hand side of the road. Foreign visitors may drive in France if they have a valid driver's license from their home country (an international license is not required), valid passport or other identity papers, and an international green insurance card. Insurance is compulsory in France for all overland motor vehicles, including those driven by visitors from abroad. On arrival, if a motorist cannot present an international green insurance card, he or she must take out a temporary *assurance frontière* policy at customs. This policy may be issued for 8, 15, 30 days; it cannot be renewed. Visitors staying longer than 30 days must either contact their insurer at home for a green card or take out a temporary policy with a French firm.

Vehicles used in France are required to have safety belts for the driver and the front-seat passenger, an external driving mirror, spare headlight bulbs, and rear warning lights or a phosphorescent warning signal (triangle) in case of breakdown. Yellow headlights are compulsory on French cars, and dazzling headlights are prohibited. The horn may be used only when absolutely necessary; in Paris and certain other cities, its use is expressly forbidden except in case of imminent danger. Children under 10 years old are not allowed to ride in the front seat of a vehicle.

If an emergency car repair is needed, a motorist can call Touring Secours (telephone 1/531-05-05), set up under the auspices of the Touring Club de France. Towing and emergency repairs are free to drivers who have joined Touring Secours. For further information about Touring Secours or driving in France in general, contact the Touring Club de France, 6-8 Rue Firmin-Gillot, 75737 Paris Cedex 15; telephone 1/532-22-15. The Royal Automobile Club of Great Britain (French headquarters at 8 Place Vendôme, Paris, Ier; telephone 1/260-62-12) is a source of additional information.

In case of accident, the drivers of both cars should find a police officer, who will fill out a report, or *constat*, that can be submitted to insurance companies. If the accident is serious, photographs should be taken, if possible. If the accident involves only one's own car, the report may be filled out by an official (*huissier*) in the nearest community. The Bureau Central Français des Sociétés Assurances contre les Accidents d'Automobiles (118 Rue de Tocqueville, 75017 Paris; telephone 1/766-52-64) should also be notified immediately.

Gasoline (petrol) is sold by the liter. An American gallon is equivalent to 3.78 liters; an imperial gallon, 4.54 liters. Distances are measured in kilometers (1 km = about .62 mile; 1 mile = about 1.61 km).

Speed limits are generally 130 kph (80 mph) on toll *autoroutes*, 110 kph (68 mph) on free *autoroutes* and other major roads, 90 kph (56 mph) on lesser roads, and 60 kph (37 mph) in developed zones. The *autoroutes* have parking and rest areas every 6 to 10 miles and emergency telephones every 11¼ miles.

SNCF offers a service, called Motorail, for drivers going toward any of several major cities. Drivers taking advantage of it are entitled to a berth on the same train that their car travels on. Once the destination is reached, retrieving the car can be done quite quickly. Contact French National Railroads (for addresses, see page 460) for more information.

Car Rental. It is quite easy for travelers from abroad to rent a self-drive car in France. The major agencies—Avis, Budget, Citer, Europcar, Hertz, Inter-Rent, and Mattei—have several offices in France. Car-rental arrangements in France can frequently be made through airlines, travel agents, or local car-rental agencies. For further information about firms in France that offer cars for hire, contact a travel agent or CSNCRA (Chambre Syndicale Nationale du Commerce et de la Réparation Automobile), 6 Rue Léonard-de-Vinci, 75016 Paris; telephone 1/502-19-10.

Renters must be a minimum of 21 years old (sometimes 25) and must be able to show that they have held a valid driver's license for at least one year.

For information about hiring a chauffeur-driven car, contact a travel agent or the Chambre Syndicale Nationale des Entreprises de Remise et de Tourisme, 48 Rue de la Bienfaisance, 75008 Paris; telephone 1/562-06-66.

By Coach (Bus)

Long-distance coach services are operated in France by Europabus and other companies. In addition, many local services and sightseeing tours are available; many of these are run by SCETA (Services de Tourisme SNCF-Europabus), 7 Rue Pablo-Neruda, 92532 Levallois-Perret Cedex; telephone 1/270-56-00, ext. 536. Contact SCETA or a travel agent for more details.

By Water

France has a great network of inland waterways—not only famed rivers such as the Seine, the Loire, and the Rhône, but also canals that connect them—and it is possible to rent a boat equipped with living accommodations to explore these byways or to take an organized inland cruise. For further information, you can contact a travel agent or the Syndicat National des Loueurs de Bateaux de Plaisance, Port de la Bourdonnais, 75007 Paris; telephone 1/555-10-49. This organization can also provide information about berthing yachts along France's beautiful Atlantic and Mediterranean coasts and about renting small craft to sail these waters.

By Bicycle

Thousands of miles of bicycle routes throughout France may be explored by energetic travelers. Fixed itineraries are offered by the following organizations:

La Fédération Française de Cyclotourisme
8 Rue Jean-Marie-Jego
75013 Paris
1/580-30-21

Le Bicyclub de France
8 Place de la Porte-Champerret
75017 Paris
1/766-55-92

Loisirs Accueil Loiret
3 Rue de la Bretonnerie
45000 Orléans
38/62-04-88

Loisirs Accueil Loir-et-Cher
11 Place du Château
41000 Blois
54/78-55-50

In addition, the French Government Tourist Offices (see page 459) and local bureaus (*syndicats d'initiative*) provide lists of suggested itineraries. Bicycles may be rented at more than 200 SNCF stations throughout France, and through other outlets as well.

On Foot

France can be crossed on foot on an excellent system of long-distance footpaths and hiking trails. The Fédération Française de la Randonnée Pédestre, Comité National des Sentiers de Grande Randonnée, 8 Avenue Marceau, 75008 Paris, will send out a list of these routes on request.

DOCUMENTS AND REGULATIONS

Passports

Visitors to France from the United States, the United Kingdom, and Canada are required to hold valid passports. No visa is necessary.

Currency

Visitors may bring an unlimited amount of French or foreign currency into France. Visitors who arrive with more than 5,000 francs (or the equivalent sum in other currency) are advised to fill out a special form (declaration of entry of foreign banknotes into France) that customs will provide on request and countersign. Visitors leaving France may not take out more than 5,000 francs (or the equivalent) unless they present this duly certified declaration.

Duty-Free Goods

In addition to personal clothing, jewelry, and effects such as cameras and sports equipment, visitors who are over 17 years old may bring the following goods into France duty-free (see list).

For information, contact the French Government Tourist Office (addresses on page 459) or the French customs office: Bureau IRP, Direction Générale des Douanes, 8 Rue de la Tour-des-Dames, 75436 Paris Cedex 09; telephone 1/280-67-22.

Item	From United Kingdom/ Ireland	From United States/ Canada
Alcoholic beverages:		
Table wines	4 liters (3½ quarts)	2 liters (1¾ quarts)
and either		
Spirits with over 22% alcohol content	1½ liters	1 liter
or		
Spirits with 22% alcohol content or less	3 liters	2 liters
Tobacco:		
Cigarettes	300	400
Cigarillos	150	200
Cigars	75	150
or		
Pipe tobacco	14 ounces (400 grams)	17 ounces (500 grams)
Perfumes and toilet water	2½ ounces (37.5 centiliters)	1¾ ounces (25 centiliters)

Prohibited Goods

Narcotics, goods that constitute copyright infringements, gold (other than personal jewelry), and firearms (other than for hunting or target shooting) are forbidden.

Dogs and Cats

Animals less than 3 months old are not allowed into France. A visitor may bring in up to three animals, only one of which may be a puppy. For each animal that comes from a country that has not recorded a case of rabies for at least three years, a certified veterinafian must complete a certificate of origin and health within five days of the animal's departure from home; the certificate confirms that the animal is in good health, that its country of origin has been free of rabies for at least three years, and that the animal has not left that country since birth or for the six months prior to entering France. Otherwise, owners must show a rabies vaccination certificate for each animal, completed by a veterinarian in the animal's home country, stating that it has been vaccinated more than a month but less than a year before entry into France or that it has been revaccinated within the past year.

Owners of all other animals must apply in advance to the Ministère de l'Agriculture, Bureau de la Règlementation Sanitaire aux Frontières, 44-46 Boulevard de Grenelle, 75732 Paris Cedex 15.

Acquisition of Valuables

Special regulations apply to precious metals, jewelry, artworks, and antiques acquired in France. Visitors who cannot prove that they purchased such items from a standard dealer may, on leaving the country, be required to pay a duty equal to 3 to 4 percent of the item's value.

Staying More Than 3 Months

Visitors who stay in France for more than 3 months must obtain a residence permit from the Service des Étrangers, Prefecture de Police, Place Louis-Lépine, Paris, IVᵉ; telephone 1/277-11-00 (open daily except Saturday, Sunday, and holidays, 8:30 A.M. to 5:00 P.M.). A visitor who fails to register at this office after 3 months in the country is subject to a heavy fine.

GENERAL INFORMATION

Money

France's unit of currency is the French *franc*, which is divided into 100 *centimes*. Coins exist in the following denominations: 5c, 10c, 20c, ½F (50c), 1F, 2F, 5F, 10F. There are paper notes for denominations of 10F, 20F, 50F, 100F, and 500F.

Major international credit cards—Access, American Express, Diner's Club, MasterCard, Visa—are honored by many establishments throughout France.

Tipping

Station or airport porters. Usually about 5F, depending on the number of bags.

Taxi drivers. 10 to 15 percent of the fare shown on the meter.

Hotel staff. 10F per piece of lúggage to the hotel porter; 10F per-day to the chambermaid.

Waiters. In cafés and many restaurants, service is generally included in the bill (*service compris*). If service is not included, tip 15 percent. About 10F should be given to the sommelier.

Coatroom attendants. At least 5F per item; at least 5F for toilet attendants.

Tour guides. About 5F per person in the group.

Public Holidays

By law, France recognizes ten major civil and church holidays, the so-called *jours féries.* These are:

New Year's Day (January 1)

Easter Monday

Ascension Thursday (Sixth Thursday after Easter)

Whit Monday (second Monday after Ascension)

Labor Day (May 1)

Bastille Day (July 14)

Assumption (August 15)

All Saints' Day (November 1)

Armistice Day (November 11)

Christmas (December 25)

On these days, banks and many shops, museums, and restaurants are closed. Check local listings.

Although not a *jour férie,* VE Day (May 8), commemorating the Allied victory in World War II, is also celebrated widely.

Time Zone

France, like most of Western Europe, is 1 hour ahead of Greenwich Mean Time (2 hours ahead in summer). Therefore, for the best part of the year, it is ahead of the following locations by the number of hours indicated:

London, Dublin:	1 hour
Halifax:	5 hours
New York, Montreal, Toronto:	6 hours
Chicago, Houston, Winnipeg:	7 hours
Denver, Calgary:	8 hours
Los Angeles, Vancouver:	9 hours

Banking and Shopping

Banking and business hours vary in different parts of France. In Paris, for example, banks are open Monday through Friday, 9:00 A.M.–4:30 P.M., and they close at 12:00 M. the day before a holiday. In major cities in the South of France, such as Nice and Marseille, many banks are closed between 12:30–1:30 P.M., and in smaller communities, banks are closed 12:00 M.–2:00 P.M.

Store hours also reflect these regional differences. Most Parisian stores and shops are open 9:00 A.M.–6:00 or 7:00 P.M. (many are open Saturday but closed Monday); the fashion boutiques and perfumeries open at 10:00 A.M. and close 12:00 M.–2:00 P.M. In the South of France, department stores and supermarkets do not close for lunch, but smaller shops do—for up to 3 hours (12:00 M.–3:00 P.M.); however, these businesses may open as early as 7:00 or 8:00 A.M. and may close at 7:00 or 8:00 P.M. Food shops remain open on Sunday (during the morning only).

Visitors to France who are at least 15 years old and who stay for less than six months may deduct the value-added tax (VAT) from the price of goods bought in France that are being taken out of the country as personal luggage. The goods must have a certain value to qualify for this deduction. For further information, contact the French Government Tourist Office (addresses on page 459).

The following table lists French clothing sizes and their American and British equivalents. Sizes, of course, may vary slightly among manufacturers, and a prospective buyer should try clothes on whenever possible before buying them.

Women

Dresses,	France	40	42	44	46	48	50	
Suits,	UK	32	34	36	38	40	42	
Overcoats	US	10	12	14	16	18	20	
Blouses,	France	38	40	42	44	46	48	
Sweaters	UK/US	32	34	36	38	40	42	
Shoes	France	35½	36	36½	37	37½	38	39
	UK	3	3½	4	4½	5	5½	6
	US	4	4½	5	5½	6	6½	7½
Stockings	France	1	2	3	4	5		
	UK/US	8½	9	9½	10	10½		

Men

Suits,	France	36	38	40	42	44	46	48
Overcoats	UK/US	35	35	37	38	39	40	42
Sweaters	France	46	48	51	54	56	59	
	UK/US	36	38	40	42	44	46	
Shirts	France	36	37	38	39	40	41	42
	UK/US	14	14½	15	15½	16	16½	17
Shoes	France	41	42	43	44	45	46	
	UK	8	9	10	11	12	13	
	US	8	8½	9½	10	10½	11	
Socks	France	39–40	40–41	41–42	42–43	43–44		
	UK/US	10	10½	11	11½	12		
Hats	France	53	54	55	56	57	58	59
	UK/US	6½	6⅝	6¾	6⅞	7	7⅛	7½

Post Offices

Post offices are usually open Monday through Friday, 8:00 A.M.–7:00 P.M., and Saturday, 8:00 A.M. to noon. However, small branches may close for lunch and may have shorter hours. Stamps may also be bought at tobacconists', hotels, cafés, and news agents and from yellow vending machines. Mailboxes (*bôites aux lettres*) are yellow as well.

Telephones

Except in the Paris area, telephone numbers have six digits and a two-digit prefix that is used only when dialing from outside the region. In and around Paris, telephone numbers have seven digits and a single-digit prefix ("1") for the area.

Public telephones accept 50c, 1F, and 5F coins. The ringing tone is high-pitched and periodic; the busy (engaged) tone is deeper and more rapid.

Overseas calls can be dialed direct from France to the United States, the United Kingdom, and Canada, without operator assistance. The prefix for telephoning the United Kingdom is 19-44; for the United States and Canada, 19-1. A zero at the beginning of the *local* dialing code should be ignored.

Voltage

Most electricity in France is run on a 220-volt current (50 cycles AC), although some remote areas may still run on 110 volts. American and Canadian visitors who travel with electric razors, hair dryers, and so on, should also bring along an adapter. (Outlet prongs are shaped differently in France as well.)

Handicapped Travelers

Facilities designed to accommodate the handicapped are becoming increasingly commonplace in France. For information, contact the French Government Tourist Office.

Hitchhiking

Hitchhiking is prohibited on major highways but permitted otherwise.

Sunbathing

Nudity is permissible on many beaches, and toplessness is virtually the norm on many others.

Police

Throughout most of France, the emergency telephone number to reach the police is "17."

USEFUL ADDRESSES

This section contains listings of addresses that may be helpful to Americans, Britons, and Canadians who are planning a vacation in France or who may need assistance or information while there. Although this listing is as up-to-date as possible, readers are reminded that addresses and telephone numbers change regularly.

French Government Tourist Offices

In the U.S.

610 Fifth Avenue
New York, NY 10020
212/757-1125

645 North Michigan Avenue,
Suite 630
Chicago, IL 60611
312/337-6301

World Trade Center, #103
2050 Stemmons Freeway
PO Box 58610
Dallas, TX 75258
214/742-7011

9401 Wilshire Boulevard
Beverly Hills, CA 90212
213/272-2661

360 Post Street
San Francisco, CA 94108
415/986-4161

In Canada

1840 Sherbrooke Avenue West
Montreal, Que. H3H 1E4
514/931-3855

1 Dundas Street West
Suite 2405, Box 8
Toronto, Ont. M5G 1Z3
416/593-4723

In the United Kingdom

178 Piccadilly
London W1V 0A1
01/493-6594

The London office has special departments dealing with Winter Sports and Youth Travel, Yachting and Canal Cruising, and Conferences. Address any inquiry about these specific areas to the appropriate department.

In Paris

Accueil de France
(Paris Tourist Office)
127 Champs-Elysées
75008 Paris
1/723-61-72
(Open daily 9:00 A.M.–10:00 P.M.)

Embassies and Consulates-General

United Kingdom

Embassy
35 Rue du Faubourg-St-Honoré
75383 Paris
(1) 266-91-42

Consulates-General
15 Cours de Verdun
33081 Bordeaux Cedex
(56) 52-28-35, 52-28-36, 52-48-86, 52-48-87

11 Square Dutilleul
59800 Lille
(20) 52-87-90

24 Rue Childebert
69288 Lyon Cedex I
(78) 37-59-67, 42-46-49

24 Avenue du Prado
13006 Marseille
(91) 53-43-32, 37-66-95

The United Kingdom also maintains consulates at Toulouse, Calais, Boulogne-sur-Mer, Dunkirk, Nice, Perpignan, Cherbourg, Le Havre, Nantes, and St. Malo-Dinard, and a vice-consulate at Ajaccio (Corsica).

United States

Embassy
2 Avenue Gabriel
75008 Paris
(1) 296-12-02, 261-80-75

Consulates-General
4 Rue Esprit-des-Lois
33000 Bordeaux
(56).65-95

72 Rue Général-Sarrail
69006 Lyon
(78) 24-68-49

9 Rue Armeny
13006 Marseille
(91) 54-92-00

15 Avenue d'Alsace
67000 Strasbourg
(88) 35-31-04

The United States also maintains a consulate in Nice.

Canada

Embassy
35 Avenue Montaigne
75008 Paris
1/723-0101

Consulates-General
24 Avenue du Prado
13006 Marseille
91/37-19-37

Croix du Mail
Rue Claude-Bonnier
33080 Bordeaux Cedex
56/96-15-61

10 Place du Temple-Neuf
67007 Strasbourg Cedex
88/32-65-96

French National Railroads

French National Railroads maintains the following offices in the United States, the United Kingdom, and Canada.

In the United States

610 Fifth Avenue
New York, NY 10020
212/582-2110

360 Post Street
San Francisco, CA 94102
415/982-1993

9465 Wilshire Boulevard
Beverly Hills, CA 90212
213/274-6934

11 East Adams Street
Chicago, IL 60603
312/427-8691

2121 Ponce de Leon Boulevard
Coral Gables, FL 33134
305/445-8648

In Canada

1500 Stanley Street, Suite 436
Montreal, Que. H3A 1R3
514/288-8255

409 Granville Street, Suite 452
Vancouver, B.C. V6C 1T2
604/688-6707

In the United Kingdom

179 Piccadilly
London W1 0BA
01/493-9731, 32, 33, 34

Britrail Travel International

Britrail Travel International represents British Rail in the United States and Canada. Travelers in these countries who want to make advance bookings on boat-train services between Britain and France, on through trains from London to Paris, or on Sealink car ferries across the English Channel should contact one of the following offices:

630 Third Avenue
New York, NY 10017
212/599-5400

510 West 6th Street
Los Angeles, CA 90014
213/626-0088

333 North Michigan Avenue
Chicago, IL 60601
312/263-1910

Plaza of the Americas
North Tower, Suite 750
LB356
Dallas, TX 75201
214/748-0860

94 Cumberland Street, Suite 601
Toronto, Ont. M5R 1A3
416/929-3333

409 Granville Street
Vancouver, B.C. V6C 1T2
604/683-6896

Reservations for any of these British Rail services may also be made at British Rail booking offices throughout the United Kingdom.

Sports and Leisure

Travelers who intend to observe or participate in sports or leisure activities while in France may obtain information from the following organizations:

Camping

Fédération Française de Camping et de
   Caravaning
78 Rue de Rivoli
75004 Paris
1/272-84-08

Riding

Fédération Equestre Française

164 Rue du Faubourg-St-Honoré
75008 Paris
1/225-11-22

Golf

Fédération Française de Golf
69 Avenue Victor-Hugo
75116 Paris
1/500-62-20

Auto Racing

Automobile Club de France
8 Place de la Concorde
75008 Paris
1/266-43-00

Ice Skating

Fédération Française des Sports de Glace
42 Rue du Louvre
75001 Paris
1/261-51-38

Flying

Aéro-Club de France
6 Rue Galilée
75016 Paris
1/720-93-02

Gliding

Fédération Française de Vol à Voile
29 Rue de Sèvres
75006 Paris
1/544-04-78

Parachuting

Fédération Française de Parachutisme
35 Rue St-Georges
75009 Paris
1/878-45-00

Tennis

La Ligue de Tennis de Paris

74 Rue de Rome
75008 Paris
1/522-22-08

Winter Sports

Association des Maires des Stations
Françaises de Sports d'Hiver
61 Boulevard Haussmann
75008 Paris
1/742-23-32

Basque Pelota

Club de Pelote Basque
8 Rue de la Cavalerie
75015 Paris
1/567-06-34

Mountain Climbing

Club Alpin Français
7 Rue La Boétie
75008 Paris
1/742-36-77

Fishing (permit required)

Conseil Supérieur de la Pêche
10 Rue Péclet
75010 Paris
1/842-10-00

Hunting and Shooting (permit required)

Office National de la Chasse
85-bis Avenue de Wagram
75017 Paris
1/277-81-75

Scuba Diving

Fédération Française d'Etudes et de Sports
    Sous-Marins
24 Quai de Rive-Neuve
13007 Marseille
91/33-99-31

Canoeing

Canoë-Kayak Club de France
47 Quai Ferber
94360 Bry-sur-Marne
1/881-54-26

Sailing

Fédération Française de Yachting à Voile
55 Avenue Kléber
75116 Paris
1/505-68-00

Water Skiing

Fédération Française de Ski Nautique
9 Boulevard Pereire
75017 Paris
1/267-15-66

Surfing

Fédération Française de Surf
Cité Administrative
Avenue Edouard-VII
64200 Biarritz

Wind-surfing

Association Française de Wind-Surf
29 Rue du Général-Delestraint
75016 Paris

Motorboating (license required)

Fédération Française Motonautique
8 Place de la Concorde
75008 Paris
1/073-89-38, 265-34-70

Cave Exploring

Fédération Française de Spéléologie
130 Rue St-Maur
75011 Paris
1/357-56-54

The Côte d'Azur

The Côte d'Azur is a legendary vacation spot—and with good reason. Apart from its remarkable natural beauty and cultural attractions, it has an exceptionally favorable year-round climate. Winters are mild and sunny—the region was first a *winter* resort—and the average January temperature along the coast is a relatively balmy 9° C (48° F). Frost is almost nonexistent. In the Alpine hinterland only a few miles inland, however, winter weather is considerably colder, and the slopes are covered with snow.

Spring and autumn are generally the best seasons for visiting the Riviera. The area is less crowded then than during the summer, and the average daily high temperatures are 20° C (68° F) in May and 21° C (70° F) in October. Autumn is the wettest season, but the heavy downpours generally do not last longer than 15 or 20 minutes. In spring, the climate is usually pleasant as well, despite brief but intense showers and occasional appearances of the mistral, a cold, fierce northwest wind that can blow for several days. The Massif des Maures and the Estérel typically act as natural barriers against this wind, so it rarely affects the Côte d'Azur east of the Var.

In summer, the area attracts hordes of vacationers for the weather is excellent. Sea breezes temper the summer heat, which averages 24° C (75° F); and there is almost no rain, leading to severe and regrettably common forest fires in the region. The average temperature of the sea during the summer is 19° C (66° F).

TOURIST OFFICES

Most French towns of even modest size have a *syndicat d'initiative*, a local tourist office. For further information about any of the major towns discussed in this guide, inquire at the appropriate address below. Address written inquiries to Office de Tourisme, unless a different office is indicated.

12 Place Général-de-Gaulle
06600 Antibes
93/33-95-64

Allées Vivien
83150 Bandol
94/29-41-35

Place de la Gare
06310 Beaulieu-sur-Mer
93/01-02-21

Place St-Louis
83170 Brignoles
94/69-01-78

26 Avenue Renoir
06800 Cagnes-sur-Mer
93/20-61-64

Gare SNCF
06400 Cannes
93/99-19-77

50 La Croisette
06400 Cannes
93/88-91-92

Place Baragnon
13260 Cassis
42/01-71-17

2 Quai Ganteaume
13600 La Ciotat
42/08-61-32

Place Calvini
83600 Fréjus
94/51-53-87

84 Avenue de la Liberté
06220 Golfe-Juan-Vallauris
93/63-73-12

6 Place de la Foux
06130 Grasse
93/36-03-56

Avenue Clotis
83400 Hyères
94/65-18-55

Boulevard Charles-Guillaumont
06160 Juan-les-Pins
93/61-04-98

Quai Péri
83980 Le Lavandou
94/71-00-61

Avenue de Cannes, B.P. 16
06210 Mandelieu
93/49-14-39

Rue Jean-Aulas, B.P. 15
06210 Mandelieu-la-Napoule
93/49-95-31

4 La Canebière
13001 Marseille
91/54-91-11

Palais de l'Europe, Avenue Boyer
06503 Menton
93/57-57-00

Direction du Tourisme et des Congrès
2A Boulevard des Moulins
Monte Carlo
MC 98030, Monaco
93/30-87-01

Gare SNCF, Avenue Thiers
06000 Nice
93/87-07-07

32 Avenue de l'Hôtel-des-Postes
06000 Nice
93/62-06-06

5 Avenue Gustave-V
06000 Nice
93/87-60-60

Centre d'Information Jeunesse
[Youth Information Center]
Esplanade des Victoires
06300 Nice
93/80-93-93

Hôtel de Ville
06190 Roquebrune-Cap-Martin
93/35-60-67

Esplanade Jean-Gioan
06190 Roquebrune-Cap-Martin
93/57-99-44

59 Avenue Dénis-Séméria
06290 St. Jean-Cap-Ferrat
93/01-36-86

Promenade Simon-Lorière
83120 Ste. Maxime
94/96-19-24

Maison de la Tour
06570 St. Paul-de-Vence
93/32-86-95

Rue Rousseau
83700 St. Raphaël
94/95-16-87

Quai Jean-Jaurès
83990 St. Tropez
94/97-41-21

8 Avenue Colbert
83000 Toulon
94/22-08-22

Avenue des Martyrs-de-la-Résistance
06220 Vallauris
93/63-82-58

Place du Grand-Jardin
06140 Vence
93/58-06-38

Square Binon
06230 Villefranche
93/80-73-68

Mairie
06270 Villeneuve-Loubet
93/20-82-82

ACCOMMODATIONS

The Riviera has a tradition of fine hotels that dates back to the eighteenth century, when European aristocrats first began to vacation there. Some of these old-style hotels—such as the famed Negresco, in Nice—still survive, but scores of newer and more modest accommodations are available as well; the low-budget traveler should not be deterred by the Riviera's exclusive reputation. About 1,000 hotels on the Côte d'Azur rank at least one star in the international classification system. (The highest category in France, four-star *de luxe*, is equivalent to the British five-star group.)

Air Inter, France's domestic airline, offers a travel package called "Weekend Côte d'Azur" that includes—for the price of a Paris-Nice airline ticket—two nights in a double room in a four-star *de luxe* hotel in Nice, Cannes, Monte Carlo, or Beaulieu. Novatours (14 Avenue de Madrid, 06400 Cannes, telephone 93/43-45-36) offers weekend packages, museum packages, and golf packages. Travel packages are also available from various other organizations.

Outside major cities and towns, travelers can stay at one of the *logis de France*, simple, well-run, and quite inexpensive country inns that usually rate one or two stars. For information about these inns and for reservations, contact Hôtel Logis de France, 55 Promenade des Anglais, 06000 Nice, telephone 93/44-70-70. Accommodations can also be obtained in a *gîte rural de France*—a house or part of a house rented for a weekend, a week, two weeks, or a month, usually in a farming area or small village—or in a *gîte chambre d'hôte*, the equivalent of a bed-and-breakfast. For further information and reservations, consult Relais des Gîtes de France des Alpes-Maritimes, 55 Promenade des Anglais, 06000 Nice, telephone 93/44-39-39.

In addition, visitors to the Riviera may choose one of its many campgrounds, caravan sites, youth hostels, or tourist apartments. For further information, consult a travel agent, the French Government Tourist Office, or another appropriate source listed in the "Introduction to France."

GETTING AROUND THE RIVIERA

By Air

From outside the region, travelers can fly into Nice, Marseilles, Cannes, Toulon, or St. Raphaël/Fréjus. Passengers who arrive in

Nice can take advantage of regular bus service from the airport to the city center, to Cannes, to Antibes, to Monaco, or to Menton. Passengers who land in Marseilles can take a bus to the Gare St-Charles downtown. The only airline service from one point in the region to another is Air-Inter's Nice–Marseilles route, although a helicopter service between Nice and Monaco is also available.

By Rail

SNCF routes connect the Côte d'Azur with Paris and other parts of France; a railroad also links the coastal towns. Trains along the coastal route are especially frequent in summer (late June–September), when a special service, the *Métrazur*, runs between Cannes and Menton at half-hour intervals.

In addition, the privately owned Provence Railway runs between Nice and Digne, through the scenic Var Valley. From Digne, travelers can proceed to Aix-en-Provence and other towns in the interior.

By Car

Travelers who want to explore out-of-the-way sights and small towns along the coast and (especially) in the hinterland should consider driving. The three roughly parallel *Corniches* that run between Nice and Menton offer spectacular views, and the inland mountain roads are excellent. In summer, traffic is very heavy throughout Provence and the Alpes-Maritimes, and parking in the larger cities can be particularly difficult and frustrating. Car rentals are offered by many agencies on the Riviera, especially at airports and major SNCF stations. For more information on car rental and driving in France, see the "Introduction to France."

By Bus

Buses generally link villages to larger towns; they tend to be infrequent and crowded. However, full-day and half-day excursion coach tours are available through SNCF and through Compagnie Transports Méditerranéens (CTM), 5 Square Mérimée, 06400 Cannes, telephone 93/39-79-40.

By Water

The Côte d'Azur is probably France's prime region for sailing. Visitors to the area can hire small craft from one of the following organizations:

Azur Yachting
Port de Bormes
83230 Bormes
94/71-19-81

Bureau Bateau
Traverse de la Tuilerie, B.P. 71
83150 Bandol
94/29-45-41

Euro-Voile
83400 Port d'Hyères
94/57-61-79

Glemot S.A.
18 Quai St-Pierre
06402 Cannes
93/99-05-50

Locazur
7 Rue Chabrier
06220 Golfe-Juan
93/63-75-88

Major Harbors of the Côte d'Azur

Harbor	Telephone	Number of Berths
La Galère	93/75-41-74	248
Théoule	93/49-97-38	255
Mandelieu–la-Napoule	93/49-80-64	1,261
Cannes–Vieux Port	93/39-61-77	786
Cannes–Port Canto	93/43-48-66	663
Cannes–La Croisette/Palm Beach	93/68-91-92	382
Golfe-Juan	93/63-96-25	858
Juan-les-Pins (La Gallice)	93/61-28-64	526
Juan-les-Pins (Le Croûton)	93/39-69-93	274
Antibes–Port Vauban	93/34-43-00	1,543
Villeneuve-Loubet	93/20-01-60	577
Cros-de-Cagnes	93/31-04-74	41
St. Laurent-du-Var	93/07-12-70	1,063
Nice	93/89-50-85	436
St. Jean-Cap-Ferrat	93/01-31-00	556
Beaulieu	93/01-10-49	790
Monaco Condamine	93/30-76-87	500
Menton–Vieux Port	93/35-78-83	485
Menton–Garavan	93/50-80-99	800

Travel agents may also be able to offer suggestions about agencies in the United States, Great Britain, or Canada through which travelers can arrange to rent craft in France.

FOOD AND DRINK

The French Riviera shares the remarkable regional cuisine of Provence—one that is surely among France's most memorable and distinctive. Provençal cuisine is far more Mediterranean in flavor than most French cooking is, and Nice offers a local variant that is strongly Italian—reflecting that city's location and history. The area is so blessed by sunny weather, ample rain, and fertile soil that it grows a prodigious supply of fruits, vegetables, and herbs. Not surprisingly, tomatoes, garlic, saffron, peppers, olives, and the local herbs—oregano, marjoram, winter savory, and thyme—all play prominent roles in Provençal fare. In fact, Provence is the only part of France where a separate vegetable entrée is presented (between the fish and roast at gala meals, between the hors d'oeuvre and main course at simple ones).

Regional specialties abound. A common appetizer is *tapenade*, a purée of anchovies and black olives. Another is the world-famous *salade niçoise*, a salad consisting of olives, tomatoes, hard-boiled eggs, and anchovies, sometimes with additional ingredients. *Soupe au pistou* is a type of minestrone to which a paste—made of fresh basil leaves, grated Parmesan cheese, olive oil, and garlic—is added upon serving, enabling each person to season the soup to taste.

Vegetable dishes native to Provence include *artichauts à la Barigoule*, artichokes stuffed with garlic and parsley; *tian de courgettes et de tomates*, zucchini (courgettes) and tomato slices covered with Parmesan cheese and baked; and *ratatouille*, a celebrated stew of eggplants (aubergines), tomatoes, peppers, and other ingredients, cooked with olive oil. *Bouilla-*

baisse, which Marseilles claims as its own, may be the region's best-known seafood dish. It is a rich, heady broth of shellfish, flavored with saffron. Sea bass (*loup de mer*), wrapped in quickly blanched lettuce leaves and cooked lightly in a white wine *fumet*, is another favorite of the area. Provence is also known for its *daubes*—stews of beef, lamb, fowl, octopus, and so on, cooked in a broth of wine and herbs and heated slowly in a *daubière*, a tightly covered casserole, for 8 or 9 hours. Other distinctive entrées of the region are *boeuf à la Gordienne*, beef stewed in red wine; and *gardiane d'agneau*, a lamb stew with olives. Local desserts highlight the Riviera's bountiful supply of fruits—which include melons, oranges, and figs—sometimes glazed, candied, or soaked in Cointreau.

Naturally, all types of restaurants are available on the Riviera, including inexpensive snack bars that serve pizza, crêpes, sandwiches, and other simple, fast fare. Meals tend to be cheaper when ordered *prix-fixe* rather than *à la carte*.

Provence is not as well known for its wines as other parts of France are, but the region produces some notable varieties nonetheless. Bellet, for instance, comes from the hills near Nice. It is a rare and admired wine that may be red, white, or rosé. Bandol produces rosé and a fruity red; nearby Cassis produces a dry white. The Côtes-de-Provence reds and rosés, light but not always superior, come from the countryside north of Toulon. The most popular local apéritif is *pastis*, an aniseed-flavored drink rather like Greek *ouzo*.

SPORTS

The Riviera's ideal climate makes it a perfect spot for year-round outdoor activities.

The region is perhaps best known for its beaches, but these are sandy only west of Antibes; they tend to be gravelly farther east. Most of the beaches are free, except in some of the more fashionable resorts, and all of the towns have a public swimming pool *(piscine municipale)*. Better-quality hotels may have pools and private beaches. Toplessness is standard on Riviera beaches.

Facilities for water skiing, wind surfing, and sailing are available all along the Côte d'Azur. Some resorts also have facilities for scuba diving and underwater fishing. For further information, consult a travel agent, the French Government Tourist Office (see "Introduction to France"), or one of the local tourist offices *(syndicats d'initiative)* listed at the end of this guide.

All towns and villages in the area have tennis courts, and 18-hole golf courses exist in Cannes-Mandelieu, Mougins, Valbonne, Biot, and Monte Carlo. Fishing is possible in the mountain lakes and rivers, and rivers such as the Tinée, Var, and Loup are suitable for canoeing and kayaking. For information about mountain climbing, consult a travel agent or the Club Alpin Français, 15 Avenue Jean-Médecin, 06000 Nice, telephone 93/87-95-41.

Other activities the Riviera offers include walking tours, speleology (cave and grotto exploration), cycling, and horseback riding. Bicycles can be rented in major towns along the coast; consult a local *syndicat d'initiative* for further information. A popular and traditional game throughout the south of France is *boules*.

Only an hour or two from the coast lie some of France's major winter ski resorts—notably Auron, Valberg, and Isola 2000. Equipment can be purchased or rented upon arrival. For further information, consult a travel agent or the French Government Tourist Office.

ENTERTAINMENT AND NIGHT LIFE

The Riviera offers many forms of entertainment and night life for the sophisticated traveler. Nice has several theaters, and its opera is in season from November through April. Nice, Cannes, Monaco, and other major towns boast several night clubs and cabarets. In season (December–March, late June–August), horse races take place at the Hippodrome in Cagnes-sur-Mer (telephone 93/20-30-30).

The area is known for its casinos, and the most celebrated is probably the Monte Carlo Casino in Monaco (telephone 93/50-69-31), which is open all year. There are others along the coast, notably in Cannes and Cassis. You must be at least 21 to enter a casino, and you should be able to produce a valid passport or identity card.

For children, there are zoos at Bandol, Marseilles, Monaco, St. Jean-Cap-Ferrat, and Toulon; a marine park at Antibes; and two safari parks at Fréjus. At some beaches —Antibes and Monte Carlo, for example— parents can leave small children with qualified supervisors while they go on their own.

SHOPPING

The Côte d'Azur is a shopper's paradise, and some of the larger towns—Cannes, for example—boast boutiques that are among the most fashionable in the world. At the other end of the spectrum, visitors can happily browse through the open-air markets in cities and villages alike, with their alluring displays of farm-fresh produce. Certain villages are known for specific manufactures: Biot for glassware and pottery; Sospel for olivewood sculpture; Tourette-sur-

Loup for ceramics and other handicrafts; and Vallauris for pottery. See the "Introduction to France" for general information on shopping hours.

MUSEUMS

Antibes

Musée Archéologique

Bastion St-André
06600 Antibes
93/34-48-01
Open daily, except Tuesday. Summer: 9:00 A.M.–NOON and 2:00 P.M.–7:00 P.M. Winter: 9:00 A.M.–NOON and 2:00 P.M.–6:00 P.M. Closed November.

Housed in the fortifications built by Vauban, this museum is devoted to the history of ancient Antipolis, from which modern Antibes derives its name. It contains ancient Greek ceramics and other relics from antiquity found in the area.

Musée Grimaldi-Picasso

Place du Château
06600 Antibes
93/33-67-67
Open daily, except Tuesday and legal holidays. Summer: 10:00 A.M.–NOON and 3:00 P.M.–7:00 P.M. Winter: 10:00 A.M.–NOON and 3:00 P.M.–6:00 P.M. Closed November. Guided tours in English by appointment.

This Baroque edifice, where the bishops of Antibes once lived, now houses more than 150 works by Picasso—paintings, drawings, gouaches, lithographs, ceramics, and so on—as well as a collection of modern art that includes works by Léger and Calder.

Musée Naval et Napoléonien

Batterie du Grillon
06600 Antibes
93/61-45-32

Open daily, except Tuesday. June 15–September 14: 10:00 A.M.–NOON and 3:00 P.M.–7:00 P.M. September 15–October 30 and December 16–June 14: 10:00 A.M.–NOON and 3:00 P.M.–5:00 P.M. Closed November 1–December 15.

One wing of this museum commemorates Napoleon, who returned from exile on Elba to nearby Golfe-Juan in March 1815. There is a bust of the emperor by Canova, figurines of soldiers and officers of his Grand Army, documents, weapons, lithographs, and other mementos. The other section of the museum honors French naval history. Paintings, drawings, and models of historic ships are on display.

Beaulieu-sur-Mer

Villa Grecque "Kerylos"

66310 Beaulieu-sur-Mer
93/01-01-44
Open daily, except Monday, 2:00 P.M.–6:00 P.M. (3:00 P.M.–7:00 P.M. in July and August). Closed November. Appointments for groups available in the morning.

A property of the Institut de France, this villa is a faithful reconstruction of an ancient Greek dwelling. It was commissioned early in the twentieth century by archeologist Theodore Reinach, and it was built of stone, wood, marble, bronze, and ivory. It contains mosaics, frescoes, and antiques from the sixth to first centuries B.C.

Biot

Musée National Fernand Léger

06410 Biot
93/33-42-20

Open daily, except Tuesday. Summer: 10:00 A.M.–NOON and 2:00 P.M.–6:00 P.M. Winter: 10:00 A.M.–NOON and 2:00 P.M.–5:00 P.M.

Constructed in the late 1950s at the suggestion of the artist's widow, Nadia Léger, this museum houses a fine collection of Leger's ceramics, gouaches, and paintings—about 350 works in all. A huge polychrome ceramic work by the artist dominates the museum's main façade.

Brignoles

Musée du Pays Brignolais

Palais des Comtes de Provence
83170 Brignoles
94/69-45-18
Open daily, except Monday and Tuesday. Summer: 9:00 A.M.–NOON and 2:30 P.M.–6:00 P.M. (Sunday, 9:00 A.M.–NOON and 3:00 P.M.–6:00 P.M.). Winter: 10:00 A.M.–NOON and 2:30 P.M.–5:00 P.M. (Sunday, 10:00 A.M.–NOON and 3:00 P.M.–5:00 P.M.). Closed September 15–October 15.

This museum includes a collection of regional art, local archeological finds, a reconstruction of a Provençal kitchen and crèche, an exhibition on the marble of Brignoles, and paintings by Parrocel de Batailles (1646–1704), who was born in Brignoles, and other local artists.

Cagnes

Château-Musée de Cagnes

Haut de Cagnes
06800 Cagnes-sur-Mer
93/20-85-57
Summer: open daily, 10:00 A.M.–NOON and 2:30 P.M.–7:00 P.M. Winter: open daily, except Tuesday, 10:00 A.M.–NOON and 2:00 P.M.–5:00 P.M. Closed October 15–November 15.

This medieval castle contains walls and guard rooms from about 1300 and elegant seventeenth-century additions—among others, a ceiling fresco, *The Fall of Phaeton*, by Carlone and Benso. It also houses the Olive Museum (a tribute to one of the Mediterranean's premier trees), the Museum of Modern Mediterranean Art, and the Suzy Solidor Donation (paintings of Solidor by forty different artists, including Foujita, Dufy, van Dongen, Cocteau, and Marie Laurencin). Since 1969, the International Festival of Painting has taken place here (every July–September).

Musée Renoir

Avenue des Collettes, Cagnes-Ville
06800 Cagnes-sur-Mer
93/20-61-07
Open daily, except Tuesday. Summer: 2:30 P.M.–6:00 P.M. Winter: 2:00 P.M.–5:00 P.M. Closed October 15–November 15.

This villa looks just as it did when Pierre-Auguste Renoir lived here from 1908 until his death in 1919. It contains paintings and sculptures by the artist, a bust of him by Maillol, and mementos of his life. The museum sits in a large garden that overlooks the Mediterranean and boasts 145 olive trees. In the garden, visitors can walk, relax, and paint.

Cannes

Musée de la Castre

Le Suquet
06400 Cannes
93/68-91-92
Open daily, except Monday. April–June:
10:00 A.M.–NOON and 2:00 P.M.–6:00 P.M.
July–September: 10:00 A.M.–NOON and 3:00
P.M.–7:00 P.M. October and December 16–
March 31: 10:00 A.M.–NOON and 2:00 P.M.–
5:00 P.M. Closed November 1–December 15.

Located in the old chateau of Cannes, on
top of the hill of Le Suquet, this museum
houses an archeological and ethnographic
collection that includes art and artifacts
from the Pacific Islands, Africa, Pre-Columbian America, ancient Egypt and Meso-
potamia, the Middle East, and the
Mediterranean region.

Monastère de St-Honorat

Ile St-Honorat
93/38-82-82
Open daily, except Good Friday. Summer:
9:40 A.M.–4:40 P.M. Winter: 10:40 A.M.–5:30
P.M.

About half an hour by boat from Cannes
(boats run about ten times daily in summer
and about five times daily in winter from
the Gare Maritime, telephone 93/39-11-
82), lie the Ile St-Honorat and its fortified
monastery. Inside its eleventh-century
donjon are a cloister (from a somewhat
earlier period), Roman cistern, and a
chapel.

Musée de la Mer

Fort Royal
Ile Ste-Marguerite
93/39-98-98

Open daily, except Monday and civil and
church holidays. Summer: 9:00 A.M.–11:45
A.M. and 2:00 P.M.–5:45 or 6:45 P.M. Winter:
10:30 A.M.–11:45 A.M. and 2:00 P.M.–3:45 or
4:45 P.M. (Closing times depend on the condition of the sea.) Closed January–
February.

About fifteen minutes by boat from Cannes
(boats run about ten times daily in summer
and about five times daily in winter from
the Gare Maritime, telephone 93/39-11-
82), this old fort contains archeological
finds from nearby sites—including Roman
and Arabic ceramics—and historical
documents.

Eze

Jardin Exotique

06360 Eze
Open daily, 9:00 A.M.–sunset.

This remarkable garden includes many varieties of cacti and other exotic plants. From
the remains of an old chateau on the
grounds, visitors can enjoy a commanding
view of the Mediterranean coastline—seeing as far as Corsica, in good weather.

Fréjus

Cité Episcopale

Place Formigé
83600 Fréjus
94/51-26-30
Open daily, except Tuesday. April–September: 9:30 A.M.—NOON and 2:00 P.M.–
6:00 P.M. October–March: 9:30 A.M.–NOON
and 2:00 P.M.–4:30 P.M.

This historic complex includes a fifth-century baptistry, a twelfth-century cloister, and an archeological museum containing such Gallo-Roman artifacts as mosaics, votive inscriptions, pottery, decorative fragments, and sculptures of deities.

Gourdon

Chateau-Musée

Commune de Gourdon
06620 Bar-sur-Loup
93/42-50-13
July 1–September 15: open daily, 11:00 A.M.–1:00 P.M. and 2:00 P.M.–7:00 P.M. September 16–June 30: open daily, except Tuesday, 10:00 A.M.–NOON and 2:00 P.M.–7:00 P.M.

A twelfth-century fortress built on the remains of a Saracen bastion, the chateau of Gourdon now houses two collections—one of furniture, weapons, documents, and paintings from the sixteenth through eighteenth centuries; the other of contemporary naïve painting. From the castle, visitors have a marvelous view of the coast.

Grasse

Musée d'Art et d'Histoire de Provence

2 Rue Mirabeau
06130 Grasse
93/36-01-28
Open daily, except Saturday and Sunday (open first and last Sunday of each month, however). June 1–September 30: 10:00 A.M.–NOON and 2:00 P.M.–6:00 P.M. October and December 1–May 31: 10:00 A.M.–NOON and 2:00 P.M.–5:00 P.M. Closed November.

This museum, located in a historic 1774 *hôtel*, contains a re-creation of a Provençal home of the past, with kitchen, salons, and bedrooms. It also features exhibitions on the art, history, and traditions of eastern Provence—furniture, porcelain, pottery, glassware, archeological finds, religious art, and so on.

Musée Fragonard

23 Boulevard Fragonard
06130 Grasse
93/36-02-71
Open daily, except Saturday and Sunday (open first and last Sunday of each month, however). June 1–September 30: 10:00 A.M.–NOON and 2:00 P.M.–6:00 P.M. October and December 1–May 31: 10:00 A.M.–NOON and 2:00 P.M.–5:00 P.M. Closed November.

Works by Rococo painter Jean-Honoré Fragonard, his son Alexandre-Evariste Fragonard and grandson Théophile Fragonard, and Marguerite Gérard are on display.

Musée International de la Parfumerie

Boulevard Fragonard
Scheduled to open in 1986.

This brand-new museum will focus on perfume and cosmetics, from their earliest beginnings to the present. It will include everything from a model perfume factory to a greenhouse of aromatic tropical and subtropical plants.

Hyères

Musée Municipal

Place Lefèvre
83400 Hyères

94/65-39-67
Open daily, except Tuesday.

This diverse collection features local archeological finds dating to the colonization of Hyères by Massalian Greeks and to the later Roman settlement of Olbia. Paintings, fabrics, and jewelry are also on display, as are natural history exhibits.

Laghet

Sanctuaire de Notre-Dame-de-Laghet

93/41-09-60
Open daily, 3:00 P.M.–5:00 P.M.

Founded in 1656, this sanctuary is a site of pilgrimages to the Virgin Mary. The cloister and the church contain thousands of votive offerings, and the museum includes several paintings on glass.

Marseilles

Musée d'Archéologie

Château Borély
Avenue Clot-Bey
13008 Marseille
91/73-21-60
Bus: 19, 44
Open daily, except Tuesday (all day) and Wednesday (morning), 9:30 A.M.–12:15 P.M. and 1:00 P.M.–5:30 P.M.

The Château Borély is an elegant residence, built in the late eighteenth century and still containing some of its original Louis XVI furniture. It has been a museum since 1863, housing one of the finest collections of ancient Egyptian treasures—statuary, sarcophagi, mummies, amulets, and so on—in France. Archeological finds from all parts of the Mediterranean and Middle East are also on display. The second floor houses a bequest of paintings and drawings by such French masters of the seventeenth and eighteenth centuries as Poussin, Watteau, Fragonard, Boucher, and Hubert Robert.

Musée des Beaux-Arts

Palais Longchamp
13004 Marseille
91/62-21-17
Métro: Longchamp–Cinq Avenues
Open daily, except Tuesday (all day) and Wednesday (morning), 10:00 A.M.–NOON and 2:00 P.M.–6:30 P.M.

The ground floor of this collection contains the Grande Galerie, featuring European painting of the sixteenth and seventeenth centuries; a hall of African sculpture; and two rooms devoted to the paintings and sculpture of Pierre Puget. The first floor houses painting and sculpture from the eighteenth through early twentieth centuries—notably thirty-six busts by Daumier, who was born in Marseilles in 1808. Works by David, Millet, Courbet, Corot, Rodin, and Dufy are also on display.

Musée Cantini

19 Rue Grignan
13006 Marseille
91/54-77-75
Métro: Estrangin-Préfecture
Open daily, except Tuesday (all day) and Wednesday (morning), 10:00 A.M.–NOON and 2:00 P.M.–6:30 P.M.

The ground floor of this late seventeenth-century hôtel boasts more than 500 pieces by the great porcelain makers of seventeenth- and eighteenth-century Marseilles and Provence. The rest of the museum is devoted to modern art, including works by

Folon, Bacon, Balthus, Hartung, Yves Klein, Arman, and Niki de St-Phalle. Major temporary exhibitions are also on display periodically; check local listings.

Galeries de la Charité

Rue de l'Observance & Rue de la Charité
13002 Marseille
91/90-26-14
Métro: Vieux-Port, Hôtel de Ville
Open daily, except Tuesday (all day) and Wednesday (morning), 10:00 A.M.–NOON and 2:00 P.M.–6:30 P.M.

Pierre Puget designed this striking seventeenth-century hospital ensemble, now being restored. Its centerpiece is the chapel, with an ovoid dome. The chapel and three adjoining galleries frequently hold exhibitions organized by the city.

Musée du Château-Gombert

5 Place des Héros
13013 Marseille
91/68-14-38
Métro: Frais-Vallon, then bus 5.
Open Saturday, Sunday, and Monday. Summer: 3:00 P.M.–7:00 P.M. Winter: 2:00 P.M.–6:00 P.M. Guided tours Wednesday at 3:00 P.M. (except during school vacations) or by appointment.

This museum contains exhibits on the arts and traditions of Marseilles and its surrounding countryside in the eighteenth and nineteenth centuries—costumes, pottery, furniture, engravings, religious art, crèches, Christmas customs, and so on.

Musée des Docks Romains

Place Vivaux
13002 Marseille
91/91-24-62
Métro: Vieux-Port, Hôtel de Ville

Open daily, except Tuesday (all day) and Wednesday (morning), 10:00 A.M.–NOON and 2:00 P.M.–6:30 P.M.

The remains of the ancient Roman docks of Marseilles form the focus of this collection, which also features Greco-Roman ceramics, statuettes, lamps, and other artifacts. Models and maps are displayed as well.

Musée Grobet-Labadié

140 Boulevard Longchamp
13001 Marseille
91/62-21-82
Métro: Longchamp–Cinq Avenues
Bus: 41, 80, 81
Open daily, except Tuesday (all day) and Wednesday (morning), 10:00 A.M.–NOON and 2:00 P.M.—6:30 P.M.

This 1873 *hôtel* was built for Marseilles industrialist Alexandre Labadié, who was an avid and eclectic collector. He amassed collections of Oriental rugs, furniture, porcelain, and musical instruments; French drawings and paintings of the seventeenth through nineteenth centuries; primitive Flemish, German, and Italian art; Flemish and French tapestries of the sixteenth through eighteenth centuries; and medieval and Renaissance sculpture.

Musée d'Histoire de Marseille

Centre Bourse
13001 Marseille
91/90-42-22
Métro: Vieux-Port
Open daily, except Sunday and Monday, NOON–7:00 P.M.

Set in the midst of a bustling commercial complex, this museum preserves the history of Marseilles in a novel way. It includes an outdoor garden, featuring remains of ancient walls, and offers audio-visual displays and temporary exhibitions on various aspects of Marseilles's past and present.

Musée d'Histoire Naturelle

Palais Longchamp
13004 Marseille
91/62-30-78
Métro: Longchamp—Cinq Avenues
Open daily, except Tuesday (all day) and Wednesday (morning), 10:00 A.M.—NOON and 2:00 P.M.—6:30 P.M.

This museum boasts not only an aquarium with Mediterranean and tropical fish, but also collections relating to paleontology, mineralogy, zoology, botany, and prehistory. The Salle de Provence features exhibits of local fossils and wildlife.

Musée de la Marine

Palais de la Bourse
13001 Marseille
91/91-91-51
Métro: Vieux-Port, Hôtel de Ville
Open daily, except Sunday, 10:00 A.M.—NOON and 2:00 P.M.—6:30 P.M. Guided tours Wednesday at 3:00 P.M. or by appointment.

The collections of this museum focus on the history of Marseilles—since antiquity and especially since the sixteenth century—as a seaport and commercial center. Paintings, engravings, models of ships, and other artifacts are on display to illustrate this rich heritage.

Musée du Vieux-Marseille

Maison Diamantée, Rue de la Prison
13002 Marseille
91/90-80-28
Métro: Vieux-Port, Hôtel de Ville
Open daily, except Tuesday (all day) and Wednesday (morning), 10:00 A.M.—NOON and 2:00 P.M.—6:30 P.M.

In the heart of old Marseilles lies this distinctive structure from the 1570s. Today, it houses many elements of the city's cultural legacy: Provençal furniture, traditional costumes, crèches, and household and religious objects. Its collection of playing cards is unique.

Menton

Musée du Palais-Carnolès

3 Avenue de la Madone
06500 Menton
93/35-49-71
Open daily, except Monday, Tuesday, and major civil and church holidays. June 15—September 15: 10:00 A.M.—NOON and 3:00 P.M.—6:00 P.M. September 16—June 14: 2:00 P.M.—5:30 P.M.

The Palais Carnolès was once the residence of the princes of Monaco. It contains Italian, Flemish, and Dutch paintings of the thirteenth through seventeenth centuries. One room features eighteenth-century works, notably Benjamin West's *The Sacrifice of Iphigenia*. The ground floor contains works by modern painters such as Max Jacob, Picabia, Suzanne Valadon, and Dufy.

Musée Jean-Cocteau

Quai du Vieux-Port
06500 Menton
Open daily, except Monday, Tuesday, and major civil and church holidays. June 15—September 15: 10:00 A.M.—NOON and 3:00 P.M.—6:00 P.M. September 16—June 14: 10:00 A.M.—NOON and 2:00 P.M.—5:30 P.M.

This seventeenth-century fortress, built to protect Menton, is now the setting for tapestries, drawings, gouaches, and ceramics by Jean Cocteau and other artists who were friends of his.

Salle des Mariages

Hôtel de Ville
Rue de la République
06500 Menton
Open daily, except Saturday, Sunday, and major civil and church holidays. June 15–September 15: 9:00 A.M.–NOON and 3:00 P.M.–6:00 P.M. September 16–June 14: 9:00 A.M.–NOON and 2:00 P.M.–6:00 P.M.

Jean Cocteau decorated this room in Menton's town hall with frescoes on the theme of marriage.

Monaco

Grands Appartements

Palais Princier
Monaco-Ville
Open daily, July 1–September 30 only, 9:30 A.M.–12:30 P.M. and 2:00 P.M.–6:30 P.M.

In summer, visitors can view the state apartments of the prince of Monaco, which is a tiny but sovereign nation. The Palais Princier includes the sixteenth-century Galerie d'Hercule, the throne room, and salons featuring ceiling frescoes, portraits of the princes of Monaco, and other rich decorations, primarily from the Baroque era.

Musée Napoléonien et des Archives du Palais

Palais Princier
Monaco-Ville

Open daily, except Monday. July 1–September 30: 9:30 A.M.–NOON and 2:00 P.M. –6:30 P.M. October–June: 9:00 A.M.–11:30 A.M. and 2:00 P.M.–5:30 P.M.

The Palais Princier also houses this museum of Napoleonic memorabilia, assembled by Prince Louis II, grandfather of the current prince, Rainier III. A bust of Napoleon by Houdon is one of this collection's treasures. The museum also displays documents and other artifacts that illustrate Monaco's rich and unusual history.

Musée de Cires

27 Rue Basse
Monaco-Ville
93/30-39-05
Open daily, 9:00A.M.–6:00 P.M.

This waxworks museum features likenesses of forty members of Monaco's ruling family, from the first prince, François de Grimaldi (1297), to Prince Rainier, Princess Grace, and their children.

Musée Océanographique

Avenue St-Martin
Monaco-Ville
93/30-15-14
Open daily. June–September: 9:00 A.M.–7:00 P.M. October–May: 9:30 A.M.–7:00 P.M.

This leading oceanographic museum was built as a "temple to the sea" by Monaco's Prince Albert I. It features an aquarium with thousands of fish and marine animals from the Mediterranean and tropical seas. The terrace of the museum offers a commanding view of the principality and the Côte d'Azur.

Jardin Exotique–Grotte de l'Observatoire–Musée d'Anthropologie Préhistorique

Boulevard du Jardin-Exotique
Monaco
93/30-33-65
Open daily, except May 1 and November 19 (Monegasque national holiday). May–September: 9:00 A.M.–7:00 P.M. October–April: 9:00 A.M.–6:00 P.M.

This striking complex includes a garden of exotic plants—notably giant cacti—set on a rocky cliff that overlooks the sea and affords a view of the French and Italian Rivieras. At the base of the cliff lies a prehistoric grotto, complete with stalactites, stalagmites, and other interesting formations. A museum here traces the course of human evolution and includes exhibits of Stone Age tools and Ice Age animals of Europe.

Musée National "Collection de Galéa"

17 Avenue Princesse-Grace
Monte-Carlo
93/30-91-26
Open daily, except January 1, May 1, November 19, and December 25. 10:00 A.M.–12:15 P.M. and 2:30 P.M.–6:30 P.M.

Charles Garnier, architect of the Paris Opera, built this villa, which now houses a remarkable collection of dolls and automatons dating from the eighteenth century through the Belle Epoque.

Nice

Musée d'Archéologie

164 Avenue des Arènes
06000 Nice
93/81-59-57
Bus: 15, 17, 20, 22 to Arènes

Open daily, except Sunday (morning), Monday (all day), and January 1, May 1, and December 25. May–September: 10:00 A.M.–NOON and 2:30 P.M.–6:30 P.M. October and December–April: 10:00 A.M.–NOON and 2:00 P.M.–5:00 P.M. Closed November. Guided tours, July 1–September 15, at 4:30 P.M.

Set on the site of ancient Cemenelum, the Roman provincial capital of Alpes Maritimae, this museum is continually being enriched as on-site excavations yield more and more archeological material. The halls and galleries are organized around major themes: daily life, history of the city and the province, Greco-Roman ceramics, trade, and funeral rites. The nearby archeological site includes Roman baths and an Early Christian baptistry and basilica.

Galerie d'Art Contemporain

59 Quai des Etats-Unis
06000 Nice
93/62-37-11
Open daily, except Sunday (morning), Monday (all day), and January 1, Easter Sunday, May 1, and December 25. 10:30 A.M.–NOON and 2:00 P.M.–6:00 P.M.

This gallery houses temporary exhibitions specifically devoted to art from the 1960s to the present. Works by new as well as established talents are featured.

Musée des Beaux-Arts Jules Chéret

33 Avenue des Baumettes
06000 Nice
93/44-50-72
Bus: 38 to Chéret
Open daily, except Monday and January 1, Easter Sunday, May 1, and December 25. May–September: 10:00 A.M.–NOON and 3:00

P.M.–6:00 P.M. October–April: 10:00 A.M.–NOON and 2:00 P.M.–5:00 P.M. Closed November (for two weeks). Guided tours in English, by appointment, to groups of ten or more; arrangements must be made a week in advance.

This museum, once a sumptuous Belle Epoque villa, now houses an important collection of European art of the seventeenth through twentieth centuries. Artists whose work is represented here include Carle Van Loo, Fragonard, Hubert Robert, Rodin, Dégas, Monet, Sisley, Renoir, Bonnard, Dufy, van Dongen, and Picasso (ceramics).

Musée International d'Art Naïf Anatole Jakovsky

Chateau Ste-Hélène
Avenue Val-Marie
06000 Nice
93/71-78-33
Bus: 8, 9/10, connection to 34, to Art Naïf
Open daily, except Tuesday and January 1, Easter Sunday, May 1, and December 25. May–September: 10:00 A.M.–NOON and 2:00 P.M.–6:00 P.M. October–April: 10:00 A.M.–NOON and 2:00 P.M.–5:00 P.M. Closed November.

A generous donation by art critic Anatole Jakovsky spurred the recent opening of this museum, which covers the history of naïve art from the eighteenth century to the present. The collection includes nearly 600 paintings and drawings; artists from twenty-seven countries are represented.

Muséum d'Histoire Naturelle—Musée Barla

60-bis Boulevard Risso
06300 Nice
93/55-15-24
Bus: 3, 4, 5, 6, 16, 17 to Barla

Open daily, except Tuesday and January 1, Easter Sunday and Monday, May 1, Whit Monday, and December 25. Weekdays: 9:00 A.M.–NOON and 2:00 P.M.–6:00 P.M. Sundays and holidays: 10:00 A.M.–NOON and 2:00 P.M.–6:00 P.M. Closed August 15–September 15. Guided tours for groups by appointment.

Exhibits focus on the primitive life forms of the animal and plant kingdoms, on stratigraphy (historical geology and evolution), and on mineralogy. The museum possesses an important collection of minerals. In addition, an entire room is devoted exclusively to mushrooms and mycology.

Muséum d'Histoire Naturelle—Galerie de Malacologie

3 Cours Saleya
06300 Nice
93/85-18-44
Open daily, except Sunday, Monday, and January 1, May 1, and December 25. 11:00 A.M.–1:00 P.M. and 2:00 P.M.–7:00 P.M.

Located in a pedestrian precinct near Nice's flower market, this branch of the Muséum d'Histoire Naturelle boasts a remarkable collection of seashells from various parts of the world and an aquarium with marine invertebrates and exotic fish.

Palais Lascaris

15 Rue Droite
06300 Nice
93/62-05-54
Bus: 1, 2, 3, 3 barre, 5, 6, 14, 16, 17 to Lycée
Open daily, except Monday. May–October: 9:30 A.M.–NOON and 2:30 P.M.–6:30 P.M. December–April: 9:30 A.M.–NOON and 2:30 P.M.–6:00 P.M. Closed November.

From the middle of the seventeenth century until the French Revolution, this building was the residence of the noble Lascaris-Ventimiglia family. It has now been completely restored and its interior set off with seventeenth- and eighteenth-century collections and décor. The *étage noble*, with its ceiling frescoes, is particularly ornate.

Musée Masséna

65 Rue de France
06000 Nice
93/88-11-34
Bus: 3, 7, 8, 9/10, 12, 14, 22 to Rivoli or Gambetta-France
Open daily, except Monday and January 1, Easter Sunday, May 1, and December 25. May–September: 10:00 A.M.–NOON. October and December–April: 10:00 A.M.–NOON and 2:00 P.M.–5:00 P.M. Closed November.

The diverse collections of this museum include Empire furniture; Italian, Spanish, Flemish, and primitive "School of Nice" paintings; Provençal and Mediterranean faïence pottery; arms and armor; and European and Oriental jewelry. Other exhibits illustrate the folklore, ethnography, and history of Nice and the surrounding region.

Musée Matisse

Villa des Arènes
164 Avenue des Arènes
06000 Nice
93/81-59-57
Bus: 15, 17, 20, 22 to Arènes
Open daily, except Sunday (morning), Monday (all day), and January 1, May 1, and December 25. May–September: 10:00 A.M.–NOON and 2:30 P.M.–6:30 P.M. October–April: 10:00 A.M.–NOON and 2:00 P.M.–5:00 P.M. Closed November.

Opened in 1963, this museum is devoted to the work of Henri Matisse. The collection is especially rich in drawings and engravings, but it also includes many of his paintings, sculptures, ceramics, and illustrated books, such as *Jazz* (1947). It traces Matisse's career from his earliest works through his triumphant maturity as an artist.

Musée National-Message-Biblique-Marc-Chagall

Avenue du Docteur-Ménard
06000 Nice
93/81-75-75
Bus: 15 to Docteur-Moriez
Open daily, except Tuesday. July–September: 10:00 A.M.–7:00 P.M. October–April: 10:00 A.M.–12:30 P.M. and 2:00 P.M.–5:30 P.M. May be closed on bank holidays. Guided tours available in English by appointment, except Sunday and on bank holidays.

This collection represents Marc Chagall's poetical and mystical vision of the world. Seventeen large paintings constitute his *Message Biblique (Biblical Message)*, and 195 preparatory sketches for this work are exhibited as well. The museum also houses gouaches, engravings, lithographs, sculptures, stained glass, mosaics, and tapestries by the artist.

Musée Naval

Tour Bellanda
Parc du Château
06000 Nice
93/80-47-61
Open daily, except Tuesday and January 1, Easter Sunday, May 1, and December 25. June–September: 10:00 A.M.–NOON and 2:00 P.M.–7:00 P.M. October–May: 10:00

A.M.–NOON and 2:00 P.M.–5:00 P.M. Closed mid-November–December.

Hector Berlioz composed his *King Lear* in the circular rooms now occupied by the Musée Naval, which focuses on the rich and often stormy maritime history of Nice and the surrounding area. The collection includes historical maps, paintings of ships and sea battles, bronze cannon, nautical instruments, and model ships.

Musée de Terra-Amata

25 Boulevard Carnot
06000 Nice
93/55-59-93
Bus: 1, 2, 7, 9, 10, 14 to Port
Open daily, except Monday and January 1, Easter Sunday, May 1, and December 25. May–September: 10:00 A.M.–NOON and 2:00 P.M.–7:00 P.M. October–April: 10:00 A.M.–NOON and 2:00 P.M.–6:00 P.M. Closed last two weeks of September. Guided tours by appointment, for groups of at least ten.

Exhibits highlight finds from Terra Amata, a well-preserved prehistoric human habitat near Nice. The Terra Amata material dates from the Acheulean era, about 400,000 years ago.

Prieure du Vieux-Logis

59 Avenue St-Barthélemy
06000 Nice
93/84-44-74
Bus: 18 to Charles de Foucault; 4, 7 to Deux-Avenues
Open Wednesday, Thursday, Saturday, and the first Sunday of each month (closed other days and January 1, Easter Sunday, May 1, and December 25), 3:00 P.M.–5:00 P.M.

This collection was established in a sixteenth-century building by Pierre Lemerre, a Dominican father who was an avid collector of fourteenth-, fifteenth-, and sixteenth-century objects.

Roquebrune-Cap-Martin

Château-Musée

06190 Roquebrune-Cap-Martin
Summer: open daily, 9:00 A.M.–NOON and 2:00 P.M.–7:00 P.M. Winter: open daily, except Friday, 10:00 A.M.–NOON and 2:00 P.M.–5:00 P.M. Guided tours: July 15–September 15, Monday and Thursday, 5:00 P.M.–7:00 P.M.

This is the only surviving Carolingian fortress in France; originally built in the tenth century, most of the existing structure dates to the thirteenth. The parapet walk leads to a terrace with an exceptional view of the village and the coast.

St. Jean-Cap-Ferrat

Fondation Ephrussi de Rothschild

06230 St. Jean-Cap-Ferrat
93/01-33-09
Open daily, except Monday. July–August: 3:00 P.M.–7:00 P.M. September–October and December–June: 2:00 P.M.–6:00 P.M. Closed November. Group visits in the morning by appointment. Gardens are also open 9:00 A.M.–NOON.

A property of the Institut de France, this lovely villa houses an impressive collection of art and decorative objects from the fourteenth through nineteenth centuries—painting (including works by Monet, Renoir, and Sisley), statues, tapestries, carpets, furniture, Sèvres and Dresden china, wrought iron work, and Chinese objets d'art. The villa sits amid French, Spanish, Japanese, exotic, and rock gardens.

St. Paul-de-Vence

Fondation Maeght

06570 St. Paul-de-Vence
93/32-81-63
Open daily, without exception. May–September: 10:00 A.M.–12:30 P.M. and 3:00 P.M.–7:00 P.M. October–April: 10:00 A.M.–12:30 P.M. and 2:30 P.M.–6:00 P.M.

The foundation has a remarkable collection of more than 6,000 paintings, sculptures, ceramics, drawings, and graphic works by twentieth-century artists, including Arp, Braque, Derain, Giacometti, Kandinsky, Léger, Matisse, Zadkine, Calder, Chagall, Miro, Matta, and Christo. Each year, it organizes special exhibitions of international significance (Chagall in 1984, for example).

St. Tropez

Musée de l'Annonciade

Place Georges-Grammont
83990 St. Tropez
94/97-04-01
Open daily, except Tuesday. June–September: 10:00 A.M.–NOON and 3:00 P.M.–7:00 P.M. October–May: 10:00 A.M.–NOON and 2:00 P.M.–6:00 P.M. Closed November.

This major museum features works by artists of the late nineteenth and early twentieth centuries, a period when St. Tropez was truly an artist's colony. Matisse's fam-

ous *La Gitane* (1906) is here, as are works by Derain, van Dongen, Braque, Vlaminck, Vuillard, Signac, Valadon, Utrillo, Camoin, Bonnard, Dufy, Rouault, and Maillol.

Toulon

Musée d'Art et d'Archéologie

20 Boulevard du Maréchal-Leclerc
83000 Toulon
94/93-15-54
Open daily, except Monday and Thursday, 10:00 A.M.–NOON and 3:00 P.M.–6:00 P.M.

Paintings on display represent the thirteenth through twentieth centuries. Among the artists included are Van Loo, Fragonard, David, and Vlaminck. One hall contains Asian art. Another portion of the museum houses Gallo-Roman, Greek, and Egyptian artifacts.

Musée Naval de la Tour-Royale

Le Mourillon
Point de la Mitre
83000 Toulon
94/24-91-00
Open daily, except Monday. March–May: 3:00 P.M.–6:00 P.M. June–mid-September: 2:00 P.M.–7:00 P.M. Mid-September–October: 2:00 P.M.–6:00 P.M. Closed November–February.

The Tour Royale was built in 1513–1524 as part of the harbor fortifications. It now contains captured British and Chinese cannon, ships' figureheads, model ships, and various items of archeological and historical interest. The terrace of the tower offers a panorama of Toulon's harbor and the coast.

Musée du Vieux-Toulon

69 Cours Lafayette
83000 Toulon
94/92-29-23
Open Monday, Wednesday, and Saturday,
afternoons only.

Local and regional history is illustrated in
paintings, drawings, and engravings by
Toulon artists. Maps of the city drawn at
different periods, weapons, and other artifacts relating to the city's past are also on
display.

Mémorial du Débarquement

Fort de la Tour-Beaumont
Mont Faron
83000 Toulon
94/93-41-01
Open daily, 9:00 A.M.–11:30 A.M. and 2:00
P.M.–5:15 P.M.

This memorial recalls the Allied invasion of
Provence in August 1944. It features mementos of the commanding officers, uniforms, insignia, and a diorama of the attack.

La Turbie

Trophée des Alpes

06320 La Turbie
Open daily. May–September: 9:00 A.M.–
12:30 P.M. and 2:00 P.M.–7:30 P.M. October–
April: 9:00 A.M.–NOON and 2:00 P.M.–5:00
P.M.

This huge Roman monument was built in 6
B.C. and topped by a statue of Augustus. History has not treated it kindly, but it has
been partially restored in this century. A
museum at the site contains a replica of the
trophy as it originally appeared, as well as
exhibits on the Roman province of Alpes
Maritimae.

Vallauris

Musée Municipal de la Céramique et d'Art Moderne

Place de la Libération
06220 Vallauris
93/64-16-05
Open daily, except Tuesday, 10:00 A.M.–
NOON and 2:00 P.M.–5:00 P.M.

Set in a striking Renaissance chateau built
in 1568, this museum emphasizes modern
ceramic art (Vallauris is a ceramics and
pottery center).

Musée National-Picasso

Place de la Libération
06220 Vallauris
93/64-18-05
Open daily, except Tuesday and legal holidays. April–September: 10:00 A.M.–NOON
and 2:00 P.M.–6:00 P.M. October–March:
10:00 A.M.–NOON and 2:00 P.M.–5:00 P.M.

Picasso came to Vallauris in 1947 and
stayed for six years, becoming involved in
ceramics and pottery. While he was living
here, the town asked him to decorate this
deconsecrated twelfth-century chapel. The
result was Picasso's War and Peace, often
considered among his most important
works.

Vence

Chapelle du Rosaire

466 Avenue Henri-Matisse
06140 Vence
93/58-03-26
Open Tuesday and Thursday, 10:00 A.M.–
11:30 A.M. and 2:30 P.M.–5:30 P.M., and by
appointment (at least 24 hours in
advance).

Matisse planned and decorated this chapel in 1949–1951. An adjacent gallery includes studies he made in the early stages of the project.

Villeneuve-Loubet

Musée de l'Art Culinaire

Fondation Auguste-Escoffier
06270 Villeneuve-Loubet
93/20-80-51

Open daily, except Monday and civil and church holidays, 2:00 P.M.–6:00 P.M.

This museum of the culinary arts is located in the birthplace of Auguste Escoffier (1846–1935), who was called "the king of cooks and the cook of kings." It contains papers belonging to the Escoffier family; busts, portraits, documents, and mementos of the great names of French cuisine; a dining room arranged and set in the Provençal style; a Provençal-Niçois kitchen of the eighteenth and nineteenth centuries; a room featuring hundreds of menus from all over the world; and other related exhibits.

CALENDAR OF FESTIVALS AND MAJOR EVENTS
IN THE FRENCH RIVIERA

January	International Record and Music Publishers Fair (MIDEM), Cannes
	Mimosa Festival, Mandelieu
	Motorcar Rally, Monaco
	Festival of St. Devoté, Monaco
February	Carnival, Nice (begins two weeks before Lent)
	Lemon Festival, Menton (begins one week before Lent)
April	(first two weeks) Wine fair, Brignoles
	International Open Tennis Championships, Monaco
	(Good Friday) Procession of the Passion, Roquebrune
May	International Film Festival, Cannes
	Rose Festival, Grasse
	"Grand Prix" Formula 1 racing cars, Monaco
	(May 16–18) *Bravade*, St. Tropez
June	(June 15) Spanish *Bravade*, St. Tropez
	Haut Pays en Fête ("feast day of the hinterland"), in a different village each year
	(late June) Horse racing begins, Cagnes-sur-Mer (through August)
July	(first Sunday) Festival of St. Peter, Antibes
	(July 14) Bastille Day (parades, fireworks)
	Jazz Festival, Juan-les-Pins
	"Nights of Lérins," *son-et-lumière* on the Iles de Lérins
	Music Festival, Menton (chamber music concerts in front of the church of St. Michel, through August)
	International Festival of Painting, Cagnes-sur-Mer (through September)
	Painting Biennale, Menton (through September, in even-numbered years)
August	Jasmine Festival *(Jasminades)*, Grasse
	(August 5) Procession of the Passion, Roquebrune
	(August 15) Harbor festival, Villefranche
September	Royal regatta, Cannes
November	Opera season begins, Nice (through April)
	(November 19) National holiday, Monaco
December	Horse racing season begins, Cagnes-sur-Mer (through March)
	(last two weeks) Fair of *santons*, Marseilles

Consult local publications or *syndicats d'initiative* for more detailed information.

INDEX

Index of Places

(Entries and numbers in boldface indicate the main points of interest and main discussions of the place cited. References to color plates are in italics.)

The Publisher has made every effort
to verify that the information in this book
is accurate and up to date.
Readers are invited
to write with more recent information.

The text was set in ITC Garamond by TGA Communications, Inc.,
New York.
The book was printed and bound by Novograph, S.A.
Madrid.